GRAND CANYON WOMEN

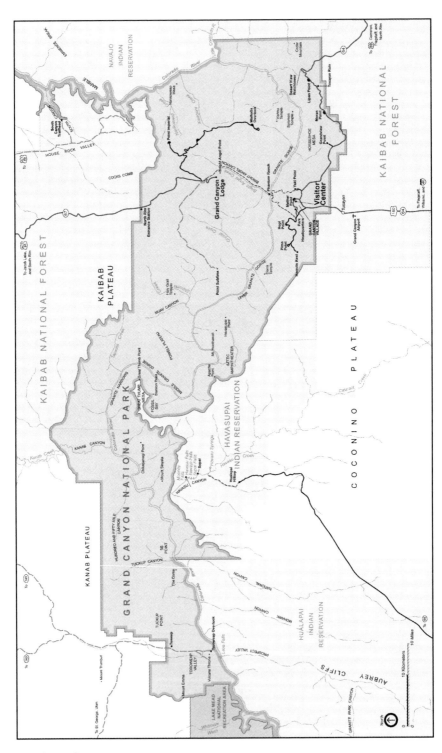

The Grand Canyon.

GRAND CANYON
WOMEN

LIVES SHAPED BY LANDSCAPE

Betty Leavengood

Designed by Rudy Ramos
Edited by Rose Houk

Printed in USA

Third Edition
18 17 16 15 14   1 2 3 4 5 6

ISBN: 978-1-934656-54-9

Library of Congress Cataloging-in-Publication Data

Leavengood, Betty, 1939-
   Grand Canyon women : lives shaped by landscape / Betty Leavengood. — Third edition.
      pages cm
   1. Grand Canyon (Ariz.)—Description and travel. 2. Grand Canyon
   (Ariz.)—Biography. 3. Women—Arizona—Grand Canyon—Biography. I. Grand
   Canyon Association. II. Title.
   F788.L398 2014
   917.91'32--dc23
                              2013050754

The Grand Canyon Association is the National Park Service's official nonprofit partner raising private funds to benefit Grand Canyon National Park, operating retail shops and visitor centers within the park, and providing premier educational opportunities about the natural and cultural history of Grand Canyon. Proceeds from the sale of this publication will be used to support research and education at Grand Canyon National Park.

Grand Canyon Association
P.O. Box 399
Grand Canyon, AZ 86023
(800) 858-2808
www.grandcanyon.org

**Grand
Canyon
Association**

Contents

Acknowledgments

I would like to thank first and foremost all the women profiled in this book who shared their lives with me:

Gale Burak invited me to her New Hampshire home for three glorious autumn days of talking and hiking. At her lovely home in Sedona, Arizona, Louise Hinchliffe showed me the picture of the Grand Canyon that had inspired her to leave Massachusetts and travel to the canyon. I met Lois Jotter Cutter at the Grand Canyon River Guides spring meeting in 1995 and later at her home in Greensboro, North Carolina. Denise Traver and I first met at the Rock Springs Café, and in the spring of 1998 I joined her all-women's backpacking trip to Supai in the canyon. I spoke with Polly Patraw by phone at her home in Santa Fe, New Mexico. She ended our conversation with, "For ninety-two, I'm doing real well!"

I traveled to Durango, Colorado, to meet Louise Teal in the beautiful Strater Hotel. Katie Lee welcomed me to her home in Jerome, Arizona. Patty Nolan let me pitch a tent in her yard on the South Rim. I met Bernice Reeve and Kitty Marr on several visits to the North Rim, and they helped me with packs and a mule ride down the North Kaibab Trail. Elizabeth Kent Meyer shared her album of her years as a Harvey Girl at the Grand Canyon.

I hiked to Supai to meet with Bernice Watahomigie and talk with her about her mother, Ethel Jack. Jean Mann welcomed me to her home near Cameron and demonstrated how to weave. I met Loretta Jackson-Kelly at her office in Peach Springs and learned of her efforts to preserve the culture and history of the Hualapai tribe. I was fortunate to attend presentations by park interpretive ranger Phyllis Kachinhongva.

Ila Bulletts and I exchanged many e-mails and telephone calls as I learned about her efforts to preserve the culture and history of the Kaibab Paiute tribe. Mary Aiken and I went to dinner at El Tovar and exchanged many e-mails while I learned about her experiences living in the canyon for thirty years.

Thanks also to historian Michael F. Anderson, Ph.D., who contributed the chapter on Elizabeth Wiley McKee, of Wiley Way Camp on the North Rim.

Diane Grua, Karen Underhill, and Richard Quartaroli at Northern Arizona University's Cline Library Special Collections and Archives helped me sort through the library's wealth of material about women of the Grand Canyon, and Jess Vogelsang supplied photographs for the book's latest edition. Colleen Hyde, Carolyn Richard, Kim Besom, and Mike Quinn of the Grand Canyon National Park Museum Collection were unfailingly helpful and cheerful during my visits to the park and in responding to frequent e-mails. Susan Eubank of the Grand Canyon National Park Library loaned me many books. Jan K. Davis helped me find the original Phantom Ranch Register at the University of Arizona Library Special Collections in Tucson, and William Frank of the Huntington Library in San Marino, California, guided me through the extensive Marston Collection.

I owe special thanks to Stephen Hirst, author of *Havsuw 'Baaja: People of the Blue Green Water*, for helping me understand the struggle of the Havasupai to regain their rim lands.

When I learned that Bessie Haley Hyde had attended my high school in Parkersburg, West Virginia, my mother, Gladys Marshall, went to the Parkersburg library and copied Bessie's photos and artwork from the 1924 high school yearbook. A longtime friend, Bill Bee, examined local records, obtaining pertinent information and locating the Haley's Parkersburg home on Oak Street. The late Dan Davis, the first river ranger at the Grand Canyon, told me of his boat trips with Georgie White Clark.

I thank all the wonderful people who have hiked the Grand Canyon with me, sharing the beauty, the adventure, the catastrophes, and the fun, especially Don and Ginny Fisher, Ruth Butera, and Jo Haslett. The Fishers kept coming back to the canyon with me. Although Ruth refused to wear the "My Age Is None of Your Business" T-shirt I gave her, she has never turned down a chance to return to the canyon. Jo Haslett and I were drenched while camping on the Esplanade near the North Bass Trail, nearly flooded out at Hermit Camp, and spotted the "high ground" signs at the Supai campground with our flashlights during a midnight storm. But Jo never complained.

Special thanks to my three children, to whom having a mother who hikes the Grand Canyon seems perfectly normal. My son, Rodney Graham, has made five trips into the canyon with me. My daughters, Cheryl and Christy, who share my love of the outdoors and the canyon, are working to catch up.

A special thank you to Pam Frazier, editor at the Grand Canyon Association for her work on the second edition of *Grand Canyon Women,* for her idea to add chapters on Native American women, and for her incredible patience. For the minor revisions to text and design for this third edition, I thank Lillian Santamaria, publishing manager for Grand Canyon Association; graphic designer Rudy Ramos; and editor Rose Houk.

—BETTY LEAVENGOOD

JULY 20 '11
60.

A group of women join a party of mule riders on the Bright Angel Trail into the Grand Canyon in 1911. *Photograph courtesy of National Park Service.*

My Grand Canyon Calls: An Introduction

I first saw the Grand Canyon as the typical tourist. Over spring break in 1970, my husband and I decided to show our seven- and eight-year-old children the canyon. We were moving from Tucson, Arizona, back east in the summer and wanted to see the canyon before we left.

I don't remember much except the impact of that first amazing view as we approached Mather Point on the South Rim. After driving for miles on the high, flat mesa, we pulled into the parking area and the earth opened up below. I stared in amazement as postcards became reality and a deep gorge with endless buttes spread before me. I certainly never thought then that I would return again and again to this place, to hike its trails and to write a book about its women.

But I did. Nine years later, back in Arizona, I headed again for the Grand Canyon, this time to meet some friends from Ohio on the South Rim. I arrived a day early to hike. A total novice, I hiked the four and a half miles down the Bright Angel Trail to Indian Garden, once home to a small band of Havasupai who used the reliable water source to grow crops, but now a National Park Service campground.

Sitting in the shade of the cottonwoods, I realized that because I'd started out so late in the day I could not make my way back to the rim before dark. I had to spend the night below the rim at the campground, attempting to sleep on a jacket I had in my daypack. The braying of feral burros woke me up at 4:00 A.M.

I started up Bright Angel Trail at daybreak and, without breakfast or snacks to sustain me, had a miserable hike back to the rim. When I finally reached the top, a young man asked me to take his picture. He held up seven fingers. "What's that for?" I asked. "I've hiked in the Grand Canyon seven times," he laughed. He offered to take my picture, and at the last second I held up one finger. Now I've run out of fingers to count the number of times I've hiked the canyon.

I have since been on many other trips to the Grand Canyon, some idyllic, others with an adventuresome twist. Always, I am struck by the changing beauty of the canyon, the crisp light of a late fall sunrise, the hazy shroud of a summer sunset, and a touch of winter's snow along the rim. Always, I am drawn back. I'm not sure I can articulate why, exactly, I am drawn to the place. Surely it is for the obvious reasons—its ever-changing beauty, its immensity, but mostly the satisfaction I feel as I drag my weary bones up one more switchback to the rim. This gives me an "I can do it!" attitude that has served me well in life.

Over the years, I thought about other women and their relationship to the Grand Canyon. In a world traditionally given over to the domain of men, women have had their place and purpose amidst the canyon's walls. The canyon does not discriminate by gender. As with any wild place, it has practiced equality through time. It tests both men's and women's mettle against scorching heat, blinding snow, treacherous terrain, and deadly waters. Survival is often dependent merely on the level of one's own resourcefulness.

Ancestral Pueblo women (formerly known as Anasazi) were probably the first to develop and survive by this brand of resourcefulness. Remnants of their adobe and masonry dwellings remain under cliffs in many areas of the Grand Canyon, where from ca. 700 to 1200 A.D. they carried out their daily tasks. No one knows precisely why the Ancestral Puebloans left their Grand Canyon homes, but some theorize an extended drought forced the population to move on. Scholars and Native Americans today believe that some Ancestral Puebloan clans are the ancestors of the modern-day Hopi who settled 100 miles east of the Grand Canyon. Along with a Hopi, women from four other Indian tribes—Havasupai, Hualapai, Navajo, and Kaibab Paiute—are profiled in this book. Their people have a long history and close ties with the canyon.

Reading about the Grand Canyon, I came to realize that most of the available books and articles concern men—John Wesley Powell, Robert Brewster Stanton, Ellsworth and Emery Kolb, and many others. Where were the women? I remembered that a woman had designed Phantom Ranch. I set out to find the Grand Canyon's women. I asked questions at the Grand Canyon National Park museum collection and library and delved through books and articles. What follows are the stories of more than twenty women whose lives were entwined, some for only a brief period, with the Grand Canyon.

Ada Diefendorf first came to the Grand Canyon in 1894. She married her tour guide, William Wallace Bass, and became a reluctant partner in his tourist business. Mary Elizabeth Jane Colter designed six structures at the Grand Canyon at a time when women were not generally accepted as architects. Elizabeth Wiley McKee owned and managed a tourist camp on Bright Angel Point on the North Rim from 1917 to 1927.

By 1905, Fred Harvey had two hotels on the South Rim. His "Harvey Girls," dressed in crisp black-and-white uniforms, worked and lived at the Grand Canyon. Among them was Elizabeth Kent Meyer, a Harvey Girl who began working at the Grand Canyon in 1926. Then there was Bessie Haley Hyde, the first woman to attempt a boat trip through the Grand Canyon, who graduated from my high school in Parkersburg, West Virginia.

In 1930, Pauline Mead Patraw convinced the National Park Service that a woman could be a ranger-naturalist. Ruth Stephens Baker grew up at the Grand Canyon, and in 1937 she accompanied Emery Kolb on his infamous climb of Shiva Temple. Botanists Elzada Clover and Lois Jotter collected specimens on a river trip in 1938 and became the first women to successfully complete a boat trip through the Grand Canyon.

Gale Burak began hiking the Grand Canyon in 1942 and finished her last stint as a ranger in 1991. Georgie White Clark ran "Share the Expense" river trips for forty years and introduced thousands of people to the Colorado River. Louise Hinchliffe left Massachusetts in 1951 to work for the National Park Service at Grand Canyon and stayed for nearly thirty-four years. Today the Grand Canyon library is named in her honor. Katie Lee's songs of protest challenged the building of the Glen Canyon Dam in the 1950s.

Phyllis Yoyetewa Kachinhongva, a member of the Hopi tribe and an interpretive ranger, has lived at the Grand Canyon all her life. Jean Mann, a master Navajo weaver, demonstrated weaving at the Grand Canyon Visitor Center from 1970 to 1980. In 1972 Louise Teal became one of the first women to handle the job of boat guide on the Colorado River through the Grand Canyon. Mary Aiken carried her baby into the canyon in 1973. She stayed to raise three children while her husband, artist Bruce Aiken, ran the pumping station at Roaring Springs. Havasupai Ethel Jack lobbied in Washington, D.C. for the return of her people's plateau lands.

Patty Nolan, Kitty Marr, and Bernice Reeve have wrangled mules off both the South and North Rims. Loretta Jackson-Kelly, as Hualapai Historic Preservation Officer, works to preserve and protect her tribe's culture. Denise Traver started a women-only backpacking program for the Grand Canyon Field Institute and introduced scores of women to the canyon experience. Ila Bulletts educates the public about the Kaibab Paiute culture and her tribe's history in the canyon.

These women are representative of countless others whose lives have been deeply touched by the Grand Canyon. They are exemplary Grand Canyon women who have carved the path and made it easier for other women to follow in their footsteps. If you embark on a mule ride, raft the Colorado River, take a nature walk along the rim, or participate in a ranger program, today a woman is as likely to be in charge as a man. As for me, I have returned again and again, ready to meet my next challenge.

CHAPTER ONE

A Lady's Rough and Tumble Life

ADA DIEFENDORF BASS

(1867–1951)

A da Diefendorf held on to her seat as the stagecoach carrying a group of six tourists bounced along the rough road from Williams, Arizona Territory, to the Grand Canyon. She wondered how she would manage the seventy-mile ride to Bass Camp, where their guide, William Wallace Bass, promised grandeur such as they had never seen. This vast, unsettled land contrasted sharply with the neat, rolling farmland surrounding her home in East Worcester, New York. The year was 1894.

Born August 29, 1867, in Charlotteville, New York, Ada grew up in East Worcester, where her father ran an undertaking and wagon business. As a child, she would rather practice her piano and organ, teach herself to play the violin, or read books than play with other children. In 1883, at age sixteen, she passed the teachers' exam and spent the next several years either teaching or studying music at the seminary in Stamford, New York, and the Boston Conservatory of Music. She was a tall, serious young woman with a stern countenance and a dry sense of humor.

When Ada traveled cross-country by train late in 1893 to visit an aunt who managed the Commercial Hotel in Prescott, Arizona Territory, she would have been, at twenty-six, considered a spinster. In that era society measured a woman's worth by her husband and children: to be unmarried was a disgrace. But the odds of marriage were stacked against her. In New York in 1894 women outnumbered men by a ratio of two to one. Perhaps Ada hoped to meet an eligible man in the West,

Portrait of Ada Bass, ca. 1908.
Photograph courtesy of the Arizona Historical Society, Tucson, Arizona, Bass Collection.

where the ratio was switched, two men to every woman. She stayed in Prescott for several months, giving music lessons during the spring and summer of 1894. While in Prescott, Ada learned of Bass's excursions to the Grand Canyon and decided to join an August trip.

William Wallace Bass had been a dispatcher for the elevated railroad in New York City. After he suffered a nervous breakdown, his doctor recommended that he go West to live a more physical, less stressful life. Bass established a camp on the South Rim of the Grand Canyon in 1884 and took up the life of a miner, locating several mining claims—including ones for zinc, lead, and silver—in the canyon. Although he continued to prospect and mine, Bass soon realized that people would pay to see the canyon; in 1885 he organized the Grand Canyon's first tourist excursion from the town of Williams to his camp, which became known as Bass Camp. The camp consisted of a small cabin that served as a kitchen and a large white canvas tent where guests slept and ate. Assorted sheds, outbuildings, and corrals completed the compound.

So that his customers could arrive in relative comfort, Bass built a road from Williams and one from the nearby town of Ash Fork to his camp. Once there, tourists would accompany him on horseback down the Mystic Springs Trail to see the Grand Canyon and occasionally venture along the Topocoba Trail to the Havasupai village of Supai. Guests came to Bass Camp as much for the charms of their host as they did for the scenery, for Bass was charming, a visionary, and able to keep tourists amused with his stories. He liked to have fun and thrived on adventure. He played the violin and wrote poetry, which impressed Ada.

The night before embarking on her stagecoach ride to the South Rim, Ada went by train from Prescott to Williams and spent the night at the Hayward Hotel. She and her companion travelers left early the next morning; by evening, after thirty-two miles of jostling in the stagecoach, they faced a flooded Cataract Creek. Ada wrote, "Twilight was just deepening with the gloom of night, and the murky waters as they rolled by with a rush and roar had an ominous look. The driver of the stage load of provisions had reached there before the flood came and succeeded in crossing the stream."

Bass drove the stage downstream to a better crossing. While his passengers walked down to the banks of the stream to look through the darkness at the raging water, Bass built a large bonfire on the bank. Despite the protests of one man, who was certain his bones would be washed up on a beach in California, everyone crossed the creek by the light of the fire. Relieved and safe, the party camped there for the night.

They traveled by stage all the next day, arriving at Bass Camp just as the sun was setting. Traveling was hard work in those days, which perhaps made the tourist experience all the more rewarding. Ada marveled at the Grand Canyon, writing in her diary, "Our party got its first view of this great panorama just as the light of day was being shaded by the curtain of night. Bright and early, before the sun was out the next morning, the entire party was out again to feast their eyes on what we had briefly looked upon the night before."

The Grand Canyon fascinated Ada, but not as much as the man who was already known as the "Grand Canyon guide." Bass apparently reciprocated, for following her visit, Ada traveled back to East Worcester to collect her personal possessions and returned to marry him. She was leaving the East's civility for the wilds of Arizona Territory. Though she planned to marry a man her parents had never met, they were no doubt relieved that she would not end up an "old maid."

Only five months after they met, Ada became Mrs. William Wallace Bass at the Methodist Parsonage in Williams on January 6, 1895. That evening Bass's friends threw a "shivaree," a frontier custom where friends gathered outside the couple's nuptial quarters and made noises with bells, tin pie plates, and shotguns until the couple came out and acknowledged their presence. Ada, unaccustomed to such raucous affairs, noted that they "were serenaded by a band and nearly drove crazy."

The man she married, almost twenty years her senior, had no permanent home and little money, but he was intelligent, ambitious, and determined to succeed with his plans to make money by showing people the Grand Canyon. Ada may have shared that plan initially, but the harsh realities of frontier tourism soon cast shadows on her dreams.

Within a week of their marriage, the couple left Williams for Bass Camp, accompanied by a paying customer—a photographer who hoped to sell his pictures of the Grand Canyon—and a man they had hired to look after the horses. Ada looked forward to her "honeymoon," writing in her diary, "I thought it would be fine to go along with them and get a taste of camping outside."

Bass drove a four-horse stage heavily loaded with a month's supplies and pulled by two mules and two horses. Not long after they started out, black thunderheads appeared on the horizon and the wind changed directions, now roaring out of the southwest. Bass urged the animals forward, hoping to cross Cataract Creek before the storm sent water rushing down the normally dry creek bed. They were too late. The creek churned with muddy, swirling water.

Ada watched as the horses and mules were unharnessed and taken to the bank to drink. Bass explained that this would prevent them from stopping to drink in midstream and allowing the wagon to settle, becoming mired in mud. The tactic didn't work, as Ada wrote: "Old Jerry, one of the mules, refused to drink when he had a chance, but, when the outfit reached midstream he suddenly became thirsty and halted, stopping the rest of the animals and we were stuck in the deep mire in the stream which was gradually rising and nearly reaching the box of the wagon."

The men jumped into the stream, urging the mules to move; the mules remained steadfast, and so they were loosened and led to the bank. Ada struggled to save the flour, sugar, and other perishable supplies from the water seeping into the box of the wagon. One of the men propped a piece of lumber under the wagon tongue, and Ada walked to the opposite bank.

The men finally coaxed the horses across Cataract Creek, and the party was able to make it to a camp Bass called The Caves. They built a fire, dried their bedding, and made some coffee before turning in for the night. The storm's persistence the following morning meant that they'd be stranded at The Caves for at least a few days. The men shot several rabbits for breakfast. Ada fried the rabbits and made some biscuits and black coffee; the food, she noted, "made us feel like a million, after the incidents of the day before."

The start of Ada and Will's life together was humble enough. Ada described her temporary home: "A tent erected over a wood floor was used for sleeping and warmed by a sheet iron stove when fuel was available. The kitchen and dining room combined was reached by going down a ladder into the cave. An old cook stove had been installed and the stove pipe emerged through a natural opening in the roof of the cave. A rough table of boards and dry goods boxes for seats and also for cupboards were the main furnishings of the underground kitchen." This set-up was adequate during dry weather, but, wrote Ada, "when it rained, streams of water trickled down the crevices of the rocks, and on down to the next cave below."

Those few days at The Caves turned into weeks as the rain persisted, keeping roads soft and impassable. Late in January Ada became ill. "I was sick two days in this godforsaken place," she wrote in her diary, and she was more than ready to leave. The civility of the East was far away indeed. It was nearly a month before conditions permitted them to leave for Bass Camp. "What a honeymoon," she wrote.

Had Ada known this trip foreshadowed times to come, she might have opted to stay single, old maid status and all. Ada's diary that first year records a rather gypsy-like existence: to The Caves, to Bass Camp, to Ash Fork, to Williams, and back to The Caves to start again. She would later write that she had either cooked a meal or slept under every tree and beside every bush between Bass Camp and Ash Fork. No sooner would she get settled than her husband would say it was time to move again. Time for a new group of tourists. Time for Ada to cook their meals, make their beds, and do their laundry.

Six months into their marriage, Ada began using the abbreviation S.O.S. in her diary. It most likely means "Same Old Stuff," a phrase she used in later years to comment on the drudgery of her life and perhaps a not so cryptic plea for help. On August 11, she commented, "S.O.S. hunting horses and cleaning up dirt." Her September 6 entry is simply, "S.O.S. S.O.S."

Exacerbating the constant moves and workload was the lack of financial resources. When Will did make money, he often celebrated with a drinking binge in town. Because the couple had no permanent home, they relied on boarding houses or friends when they were in Williams or Ash Fork. Will often left Ada to fend for herself for extended periods while he worked in his mines or explored new routes for trails into the Grand Canyon or just "disappeared." When she ran out of money to pay for her board, she slept in the stage and washed dishes for meals. "I am putting in a wretched existence," the new bride wrote, and by November she was forced to sell personal items to make ends meet. On Thanksgiving Day Ada even played for a dance to earn a few extra dollars. Just a week shy of her first wedding anniversary, Ada wrote, "Thus endeth this horrible year, can the next be worse?"

The answer? Yes. Ada, now pregnant, spent most of January and February in Williams alone, struggling to make ends meet. When Will finally returned in late February, she accompanied him to Bass Camp to check on the water supply and

William Wallace Bass and Ada Bass at Cataract Camp (The Caves). *Photograph courtesy of the Arizona Historical Society, Tucson, Arizona, Bass Collection.*

help get the camp in order for a small group of tourists due to arrive within the week. In the rock cisterns near the trail into the Grand Canyon enough water had accumulated for the animals and house use. Will decided that with an extra barrel of water for drinking and cooking, the supply would be sufficient for the group. What luck! They would not have to haul water.

But while they slept, a group of Havasupai Indians came to their camp with horses whose thirst emptied the cisterns. Bass awakened, lectured the group, and ordered them off his property. Ada and Will now had to return to The Caves and haul water back to Bass Camp. They arrived at The Caves after 10:00 P.M., watered their horses, and turned them out to graze before going to bed.

By morning a strong wind whipped snow flurries through the camp as Will searched for the horses. Ada grew apprehensive with the memory of her stay at The Caves just a year before. Unable to find the horses, Will returned, exhausted and feeling ill. Ada, now four months pregnant, watched as Will suffered from chills and grew progressively weaker. Ash Fork was thirty-five miles away, and she began to panic. "The days passed and no one came our way," she wrote. "There was a cold wind blowing and no wood for fuel to keep him warm. I had to saw down the logs of the corral and cut them up. The water in the cistern was getting very low. In fact, it was not fit to use. Our food supply was dwindling and the situation growing very serious. I walked, in different directions from the camp each day, hoping to find a horse I could use to ride for help. I wrote notes and fastened them on bushes along the road telling of our plight and I hoped someone passing would find them." They had been stranded at The Caves for nearly eight weeks. Not a living soul passed by. Ada's imagination ran wild. Would they starve to death? Freeze to death?

Will's condition worsened with each day, and Ada grew desperate. "One day I walked to the old dam, about three miles down the Cataract. Here, I found an old grey horse blind in one eye. I herded him back to Camp and began to plan for the trip to Ashfork for help. Mr. Bass was too sick to get out of the bed and I knew we could not subsist very long on what food we had."

Ada put all available food and water within Will's reach in preparation for her departure. She packed her blankets on the horse and was getting ready to leave when their dog began barking and leaping at the door. "I stepped quickly to the door. I looked in the direction of the dog's bark, and, behold a man coming on horseback, leading a pack horse. I waved him to come our way and told him of our terrible plight." The man rode into Ash Fork to seek help. Ada waited two more days. "The second night I heard the rattle of the wagon and horses' hooves. He brought us food. The next morning we left early for Ashfork, stopping once for lunch."

Safe, warm, and comfortable at last, Will began to recover, but the ordeal left him and Ada without any financial resources. "Our money is all gone and old Cervis, the only store in town, don't like to trust us for groceries. God Help Us," she wrote. In early April, Ada sold her embroidered bedspread, a fine pieced quilt, and pillow slips with lace to pay their rent. Two days later, she sold her silverware and music book to buy something to eat.

By May of 1896, Ada had had it. "Began packing my trunk to beat it, back to home and mother," she wrote, and in mid-May she arrived by train in East Worcester. Surrounded once again by the comforts of a civilized home, Ada showed little interest in returning to the Grand Canyon or to Will. Her first child, Edith Jane, was born that August 20. "Dr. Smith and Mrs. Leape attended," Ada wrote. "It's a wonder I'm alive to copy this. Such help."

Will wrote occasionally, keeping her informed of events "at home." Meanwhile, she renewed her teaching certificate and taught school in West Richmondville for the 1898–1899 school year. Then, whether absence made the heart grow fonder or time eased the wretchedness of hardship, somehow Will persuaded Ada to return to him after a three-year separation. By fall of 1899, she and Edith were living at Bass Camp, and Will was in the process of adding a kitchen to their one-room building.

Just why she returned to this "godforsaken place" is unclear. Did her life at the Grand Canyon look better from afar? Did the social mores of the day require that she stay by her husband's side? Did she feel an attraction to the place called Grand Canyon? Or, did she once again succumb to the charms of William Wallace Bass? Whatever the reason, her nomadic existence resumed, this time with the added responsibility of little Edith.

The winter of her return was harsh and unrelenting. Will decided to move the family to his newly built camp on Shinumo Creek in the depths of Grand Canyon. On January 9, 1900, the Basses opened the new century with a ride into the canyon down the Mystic Springs Trail. Ada, now pregnant again, proudly wrote that three-and-one-half-year-old Edith was "probably the first child to ride a horse to the river alone."

With warmer temperatures, protection from the wind, and ample water, Shinumo Camp was a refuge from winter. Bass had a vegetable garden and an orchard along the creek. He repaired prehistoric irrigation ditches (Shinumo is a Paiute Indian word for "old people") to water his trees and crops. Ada happily took care of the tent house and little Edith, who loved playing on the sandy beach near the river. It was late March before the weather had warmed enough for the family to return to Bass Camp and the drudgery of a tourist leader's wife.

Ada found that the kitchen roof had been damaged by the hard winter. Before Will had time to make repairs, he escorted a tourist party, the Winegards, around the Grand Canyon. As Ada prepared their food, it began to rain. "I had to hold an umbrella over my head to cook meals," she wrote, and when the Winegard party left, Ada wrote, "I was happy to get rid of the cussed outfit." By now any enthusiasm Ada once had for the tourist business had disappeared. The reality of Will's enterprise meant hours of extra cooking and cleaning for her—and little else.

Ada had planned to return to East Worcester for the birth of their second child, and her father sent her money for the trip. But the baby, William Guy, arrived early, on July 26, 1900, in Williams. To celebrate the birth of his son properly, Will used Ada's travel money to get drunk.

As soon as she was able, Ada borrowed money and left on the midnight train for East Worcester with Edith at her side and little Willie in her arms. Although it is clear what Ada's life with William Wallace Bass entailed, her diaries reveal nothing to explain why she chose again to return. The following summer, after nearly a year in East Worcester, she journeyed back to Bass Camp to take up what she surely knew was a difficult life. On top of caring for two young children, cooking and cleaning for tourists, and living in a harsh land, she also had to endure the whims and peccadilloes of her charismatic husband. By early 1903, Ada was once again pregnant.

To be near the doctor for the birth of their third child, Ada left the Grand Canyon that July and rented a cottage in Williams. Hazel Canyonita arrived on October 5, 1903, weighing barely five pounds fully clothed. Will came to meet his new daughter a few days later, "half drunk as usual," as Ada remarked in her journal.

Ada's brief "maternity leave" ended in early November, when Will picked her up in a four-horse stage so as to have room not only for Ada and little Hazel, but for the latest group of tourists bound for Bass Camp. That year ended with Will absent again, this time off to give lectures about the Grand Canyon in Chicago, Washington, and New York, leaving Ada alone to care for the children and an occasional tourist. Christmas passed without celebration. On the last day of the year she wrote, "This sure is a fine place to be marooned in for the winter. God help us all, this next year."

Nearly five months would pass before Will returned from the East. When she unpacked his suitcase she "found all his ladies letters which he forgot to destroy and other interesting information." Now added to the strain of hard work, the harsh land, and the care of the children was the humiliation of Will's infidelities. What did Victorian women do in the face of such realities? To whom could they turn with the shame or guilt? Ada did what women of her age were compelled to do. She swallowed rage, bit back tears, harbored bitter resentment, and stayed with her husband. And she became pregnant again in the summer.

To make room for his growing family—and perhaps to assuage his guilt—Will enlarged the house at Bass Camp. It now had three bedrooms, a living room, dining room, kitchen, pantry, and storage room. Porches were added on the west and east sides. Guests still stayed mostly in tents, but occasionally, despite Ada's objections, they were allowed to sleep in the main house. Ada rarely had time to enjoy the new addition or to play the piano, her one tie to her former life. Business was improving, and Ada was kept busy. She wrote on July 18, "All this gang on my hands to cook and fix beds for and all the children to wash for. I'm tired enough to die and can't stand this much longer and no one to help me."

With the end of the summer tourist season, Ada once again escaped to East Worcester in September to await the birth of her fourth, and last, child. Mabella

Melba arrived on April 25, 1905, weighing in at seven and one-half pounds. It was, according to Ada, "a cold, windy disagreeable day for the event."

Ada remained in the East for the summer helping her mother who had had a stroke. She did not return to the Grand Canyon until August 20. She came back to a new stop for the train, which became known as Bass Siding, and a nearly completed new house. Bass had built the siding and the house in response to changes at the Grand Canyon. Most people now came to the Grand Canyon by train, which the Santa Fe Railway extended to the canyon in 1901, and were more likely to stay at the newly opened El Tovar Hotel, just across from the railroad depot, than at Bass Camp, a twenty-five-mile stage ride away. Plus, they were increasingly more interested in short tours around the rim of the Grand Canyon than long treks into the canyon.

The new house, which because it was painted white they called the White House, suited Ada well, and she spent much time papering the walls and getting it in order. She still faced moves to Bass Camp and even to Shinumo Camp as Will's clients demanded, yet life at the White House was better than before.

Ada became concerned about the children's education and, using her experience as a teacher, gave them lessons at home. For several winters Ada took the children to Phoenix to attend school, but they usually remained only a couple of months, either running out of rent money or responding to Will's requests that she come home. Finally, when enough people were living at the Grand Canyon to start a school, Bass donated lumber for a school building, and Ada boarded the teacher part of the time. The Bass children made up half of the first class.

By 1911, Will decided that he needed to be even closer to Grand Canyon Village—the tourist complex that was home to employees of the Santa Fe Railway and Fred Harvey Company—to capitalize on the increased demands for short tours by tourists coming in on the train and remaining just for the day. He built a house on land leased from the Forest Service. As the sides were covered with pressed tin, they called it the Tin House. Ada's piano, always her most prized possession, was moved once again. This two-story house was much to Ada's liking. She was able to socialize with friends in the village, and had less work now that most tourists came just for day trips.

By the outbreak of World War I in Europe, tourism was flourishing at the Grand Canyon. Will now had four surreys and two larger wagons. Edith, now nineteen, was a natural with tourists, having inherited her father's gift of gab and love of the Grand Canyon. She was a skilled horsewoman and often took people into the Grand Canyon by herself. Willie, now called Bill, also helped, as did a couple of hired hands.

Ada and William Bass' children: Edith Jane, Hazel Canyonita, William Guy, and Mabella Melba Bass. *Photograph courtesy of the Arizona Historical Society, Tucson, Arizona, Bass Collection.*

One of them, Bert Lauzon, had an eye for Edith. Already a Grand Canyon legend for having accompanied the Kolb brothers on their 1911 trip on the Colorado River, Bert was a great asset to Will, although Will disapproved of his interest in Edith.

Bass was finally prospering after years of hard work. There was money for a new piano for Ada and a Studebaker for Will, and Ada traveled to Coronado Island and San Diego to visit relatives. In 1915 the income from Will's tourist business was $20,000, a tidy sum in those days. The next year, Will purchased property in Wickenburg, Arizona, looking toward retirement.

But the good times at the Grand Canyon did not last. Despite Will's disapproval, Edith married Bert Lauzon in 1916, the same year that Bill went to work as a driver for the Fred Harvey Company. The National Park Service was established in 1916, and in 1919 the Grand Canyon became a national park. In 1920, Fred Harvey became the park's main concessioner. This action signaled the beginning of the end for the Bass tourist business. William Bass couldn't compete with Fred Harvey's Pierce Arrows and uniformed drivers. In 1923, the Basses entertained their last guest.

Perhaps it was time. Tragedy struck when, on September 21, 1924, Edith, so vibrant and well suited for life at the Grand Canyon, died unexpectedly of complications following surgery for removal of gallstones. That same year, when William Bass was seventy-five, he did not renew his lease on the Tin House and agreed to let the Forest Service tear it down. Ada and Will moved back to the White House. In 1926 they sold their holdings to the Santa Fe Railway Company for $25,000. Will received a $5,000 option. Half of the $20,000 they received at closing was in a separate check made out to Ada. She knew her husband too well to trust him with the entire amount.

Ada and Will "retired" to Wickenburg, a small town northwest of Phoenix, in 1927. Will, ever restless, staked a gold-mining claim in the nearby hills and opened what was probably the first motel in Arizona. Under a grove of mesquite trees, he had cots and wash basins for motorists, later adding a gasoline station and a swimming pool. Son Bill moved down from the Grand Canyon to help with this new business and later built the modern La Siesta Motel that remains in business in Wickenburg to this day.

Will died in 1933 at the age of eighty-five. At his request, his ashes were scattered on the 6,703-foot-high Holy Grail Temple, known for many years as Bass Tomb, high above Shinumo Creek. Ada spent her remaining years in Wickenburg, often visiting her daughters in Phoenix and her grandchildren at the Grand Canyon. Little remains of the Bass complex: Bass Camp, the White House, and the Tin House live only in memory, but Bass Trail, which so long ago carried the footsteps of the young Ada Bass, remains. Today hikers can follow the steps of Ada Bass to the river she first descended a hundred years ago. It is still an amazing trip.

When Ada was in her early eighties, her son Bill took her to the North Rim of the Grand Canyon. Bill had always wondered why Ada stayed so long at the canyon and endured so much. As they sat on the veranda of the Grand Canyon Lodge looking across the canyon, Ada was silent for a long time; then, as if to answer all his questions, she said, "You know, I love the Grand Canyon too."

Ada died in 1951 at the age of eighty-four. She lived long enough to realize her place in Grand Canyon history. She was the first European-American woman to raise a family at the Grand Canyon. She was, albeit reluctantly, a partner in the beginnings of tourism that today has reached proportions she could not have imagined. Today Ada Bass lies finally at rest in the Grand Canyon Cemetery on the South Rim.

CHAPTER TWO

Building a Legacy

MARY ELIZABETH JANE COLTER
(1869—1958)

Mary Elizabeth Jane Colter designed and supervised the construction of eight structures at Grand Canyon National Park. As architect for the Fred Harvey Company and the Santa Fe Railway, she utilized native materials from the canyon to blend with the natural surroundings. People who worked with Miss Colter, as she was generally addressed, remembered her as a perfectionist and a stern taskmaster. We're lucky she was, for her buildings have proven timeless and inviting. They continue to delight park visitors, making their stays pleasant, comfortable, and meaningful.

Colter's Hopi House, which opened on the South Rim in 1905, resembles a traditional Hopi dwelling and is today a gift shop featuring Native American handicrafts. Hermits Rest and Lookout Studio, both built in 1914, blend so well into their surroundings that from a distance, each appears to be part of the canyon rim. Both serve today as pleasant places to relax and enjoy views of the canyon. Hermits Rest still offers tourists a cold drink and a snack, although not for the original fee of fifty cents.

Phantom Ranch, a series of stone cabins along Bright Angel Creek on the floor of the Grand Canyon, opened in 1922 and continues to welcome weary hikers with rustic accommodations and a hearty meal. In 1933 Colter completed the Watchtower at Desert View, a tour de force modeled after similar, though smaller, Indian towers. Tourists today clamber up the spiraling stairs for views of the Grand Canyon. Bright Angel Lodge, which opened in the summer of 1935, still provides moderately priced housing for guests, serves as headquarters for the Grand Canyon mule rides, and includes a restaurant, saloon, and gift shop.

Mary Elizabeth Jane Colter was born April 4, 1869, in Pittsburgh, Pennsylvania, the daughter of William and Rebecca Colter. In 1880 the family moved to St. Paul, Minnesota. Mary became fascinated by the Sioux, the first American Indians she had ever seen. A friend gave her some Sioux drawings, and so dear were they to her that when a smallpox epidemic swept the Sioux population and Mary's mother burned all of the Indian articles in the house, Mary hid them. Collecting Native American art became a lifelong passion for her.

When Mary's father died suddenly in October 1886, leaving the family to survive on a small inheritance, Mary persuaded her mother to use some of the money to send her to the California School of Design, where she could earn teaching credentials to support the family.

Mature at seventeen years of age, Mary traveled alone to San Francisco, determined to succeed. Despite what she told her mother, her dream was not to teach but to design and decorate buildings. While in school, she worked as apprentice in a San Francisco architect's office. Local architects then were developing a new building style more suited to California's landscape and heritage than copies of the latest European styles. By the time Colter graduated in 1890, many California architects were patterning their designs after the early Spanish missions, a trend that deeply influenced her work.

Colter's impressive Lookout Studio. *Photograph by Betty Leavengood.*

Mrs. Harold Ickes (left), wife of President Franklin Roosevelt's Secretary of the Interior, with Mary Jane Colter, looking over Colter's plans for the Bright Angel Lodge, 1935. *Photograph courtesy of National Park Service.*

Colter returned to St. Paul and taught freehand and mechanical drawing over the next fifteen years. During this time, she also gave lectures on world history and architecture at the University of Michigan, reviewed books as literary editor of the *St. Paul Globe*, took courses in archeology, and traveled. On a trip to San Francisco, Mary visited a friend who worked in a Fred Harvey gift shop. Recognizing opportunity, she indicated to the manager of the shop that she would be interested in working for Fred Harvey, perhaps as an interior decorator or designer.

The Fred Harvey Company, already well known for excellent hotels and food service at railroad stations, was considering featuring Native American crafts in their gift shops. The company noted the way train passengers would crowd around the Indians selling their crafts at the stations. Herman Schweizer, a buyer for Fred Harvey, urged the company to merchandise Native American jewelry and crafts in its gift shops and hotels.

In the summer of 1902, Mary looked down from the roof of her cabin in the Minnesota backcountry, where she was making repairs, to see a Western Union boy waving a telegram. The Fred Harvey Company wanted Mary to decorate an Indian museum and salesroom for Native American handicrafts adjacent to its new

Alvarado Hotel in Albuquerque, New Mexico. Mary accepted immediately. She traveled to Albuquerque and began working long days painting, building display tables and shelves, and arranging then rearranging merchandise until she was satisfied with the results.

Navajo rugs covered the floors, baskets hung on the walls, and pots of all sizes filled tables and shelves. A log burned in the fireplace, adding atmosphere and the aroma of a wood fire to the rooms. Native American craftspeople worked in the shop during business hours, weaving, making baskets and jewelry, and attracting buyers. The shop was the first of its kind, and judging from the preponderance of such shops today, it's safe to say that Colter's project was a tremendous success. But, once the job was complete, there was no more work for her. She returned to St. Paul and her teaching job.

Mary did not hear from Fred Harvey again until 1904, after the Santa Fe Railway extended its line north from Williams, Arizona, to the South Rim of the Grand Canyon and commissioned Charles F. Whittlesey, the architect responsible for the Alvarado Hotel in Albuquerque, to design a new hotel at the South Rim. As the Harvey Company had specified at the Alvarado, plans called for an "Indian building" near the new hotel. The Santa Fe Railway hired Mary to design the entire building, exterior and interior.

Drawing on her training and instincts, Colter designed a building that belonged to the area. Hopi House, as it came to be called, was built of wood and stone native to the area and constructed primarily by Hopi workers.

Just as the Hopi had done for centuries, Mary built a solid square building on several levels, with stone steps and wooden ladders connecting one rooftop to the other. Massive interior rooms were covered with a light brown adobe-like plaster, and strong ceiling log beams supported smaller branches lying across them. The mud-like floors were actually cement. Hand-hewn tables laden with Indian baskets, pots, and other crafts filled the rooms. Brightly colored Navajo rugs dressed the floors, and a Totem Room displayed carved masks and bowls made by Indians from the Pacific Northwest. A special exhibit featured the Harvey collection of old Navajo blankets, winner of the grand prize at the 1904 St. Louis Exposition.

Hopi House opened on January 1, 1905. As she had done at the Alvarado, Colter arranged for Native American artisans to work daily in the shop, making pottery, blankets, jewelry, and baskets. Among them was the famed potter Nampeyo. Every evening at five o'clock, Hopi dancers entertained on the patio.

Although Hopi House was a tremendous success, the Harvey Company once again took its time before offering Colter another project. In 1910, the Fred Harvey Company and the Santa Fe Railway jointly offered Mary, now forty-one, a permanent position as company architect and designer. Impressed with her work at the Alvarado Indian Building and Hopi House, the companies believed she had the style, imagination, and strength of personality to see her ideas through to completion.

Colter's position was really quite remarkable, for at the time it was unheard of for a woman to excel professionally with such a large company, let alone be successful in a field almost exclusively male. The job required serving two masters. The Fred Harvey Company operated the restaurants and hotels of the railroad, but it owned only the furnishings; the buildings were owned by the railroad. Often her plans would be approved by the Harvey Company only to be altered by the railway engineers. Colter's will and strong personality helped her navigate the waters between these two powers. Admirers recall her as a "determined, positive person" who knew how to get her way. Critics remember her as "outspoken and sometimes even cruel."

Colter moved to the Harvey Company headquarters in Kansas City, Kansas, and began work on various projects unrelated to the Grand Canyon. In 1914 she was sent back to the Grand Canyon on orders from the company, which had recently completed the building of the Hermit Rim Road along the edge of the Grand Canyon. The eight-mile roadway was designed to accommodate horse-drawn touring stages; Fred Harvey wanted a building at the end of the road where tourists could have refreshments and enjoy the views.

Colter considered various designs, including the then-popular Swiss chalet style with gingerbread trim, but she decided to continue the indigenous style she'd used with Hopi House. When completed, Hermits Rest looked as if it had been haphazardly designed by someone hurriedly piling rocks for shelter. Railroad men teased her about the structure's appearance, saying, "Why don't you clean up this place?" to which Colter replied, "You can't imagine what it cost to make it look this old." An arch of uneven stones formed the entrance, a broken mission bell Colter found in New Mexico swung under the arch, and a lantern hung from one of the projecting stones.

Tourists sat on chairs made from twisted tree stumps and sipped coffee and lemonade on a porch extending to the edge of the Grand Canyon. Crude hand-hewn wooden posts supported the log beams of the porch. On cold days a fire burned in the massive fireplace, warming the interior. Tour participants relaxed by the fire, their feet on a bearskin rug, enjoying free tea and cookies as they viewed

Mary Elizabeth Jane Colter and unidenti-
fied man examine an oval twin tower
at Hovenweep, Utah, in preparation
for designing the Watchtower, 1931.
*Photograph courtesy of National Park
Service.*

the Grand Canyon through a row of large glass windows. Visitors not on a Harvey tour had to pay fifty cents for the refreshments and view.

Later in 1914 Colter designed Lookout Studio in similar fashion. Built on a point west of El Tovar, the Lookout provided outstanding views of the Grand Canyon. Stairs descended to the very brink of the canyon, and high-powered telescopes on the porch gave visitors a close-up glimpse of the Inner Gorge. Viewed from a distance, Lookout Studio seemed to be part of the Grand Canyon itself. Built of native stone with an uneven, ragged construction, Lookout Studio could be mistaken for an ancient Indian dwelling.

The Grand Canyon became a national park in 1919, and with World War I over and tourism on the rise, the Fred Harvey Company and the Santa Fe Railway received permission from the National Park Service to build tourist lodging at the bottom of the canyon along Bright Angel Creek. This facility, to be named Roosevelt Chalet, would permit mule riders to spend a night in the Grand Canyon. A swinging bridge across the Colorado River was completed in 1921, allowing easier passage across the river.

Mary, now fifty-two, rode a mule into the depths of the Grand Canyon to work on the design. Building the facility proved an onerous task. Although builders were able to use native stone, all other materials had to be hauled in by mule. Mules carried wooden crossbeams down the Bright Angel Trail and across the swinging bridge. No piece could be longer than six feet, and construction of longer beams to hold up the roofs took some careful calculations. When all was completed, the small lodge—containing a kitchen, dining room, and a storage area—and four individual cabins stood solidly along Bright Angel Creek.

Colter called the complex Phantom Ranch, naming it after nearby Phantom Creek, a far more intriguing moniker than Roosevelt Chalet. Gale Burak, who began hiking in the canyon in 1942 (see chapter nine), remembered Colter as "a very imaginative and intelligent person who was quick to get the romanticism and impact of a name that would lend intrigue to somebody. Certainly they wanted people to come down, and Phantom would be a very nice name for something down in the deep recesses, out of general sight on the rim of the Grand Canyon."

The origin of the creek's name remains a mystery, giving rise to some good stories. Some say the cliffs near the creek look like a phantom in the moonlight, and others contend that the ghost of John Wesley Powell wanders the canyon at night. It could be because cartographers in 1902 found this part of the Grand Canyon so narrow that its convolutions would appear and disappear on their topographic maps like a phantom. Whatever the origin of the name, Mary Colter liked it, and Phantom Ranch it remains.

On opening day, November 9, 1922, Colter rode a mule to Phantom Ranch and signed the register with a firm hand. Phantom Ranch today remains much as Colter designed it. The cottonwood trees have matured, the dining hall has been expanded, and more cabins and bunkhouses have been added, but the atmosphere persists. On a quiet evening, sitting on the porch of a cabin, one still hears the sound of Bright Angel Creek rushing to the Colorado. Too, the happy sound of laughter drifts from the beer hall each night, as people from around the world gather to celebrate their journey into the Grand Canyon.

Other projects kept Colter away from the Grand Canyon until 1931, when she returned to design a rest station, gift shop, and lookout at Desert View on the east end of the park's South Rim. Colter envisioned a structure that would provide dramatic views of the Grand Canyon. In her study of archeology, she learned about prehistoric Indian towers, particularly the cliff dwellings found at Mesa Verde and Canyon de Chelly.

Colter chartered a small plane to locate and study tower ruins. She then went overland to photograph and sketch the towers. Before finalizing her plans, she had a seventy-foot wooden platform built on the site. She climbed the platform to see if the height provided the view she wanted. She then made a table-sized clay model that included the proposed tower and an exact replica of the terrain.

"She was brilliant and a perfectionist," recalls Elizabeth Kent Meyer (profiled in chapter four), who lived at the Grand Canyon while the Desert View Watchtower was being built. "When that tower was halfway up, there was one rock in she didn't like. She made them take it out and replace it!"

The finished tower was not a replica but rather what Colter called a "re-creation" of an Indian watchtower. It was, at seventy feet tall and thirty feet in diameter, much larger than any known Indian tower. It was built of carefully selected native stones with an internal frame of steel made by the bridge department of the Santa Fe Railway.

The first floor of the tower, reached by climbing the stairs out of the sunken kiva, is called the Hopi Room. Mary chose Fred Kabotie, a Hopi artist, to decorate this room because "the Hopi people are the most closely associated with the Grand Canyon of any Pueblo Indians." Years later, in his book *Fred Kabotie: Hopi Indian Artist*, Kabotie told what it was like to work with Colter:

> Miss Colter was a very talented decorator with strong opinions, and quite elderly. I admired her work, and we got along well . . . most of the time. But once and awhile she would be difficult, especially when it came to matching colors. I remember one day she kept sending me up in the tower with little dabs of oil colors, too small to match. I don't know whether you'd call her thrifty or stingy, but I finally lost my patience. "Let me have that tube," I said, and slashed it open. I squeezed everything out, and stirred in the color I felt was right. "We're through—you've ruined everything," she gasped. "And you've used up all the paint!" "But Miss Colter, we haven't tried it yet," I said. I took a little dab and ran back up in the tower. Fortunately it matched, the very color we'd been seeking. So that saved my life—and hers.

Kabotie was not alone in his assessment of Colter. Others remarked about difficulties getting along with "Old Lady Colter." One employee recalled, "Everyone hated to see her come on the job." A co-worker, Harold Belt, said, "Like most creative people and people of large accomplishment, she was very demanding of those over whom she had authority." Her habit of calling the draftsmen and engineers who worked for her "boys" irritated workers. Yet, over the years, those who clashed with her came to respect her tremendous talent and determination.

The dedication of the Watchtower on May 13, 1933, was done with typical Harvey flourish. The kiva and tower were blessed by Hopi dancers. The strange staccato chant of the "Keeper of the Kiva" could be heard above the rattle of gourds, the clatter of tortoise shells, and the rhythmic thuds of the drums as he thanked the spirits for their presence. This was the first time such a blessing had been done away from the Hopi villages. Paramount News filmed the dedication and showed it in theaters across the nation. Radio networks broadcast live reports, and more than six hundred newspapers in forty-five states detailed the festivities. The Watchtower remains today as the most striking example of the genius of Mary Elizabeth Jane Colter.

The design and construction of Bright Angel Lodge on the South Rim was Colter's final major Grand Canyon project. When the Santa Fe Railway completed its line to the canyon, it had acquired the old Bright Angel Hotel, built in the 1890s by James Thurber. In 1934 the Fred Harvey Company decided to replace most of

Colter's Desert View Watchtower was completed in 1932. *Photograph by Betty Leavengood.*

the old structure. Colter first made models of stone buildings close to the rim, but the National Park Service did not approve of a building that blocked views of the Grand Canyon. She then designed a pioneer-style building in natural wood set back from the rim which met with park service approval.

A distinctive feature of Bright Angel Lodge is Colter's "geological" fireplace, designed to represent the rock layers of the Grand Canyon, from the water-smoothed stones of the Colorado River to the Kaibab Limestone that forms the top rim of the canyon. In typical Colter perfectionism, Mary was determined to have each stone personally selected by an expert on Grand Canyon geology, then packed up by mule and reassembled on site. Edwin D. McKee, park naturalist and expert on geology, agreed to help her. When he was unexpectedly called away from the canyon for several weeks, he turned the job over to a younger associate. Colter was furious. She excoriated McKee in an April 1, 1935, letter and informed him that she had to halt all construction until his return. McKee came back to help finish the fireplace. Today the geological fireplace is in the "history room" of Bright Angel Lodge.

A small village of individual cabins and several historically significant buildings share the grounds with the main Bright Angel Lodge, including the first post office at the Grand Canyon, a one-story log building of hand-squared log construction, and a cabin that belonged to Buckey O'Neill, a colorful, early-day sheriff who died fighting with Teddy Roosevelt's Rough Riders in the Spanish American War. Colter's plan protected both structures. On June 22, 1935, two thousand people attended the barbeque celebrating the opening of Bright Angel Lodge.

Mary Jane Colter retired from the Santa Fe Railway Company on January 1, 1944, at the age of seventy-five. In 1946, when tourism surged at the Grand Canyon, Colter rode a mule into the canyon at age seventy-seven to make some alterations to Phantom Ranch. Two years later, she officially retired from the Fred Harvey Company.

Colter traveled extensively in her later years, thanks to pensions from the Fred Harvey Company and the Santa Fe Railway, and a lifetime pass on the Santa Fe Railway system. She wore false teeth that didn't fit properly, and comments about her in her later years invariably refer to her clicking teeth. One day Earl Shirley, the manager of Fred Harvey Transportation, was driving Colter from the canyon to the Del Rio Ranch in Chino Valley. At one point, unable to bear the clicking of her teeth further, he stopped the car and said, "Miss Colter, you are just going to have to remove your teeth or else you will have to walk the rest of the way."

Before her death in 1958 at age eighty-eight, Mary donated her magnificent collection of Indian jewelry to Mesa Verde National Park, in addition to $2,000 to buy glass cases for the collection. She bequeathed her large estate, $150,000, to over fifty persons and organizations.

Today, when women enter most professions with relative ease, it is hard to appreciate the difficulties Mary Elizabeth Jane Colter faced. To be on a construction site, ordering male workers to redo their work and to get it right, required strength of character and belief in herself. Colter left no diaries and gave no interviews, leaving us to speculate on just how deeply the canyon affected her. We do know she was somewhat ahead of her time in her recognition of the beauty and talent of indigenous peoples' craftwork. How lucky we are that her genius remains a part of the Grand Canyon and that she had the foresight to procure and maintain the canyon's natural elegance through her work.

CHAPTER THREE

Summers on Bright Angel Point

ELIZABETH WYLIE MCKEE
(1872—1957)

by Michael F. Anderson, Ph.D.

L ong before Xanterra, Delaware North, and other corporations evolved to accommodate the late twentieth century's tourism industry, entrepreneurs arrived at western national parks to test the viability of tourism as a regional economy. These pioneers appeared at Grand Canyon's South Rim following construction of the Atlantic & Pacific Railroad across northern Arizona in 1881–1883. A half dozen or more modest tourism operations took root within a decade of the first locomotives, and persisted for two generations before surrendering to the Santa Fe Railway, Fred Harvey Company, and demands of a fast-expanding market.

On the North Rim, Elizabeth Wylie McKee, her husband Thomas, and seven-year-old son Robert established a tourist camp at the very tip of Bright Angel Point in 1917. Their arrival seems late considering that small businesses on the South Rim were nearly extinct by that year. But the North Rim and larger "Arizona Strip," separated from the rest of Arizona by a very long, mile-deep crevasse and lacking a railroad or any roads other than wagon tracks, remained a mysterious landscape to all but a few Southern Paiute and Mormon residents. For example, earlier in 1917, Elizabeth's brothers, Fred and Clinton, became seriously lost while searching for Bright Angel Point in their Model-T Roadster. Taking one of many wrong turns along the rutted two-track from Hurricane, Utah, they ran out of gas in the vicinity of Mt. Trumbull and survived only because an amenable sheep herder with a wagon towed them back to civilization nearly two weeks later.

A tourism enterprise in such country seemed dubious to many, certainly to Fred and Clinton, but others disagreed. The Union Pacific Railroad, like the Santa Fe south of Grand Canyon, was eager to join the late-nineteenth-century railroad trend of building upscale tourism facilities at western national parks. In 1916 Union Pacific managers invited Elizabeth's father, William Wallace Wylie, to open primitive camps at Mukuntuweap National Monument, which would become Zion National Park in 1919, and at Grand Canyon's North Rim—with his own money, of course. Their transparent strategy was to observe his efforts, assess demand, and then replace his pioneering efforts with resort accommodations once visitation justified investment.

Elizabeth Wylie McKee operated the first tourist camp on the North Rim of the Grand Canyon. *Photograph courtesy of Martha Krueger.*

The Union Pacific chose William Wylie to lay the groundwork because he long ago had done the same at Yellowstone National Park. An educator in Lyons, Iowa, in the 1870s, Wylie moved his family, including seven-year-old Elizabeth, to Bozeman, Montana, in 1879 to become Montana's superintendent of schools. He fell in love with the nearby national park, began guiding tourists in 1881, secured his first lease for a tourism camp in 1893, and quickly developed the "Wylie Way" concept that would be adopted at Zion, Grand Canyon, and many other national parks. Distinguishing characteristics included a central services building surrounded by "tent-cabins," hybrid structures with wooden floors and walls to a height of four feet to keep out mud and snow, topped by three-foot walls and roofs of striped canvas, partitioned with sheets into several rooms, nicely furnished, and heated with a Sibly Stove. Other commonalities among camps included guided trips into the backcountry—first by horseback, later by wagon, automobile, and touring bus—and nightly campfires where the proprietor offered local lore, lectures in natural and human history, skits, and other entertainment.

While William Wylie traveled to Zion in the spring of 1917 to establish the camp that he and his wife would manage, daughter Elizabeth and son-in-law Thomas McKee agreed to open the camp on the canyon's North Rim later that summer. Like nearly all early South Rim tourism enterprises, the North Rim Wylie Way Camp promised an uncertain future for the McKees, who were by no means wealthy. They invested everything they had and borrowed more just to get started. And although they would later employ as many as a dozen young men and women from local communities, they were on their own the first few years. Who were these people, and why would they agree to enter the tourism business in such an unlikely location?

Thomas Herron McKee, born in Clarksburg, West Virginia, in 1872, moved to Bismarck, North Dakota with his parents in the 1880s, settling in Miles City, Montana, by 1888. In the 1890s he worked as superintendent of mines for the Northern Pacific Railroad, and for a number of summer seasons helped the Wylies at Yellowstone before earning a law degree at Columbia University. He practiced publications law in New York City at the turn of the century, editing some of the more libelous words from Upton Sinclair's *The Jungle* (for which Sinclair never forgave him); working for prominent publishers like Frank Doubleday and S.S. McClure; and, as president of *Hampton's Magazine*, hiring the renowned novelist Theodore Dreiser as managing editor.

Less is known of Elizabeth Wylie prior to the 1910s. She was born in 1872, perhaps in Iowa where her family lived prior to the move to Montana. She grew up in Bozeman and worked summers at Yellowstone while attending school. "Lizzie" or "Liz," as she was called by many, attended Wellesley College where she earned a bachelor's degree in biology in 1897. She also completed a year of graduate work at Wellesley in 1901, studying fungi and lichens, while teaching high school in Gallatin County, Montana. Elizabeth and Thomas, who no doubt met and worked side by side at the Yellowstone Wylie Way Camp in the 1890s, married on September 9, 1903, honeymooning—where else?—at Yellowstone. It is uncertain, but probable, that the couple then returned to New York City since Thomas was senior partner in the law firm of McKee, Frost & Company in that year.

The McKees' only child, Robert, was born in 1910, and his impending arrival together with Thomas's health (he had contracted tuberculosis) may have been catalysts for the family's return to the West. Later in life, Robert summarized his father's diaries, which indicate that they were living in the Pasadena, California, area by 1915. Thomas was still in precarious health in that year, but earning money at the occasional practice of law while trying to patent a homestead near Victorville. Elizabeth augmented their income by substitute teaching. So it is not too surprising that when the call came from W.W. Wylie to establish a camp at the North Rim, the McKees would be amenable to spending their summers in the crisp, clean air of the Kaibab Plateau while perhaps earning a little money to make ends meet.

Ends proved far apart at Bright Angel Point for the first few years. The couple had to scrape up sufficient cash to purchase materials, then build cabins and other camp structures themselves. Elizabeth arranged for supplies with the Mormon ZCMI store in Salt Lake City, hundreds of miles to the north, at a time when freight still moved in wagons at considerable cost. Transportation for any purpose, in fact, was costly, difficult, and time consuming. Over the years the McKees would try different routes and means to commute between Pasadena and the North Rim each summer and autumn. Elizabeth and Robert, like most tourists, often chose the Union Pacific's Salt Lake & Los Angeles line as far as Lund, Utah, then managed a ride by automobile to Cedar City, Zion (where they would visit Elizabeth's parents), Hurricane, and across the Arizona Strip to Kanab and Fredonia. Provisions for each season's immediate needs could be purchased at Kanab, where Edwin Dilworth "Uncle Dee" Woolley, the local Mormon stake president, operated a general store. Thereafter followed an eighty-mile journey up the Kaibab Plateau to Jacob Lake and on to Bright Angel Point via the Grand Canyon Highway, a wagon road upgraded for automobiles in 1913.

The physical labor involved in maintaining a tourist camp with little hired help made things that much more difficult. Despite occasional respiratory problems, Thomas was responsible for turning wood and canvas into buildings, as well as maintaining them throughout the season. He obtained the camp's fresh meat through an arrangement with local cattlemen, whereby he dispatched and butchered any cow he happened upon and paid later. He and Robert also had the disagreeable task of digging privies in the resistant Kaibab Limestone, using dynamite to loosen the soil. Privies had to be relocated every few weeks. When Robert wrote his memoirs in the 1980s, he recalled the interminable task of making holes for human as well as kitchen wastes, among a long list of other duties, like hauling wood for kitchen and cabins, pumping gasoline, and dumping trash.

Robert's primary responsibility, an important one, was hauling water from a spring not far below the rim in Transept Canyon. He was assisted by Bright Angel, nicknamed Brighty, a gray, gelded burro made famous years later in a children's book by Marguerite Henry. Thomas McKee did considerable research into Brighty's long life (1884–1921) and published his biography, which prompted Henry's book. The real Brighty was an intelligent animal, fastidious in his personal habits, owned by none and loved by all, including local cowboys, tourists, and especially Robert McKee. Abandoned by prospectors who probably drowned at the mouth of Bright Angel Creek in the early 1890s, the burro chose to winter at the Colorado River for the rest of his life, but each spring ambled up to the rim to greet his friends. With the wisdom and perhaps arthritis of advancing age, Brighty was not especially fond of work, but accepted his role as water carrier, for a price. Each day the duo made four to seven trips down to the spring, the boy loading twenty gallons of water into carriers, the burro taking his sweet time climbing back up to camp, where he insisted that unloading take place in the shade and he be paid in pancakes.

While Brighty and the boys occupied themselves with assorted chores and what little guiding was required in these early years, Elizabeth directed operations. Not only did she manage the few workers they employed and perform sundry tasks expected of women at the turn of the twentieth century, she was the effective and *official* manager, her name and title displayed prominently on formal stationary. Her position was owed to her father, who had arranged for the business, "owned" the permits issued first by the U.S. Forest Service and later by the National Park

Wylie Way Camp's brightly striped tent cabins offered relative comfort for the time on the North Rim. *Photograph courtesy of Martha Krueger.*

The camp "family" at Bright Angel Point: Elizabeth McKee and son Robert, far right; Thomas McKee, far left; Brighty the Burro and camp staff, center, ca. 1918. *Photograph courtesy of Martha Krueger.*

Service, and believed that his daughter could do it given her experience at Yellowstone. Robert later recalled that his mother was a "very capable and hard-working manager," ordering supplies, paying bills, handling reservations and business correspondence, banking, supervising employees, even acting as nurse for family, workers, and guests. "The lamp in her tent," wrote Robert, "burned late into the night."

Letters exchanged between Elizabeth and park officials portray her as an articulate woman who stated her business operations, desires, and complaints clearly, and that National Park Service administrators recognized her interests, authority, and value to North Rim tourism.

The years 1917 to 1921 were lean. The McKees invested $13,000 in those years, borrowing some from Elizabeth's father, while at best breaking even on operations. The Union Pacific advertised their services to its rail passengers, and the Parry Brothers of Cedar City delivered these passengers to the camp in automobile stages. But it took time for a tourist trade to develop, and few visitors braved a North Rim journey in their own vehicles. Elizabeth charged standard canyon rates for the time—$1.50 for a cabin and for each meal—but because expenses were much higher at the North Rim, they sold meals, gasoline, postcards, and other items at little more than cost.

Elizabeth, as manager and accountant, was well aware of their financial condition. Responding to Park Superintendent W.W. Crosby's request in 1922 for discount rates for park rangers, who, because there were no NPS facilities at the North Rim until 1924, lodged and took their meals at the Wylie camp, she wrote, "this camp has never yet paid its cost of operation." Shortly thereafter she wrote Crosby and Stephen Mather a letter, one of many over the years to the NPS Washington office and the park's first six superintendents, succinctly arguing the financial quandary she and other pioneer concessioners faced doing business with federal land managers. The Fred Harvey Company and other well-financed concessions used similar arguments, with hardly more intelligence but considerably more political influence, to obtain twenty- and thirty-year contracts:

We are now rather anxiously considering the problem presented by the tourist subsistence situation on the North Rim. . . .

The Wylie Company, of which I am Manager, has gone on from season to season since the creation of the Park, taking care of the tourist travel pending the grant of a long term lease. . . .

We went there in 1917 under promise from the Forest Service of a twenty year lease, to contain a monopoly clause, . . . the written lease to be delivered as soon as the necessary formalities could be complied with. We established the camp, but the lease never came. . . . [T]he plans of your Department not having matured, we have been simply bridging the gap. . . .

To meet the needs of the coming season the capacity of the camp must be doubled. This will require new money in substantial amount, which we do not feel like putting in . . . .[T]he business itself cannot borrow a cent. Operating as we are under short term leases, banks and other lenders do not consider the enterprise a good business risk.

If we had a twenty year license, guarded against ruinous competition, we should be most glad to go on, and the enterprise could then be easily financed.

North Rim tourism had begun to catch on by 1922, when nearly a thousand private vehicles and three thousand people managed to reach Bright Angel Point.

But, as any business owner knows, growth poses challenges. Elizabeth found herself between a rock and a hard place, the same conundrum that had caused many early tourism operators to exit the South Rim. Mather, a millionaire businessman, well understood the need to borrow to facilitate cash flow, but refused to work with small operators who had a difficult time financing his vision and often proved "a pain in the posterior" with their demands and squabbles amongst themselves. It is clear by his correspondence that he considered Elizabeth a competent manager, but he preferred to extend the cooperation she sought to large investors like the Fred Harvey Company, which received one of the first twenty-year exclusive contracts issued by the National Park Service in 1920. Elizabeth also worried about competition from the Kaibab Lodge, which opened in 1922 at VT Park, north of the park boundary, and other enterprises that might take root at the North Rim unless administrators ensured her exclusivity. Rejected by park administrators, she nonetheless found the money to upgrade facilities for the 1923 season, and again in 1925–1926, through loans and earnings.

W.W. Wylie sold his Zion interests to the Union Pacific in 1923, and then transferred ownership of the North Rim camp to Elizabeth the following season. By 1926 the McKees could lodge, feed, and entertain as many as 120 people, and had built a new central services building, installed "fly-free" privies and electric lights, augmented their line of products, and increased the number of guided tours, conducted almost daily to Cliff Spring, Cape Royal, Point Imperial, and Point Sublime. These were good years when the couple might have realized return for past labors, but because visitation had increased steadily to 14,500 in 1926, the Union Pacific and National Park Service decided that the time had come for real investment. The corporate-federal partnership envisioned a "grand circle" tourism loop for Zion, Bryce, Pipe Spring, and Grand Canyon's North Rim, one that included new regional and in-park automotive roads, a bridge at Marble Canyon, and re-engineered park trails. At Bright Angel Point they wanted a grand lodge, new NPS facilities, and very expensive water and power developments that the concessioner would have to finance.

The plan, which Elizabeth did not learn about until late 1926, was far beyond what she could afford. Its dimensions were written into a prospectus, or "request for bid," with the certainty that there would be only one bidder: the Utah Parks Company, a recently formed concession subsidiary of the Union Pacific Railroad. NPS policy then, as now, required that the successful bidder pay existing concessioners

Robert McKee and his pal Brighty worked together to supply the camp with water from a spring below the canyon rim. *Photograph courtesy of Martha Krueger.*

the value of their improvements, but nothing for business value. Stephen Mather took an interest in the sale but left negotiations to Utah Parks' managers and the McKees, who grudgingly settled for $25,000 in May 1927. Utah Parks managed the Wylie Way Camp for the 1927 season while building Grand Canyon Lodge and its other facilities on the North Rim, which opened in June 1928—a date that marks the very end of the pioneer era at Grand Canyon National Park.

Despite their disappointment at the sale price, a decade of little profit, and a lot of hard work, the McKees retained their interest in tourist camps. By 1928 they purchased the Cherokee Lodge at June Lake, near Mammoth, in Mono County, California, and were at work building another lodge similar to a Wylie Way Camp at nearby Gull Lake. If Thomas's diary is any indication, the couple worked even harder at their new facilities, with equal reward or lack thereof, until selling the Cherokee in 1940 for $15,000. They continued at Gull Lake until the outbreak of World War II at least, when Thomas went to work for the defense industry in Los Angeles.

William Wylie died in southern California in 1930 (his wife in 1928), after a long, productive life as an educator and trend-setting tourism operator of the western national parks. Thomas and Elizabeth McKee retired to their home in Alhambra, California, where they spent the rest of their lives. Thomas turns up in the 1950s in park service correspondence with Lon Garrison, assistant superintendent of Grand Canyon National Park; with Marguerite Henry; and with *Arizona Highways Magazine*, as an expert on the early years at Grand Canyon's North Rim. Despite his bout with tuberculosis, he survived to age ninety, dying at San Gabriel, California, in 1961, and adding substance to the adage, "go west young man." What Elizabeth did in retirement until her death in 1957 is unclear, but she had certainly earned her rest working so many years for her parents and then with her husband and son in the early years of western tourism. Records indicate that Elizabeth McKee, along with Catherine Verkamp in the 1940s and Suzie Verkamp in recent years, are the only women to ever formally own as well as manage a tourist concession at Grand Canyon National Park.

Robert McKee edited his father's diaries and recorded his own memoirs in the late 1980s, before dying at Sonora, California, in 1992. His experiences at North Rim and June Lake apparently dissuaded him from continuing the family tradition of running tourist camps, but he stayed close to home forging a thirty-five-year career with the telephone company in Los Angeles. Robert's daughter, Martha McKee Krueger, continued to visit the North Rim on occasion. One of her prized possessions is a painting by Gunnar Widforss, a present from the brilliant artist to his friend and Martha's grandmother, Elizabeth Wylie McKee.

CHAPTER FOUR

A Harvey Girl

ELIZABETH KENT MEYER
(1907—1999)

Crisp. Clean. Starched. Pressed. And pretty, very pretty.

Those were the first impressions anyone had upon seeing a Harvey Girl for the first time. Their long black skirts, smartly hemmed eight inches from the floor, were met at the waist with crisp white blouses that were buttoned tightly to the neck. Topping off the uniform was the attractive Harvey Girl smile, worn on a face where, by contract, makeup was prohibited. Harvey Girls were the very picture of cleanliness, their inviting demeanor the very essence of hospitality. By delivering such sharp and friendly service, these exuberant, hard-working young women helped Fred Harvey build his tourism empire.

Harvey, an ambitious English immigrant whose early work on the railroad helped him develop his reputable services for railroad customers, did not originally hire women as waitresses. The idea surfaced after a group of male waiters at the Harvey House in Raton, New Mexico, got into a drunken midnight brawl and were too battered up to report to work the next morning. A furious Fred Harvey fired all the waiters and the manager. The new manager, Tom Gable, suggested to Harvey that he hire women because they were less likely "to get likkered up and go on tears." Harvey agreed.

Critics of Harvey's plan thought the idea laughable. For one thing, female waitresses at the time were better known as "saloon girls," and they typically delivered more than a steak and a beer to those they waited on. It would be difficult to replace the "saloon girl" reputation with the wholesome, clean image Harvey wanted. For another thing, critics could not imagine how Harvey would entice women to come

Betty Kent in her Harvey Girl uniform. *Photograph courtesy of Elizabeth Kent Meyer.*

to the West, where they'd have to abandon city civility and endure the wild world of the new frontier. The men who populated the West and frequented its saloons were miners, ranchers, gamblers, cowboys, and other rough-and-ready types. No civilized woman, critics thought, would willingly subject herself to the likes of them or to a society that permitted such behavior.

The critics were wrong. Thousands applied. Why? The prospect of finding a husband was certainly one reason. The 1870 census listed 172,000 women and

385,000 men living between the Mississippi River and the Pacific Ocean. The men of the West may have been roughly hewn, but there were lots of them, and a few good ones were likely to be found in the bunch. With women outnumbering men in the East two to one, many women found their prospects of marriage slim to none and so went west eagerly, bringing with them visions of romance and the opportunity for marriage to willing frontiersmen. Women from lower-income families especially viewed this as an opportunity to improve their lives.

Harvey advertised in midwestern and eastern newspapers and in women's magazines for "young women eighteen to forty years of age, of good character, attractive and intelligent" to come and work in the West. The requirements were strict. A Harvey Girl must be educated, which at that time meant finishing high school or at least eighth grade. She must speak clearly, have good manners, and be neat in appearance. Typical contracts required a six-, nine-, or twelve-month commitment; when a young woman signed a contract she agreed to learn the Harvey system, follow instructions to the letter, obey employee rules, accept whatever location she was assigned, and abstain from marriage for the duration of her initial contract. If she broke the marriage contract, she forfeited her pay and railroad pass home.

Successfully beating the odds, Harvey hired his famous "girls," and soon they were a key part of his business. His restaurants and hotels became increasingly popular among late nineteenth- and early twentieth-century tourists, and Harvey Girls became the emblem of superior service. They wore the Harvey Girl uniform proudly, and they stood out among women.

Girls typically lived upstairs in the facility they worked in or in a nearby dormitory. Housemothers enacted a strict curfew, and when girls did go out, they were closely chaperoned. Although men were allowed to meet with the girls in the parlor, they were not allowed in the bedrooms. The rigors of such strict rules were bound to try the will of even the best-intentioned Harvey Girl. Add to this that most Harvey Girls were independent, adventurous, and resourceful, and you had a recipe for mischief. Many of them had stories to tell about climbing the trellis or bribing the cook to let them in after hours.

Elizabeth ("Betty") Priest was in many ways a typical Harvey Girl. She was fun-loving, hard-working, and above all, independent. Having been abandoned by her father at the age of fifteen, Betty was shuffled from household to household. She became self-reliant, a trait that helped make her a capable Harvey Girl.

"My mother and father separated when I was only three and a half," Betty explained, "and mother had other kids after me. My father got custody of me, then left me with a cousin. He never came back after me until I was ready for high school." Betty moved with her father and his second wife to Prescott, Arizona, where she attended school and worked part-time in a hotel. "One day before I went to school, my father asked me for my check, which I had just gotten," Betty said, "and when I came home, he and his wife were gone."

Betty was fortunate to find a job caring for the daughter of the school orchestra leader. She lived with them and finished high school. "The State of Arizona located my father, and he sent me a pass to go to Albuquerque, where he had relocated, but I was afraid to go. I told the officer about a relative, Mother Holladay, in Kansas City, so the Santa Fe Railway gave me a charity pass to go to Kansas City."

It was while she was in Kansas City that Betty took a dare from a friend to apply at the Fred Harvey Company office at Union Station. She was just seventeen. Betty was accepted into the Harvey Girl program and passed her training with flying colors.

Early on, she learned to listen for the sound of the train whistle—a sound that energized the Harvey staff into frantic activity. "The porters took orders from people on the train and radioed them ahead, so we'd know to set up the dining room. Customers could have a full meal—salad or soup, and a full dinner, and a dessert, and coffee—all for a dollar. A mile or so out, the train blew the whistle. The manager met the customers at the door and told them which way to go and where to be seated. We did all of our own set-ups. We didn't have busboys in the dining room."

Betty loved the work, especially the money, which meant freedom and independence. "I was able to pay back all Mother Holladay's charge accounts that I had bought clothes on and still was able to buy a beautiful blue coat with a genuine squirrel collar." Part of that coat money was earned in Kansas City, where she had been sent on a temporary assignment to work at the Republican Convention.

"I will never forget the biggest tip I ever got was in Kansas City at Union Station," Betty explained. "There were four men playing poker at the table. They had all ordered special steaks, so I came out with the steaks and they were piping hot. I said, 'You have to eat your steaks now.' One replied, 'We're not through here. This is a big pot,' and another one said, 'Now what'll we do with the pot? Who's going to win this pot? We're not going to divide it.' Then someone said, 'I guess the waitress wins it!' and they scraped the money into my apron pocket. I had $67! I've never forgotten that $67."

Betty jumped at an opportunity to work at the Alvarado Hotel in Albuquerque, New Mexico. "I wanted to go west because I knew that my father was the freight man on the run out of Albuquerque, and I thought I might find him." She had not seen her father since he had abandoned her two years earlier in Arizona.

She did find her father in Albuquerque. She also found a man whom she thought was her true love, a barber who worked on the Santa Fe train that ran between Albuquerque and San Francisco. They became engaged and "we made arrangements that I would come to San Francisco to get married, and then we would travel back to Albuquerque together," Betty explained. "My father was driving to San Francisco to get his wife, so I rode along with him." By this time, Betty had completed her initial contract with the Fred Harvey Company and was free to get married.

As fate would have it, Betty and her father decided to stop at the Grand Canyon on the way. "I walked into the dining room at Bright Angel Lodge, and there was the head waitress I had worked for at the Alvarado. She'd been transferred to the canyon. 'You're an answer to my prayers,' she said when she saw me. 'Can you go

A group of typical Harvey Girls, ca. 1895. *Photograph courtesy of the Kansas State Historical Society, Topeka, Kansas.*

The Bright Angel "Gang." *Photograph courtesy of Elizabeth Kent Meyer.*

to work?' Sure, Betty replied, "and the next morning I was on the floor!"

That evening, unknown to her, Betty was being "checked out." Two Santa Fe Railway workers sat on the railing outside the lodge watching the new Harvey Girl through the dining room windows. Bill Kent and John Cunningham considered it their duty to check out anyone new to the Grand Canyon, especially a Harvey Girl.

"Who's the new girl?" asked Bill.

"That's my girlfriend Alice's new roommate," John replied. "Stick around and when they get off work, I'll introduce you."

The two young men sat awhile longer, their backs to the Grand Canyon, watching as the attractive young woman in the spotless white and black uniform hurried about inside. Finally, Bill turned to John and said, "I'm going to marry that girl!"

"That's the silliest thing I ever heard. You haven't even met her yet," Johnny laughed.

"I don't care," Bill retorted, "I'm going to marry her."

Betty met Bill at the Saturday night dance. "I forgot all about the barber!" Betty laughed. Harvey regulations normally forbade dating among employees, but the Grand Canyon, a world unto itself, rendered such regulations unenforceable.

Despite the romantic diversions, Betty put in long, hard days at Bright Angel

Lodge, which was at that time a collection of cabins with a cafe-dining hall. "We worked according to how the buses and the trail trips went," Betty explained. Her day began at 6:30 A.M., when the mule riders came in for breakfast, followed at 7:30 A.M. by people taking bus tours. Once they left she'd have a short break until lunch, when the bus tours returned. Afternoons were free until dinnertime, when the mule riders and afternoon tours returned.

Betty enjoyed her afternoons. She liked to walk along the rim of the canyon, looking out over the edge. Its vast expanse made life seem full of promise and possibilities, and Betty was glad to be right where she was. Some afternoons she'd take a nap. Other days she'd sit in the sun and chat with fellow Harvey Girls about their dates and the customers.

One of Betty's favorite customers was none other than the governor of Arizona, W.H.P. Hunt. "Governor Hunt came to the canyon several times when the union was trying to organize us," she explained, "and he had a colored chauffeur that drove with him everywhere." On Governor Hunt's first trip, he got a table for lunch at El Tovar while his chauffeur parked the car. "When the chauffeur came into the dining room and sat down with the governor, the waiter said, 'No, you go in with the colored fellows where the train porters are. You have to eat in there—you can't eat in the dining room,'" Betty said. "Governor Hunt was furious. He went down to Bright Angel, and he asked the manager, 'Can my chauffeur eat with me?' The manager said, 'Yes, you both can eat any place you want to in here.' And so, he and his chauffeur always had a table at Bright Angel. He was very nice and easy to wait on."

Aside from the excitement of waiting on Governor Hunt, it was the "after hours" life that Betty remembered best. After the tours ended, the restaurants closed, and the tourists had gone for the day, the rising moon brought more than light to the canyon. Harvey employees played as hard as they worked. They went on hay rides, held dances, played cards, and brought in movies. Couples would steal away under the cover of night to take long walks (with some long pauses!) along the rim of the canyon. They'd frequent their favorite nooks tucked under the rim to look at the stars or watch a storm sweep across the horizon. This is how dating at the canyon came to be called "rimming," and between the continual arrival of Harvey Girls and the steady supply of working men, there was a whole lot of rimming going on.

Before long, Betty and Bill began "rimming" in earnest. "There are so many wonderful shelves or cave-like spots where you can sit and hang your feet over the edge," Betty remembered. "With a 3,000-foot drop below you, it really was an exciting place for spooning. One of our favorite places was under the Lookout Studio, where one could look at the peaceful moonlight in the big Grand Canyon."

Just six weeks after he set eyes on her, Bill Kent offered Betty a diamond ring. She promptly rejected it. "The fourteenth of August!" she exclaimed. "That's too soon! I don't know you that well." But Bill persisted, and ten days later Betty accepted the ring. She admitted that Bill had his own version of the engagement. "Bill loved to tell the story that I proposed while he had his back against the railing under the Lookout Studio. He'd say he had to say 'yes' or I would have pushed him 3,000 feet into the canyon!"

Betty and Bill married at Rowe's Well, a small tourist camp west of the village, on October 6, 1926. Soon after, Betty resigned from her job at the lodge, and the couple moved to a rented room in Grand Canyon Village. Their room had an oil stove, a table, chairs, bed, and a dresser. Modest beginnings, but serviceable for life together at the canyon. Making herself a proper housewife, however, proved more challenging for Betty, who was better at serving food than cooking it. "At the time I was a teenager who didn't know how to boil water, and at 7,000 feet most real cooks didn't know either," Betty laughed.

Betty rode the train into Williams twice a month for provisions. "All Santa Fe Railway wives met their husbands at the depot on paydays—the sixth and twenty-first of each month. Our husbands cashed their checks, and we got our $20 and left on the 10:00 A.M. train to buy our groceries," Betty explained. "I only spent $10 at the 'Pay and Take It' and saved the rest for emergencies. We arrived home at 3:00 P.M. Our husbands would meet us at the 'Y' where the train backed in so they'd be headed out the next morning."

Money went a long way in those days. "For $10 we bought flour in twenty-five-pound sacks, coffee, lard, and canned goods. It was all the boys could do to carry the big boxes home. We didn't know what fresh vegetables were, being so far from Phoenix and Los Angeles. I still like canned peas," she allowed. Betty purchased butter and eggs by the case from a farmer in Utah. A dairy in Phoenix delivered milk and cream once a week. The men hunted for venison and antelope on their days off.

Betty would never again eat rabbit because of all the rabbit she had in the early days of her marriage. "On Sundays, the men would have a rabbit hunt. They'd catch the little train that went into Anita and they would divide into two teams, about fifteen men on each team. They'd have shotguns and gunny sacks and hunt for about three hours. The losing team had to clean and cook all of the rabbits and serve a big meal at the Fred Harvey Mess Hall. I never knew there were so many ways to cook rabbit—stewed, fried, baked, á la king!"

As was true for most of the American Southwest, the scarcest item at the Grand Canyon was—and still is—water. All water had to be brought in by train from the Harvey Company ranch at Del Rio, Arizona, where the company pastured the mules in the winter. The train came in twice a week in the winter and every day during the summer. "We had to be careful about water," Betty explained, "because we were charged fifteen cents a hundred gallons. We put bricks in the toilet and saved the bath water to fill the

Betty Kent in her wedding dress, Grand Canyon, Arizona, 1926. *Photograph courtesy of Elizabeth Kent Meyer.*

tank. Bill took his showers at the Power House, and I took spit baths, only taking a tub bath once a week."

Betty and Bill spent the first years of their marriage happily, living amidst the canyon that had brought the Harvey Girl and railroad worker together. But 1929 was an unlucky year for most Americans, and those at the canyon were not spared the effects of the stock market crash. Bill's hours were cut, and to make ends meet Betty donned her Harvey Girl uniform and went back to work as a waitress at the Bright Angel lunch counter for thirty-five dollars a month plus meals and tips.

Tourism at the Grand Canyon dwindled as the Depression deepened, and Betty eventually lost her job at the lodge. Bill's hours were cut yet again, and he tried to offset the loss by working as a Harvey tour driver. Betty worked part-time at Babbitt's General Store near Grand Canyon Village and at the telephone company as a relief operator. The telephone office was the hub of the town as well as a source for one of Betty's more amusing stories. "The telephone office was next door to the naturalist's office," she explained. "One evening I was working relief when, to my amazement, the door of the naturalist office cracked open and a big six-foot snake crawled out and into the phone office. I climbed on top of the switchboard and called the ranger!"

Although money was tight in the mid-1930s, Betty and Bill jumped at the opportunity to move into one of the new village houses built by the Santa Fe Railway. "We couldn't afford to buy much furniture. We sent to Montgomery Ward for a pretty gray enamel cook stove and a linoleum rug for the floor and found a discarded Fred Harvey table and old chairs. Then we bought a bed and dresser from Babbitt's. The rest of the house we left empty."

Hard times seemingly made for the best times at the Grand Canyon. "If only that hall could have told stories about the parties we held there," Betty laughed. When prohibition was in full swing—1920–1933—bootleg whiskey always seemed to be available. "When Millie and Johnny Schmidtkie were married, we had a big punch bowl by the window, and everyone that came in added some whiskey. By 10:30 P.M. the punch was pure moonshine and bootleg whiskey. Bill was dancing with Millie, and they fell down. Everyone kept on dancing over them. I had to clean his suit, and there were footprints all over it!"

The Great Depression was hard on all Americans, and the stories of how people retained a positive outlook throughout its long term are remarkable. Despite Betty and Bill's financial difficulties, Betty remembered mostly good times at the Grand Canyon during the Depression years. "There was no entertainment in the village," she explained, so, typical of Harvey employees past and present, "we had to make our own. The park service built a community hall behind the Fred Harvey garage, so all social activities were held there, including Saturday night dances, Sunday morning services, and Sunday night movies. The Fred Harvey Company rented the movies, and one of the chauffeurs ran the projector. A group of guides and chauffeurs organized an orchestra."

One of the most memorable Depression parties she remembered was the unofficial dedication of the Desert View Watchtower on New Year's Eve, 1934. The tower had been officially dedicated in May 1933 but, Betty said, "Our gang decided it needed a real dedication. The evening girl stationed at the tower was one of us, so we had quite a party." "One of us" meant the girl stationed at the tower had the spirit of a true Harvey Girl, only they weren't climbing trellises this time. "We sneaked in food and liquor. By midnight, all the men that could make it up the stairs took their shotguns to the top and shot into the air." Happy New Year.

Betty recalled Christmas as being especially wonderful at the Grand Canyon. "We always had Christmas caroling throughout the town, and then we went to the community hall for Santa Claus. The Indians came in from the reservation in wagons, camping out for three days so that the youngsters could see Santa Claus and get an apple and orange and a sack of hard candy. It was such a wonderful treat, and they came every year."

The advent of World War II brought a close to Bill and Betty's Grand Canyon life. Tourism slowed to a trickle. "Anyone that didn't have children was asked to go work in the war plants," Betty said, and so she and Bill went to California, where she found a job with Douglas Aircraft.

Elizabeth Kent Meyer, Phoenix, Arizona, 1996. *Photograph by Betty Leavengood.*

Although he was forty-five years old, Bill enlisted in the army and was sent to Alaska as a mechanic. "When he left, he took a front door key. He said he wanted to know he had a place to come home to. I'll never forget the day he came home," Betty said. "He caught a plane out of Fairbanks headed for the United States, then caught a bus from the airport. I didn't know he was coming, and I worked nights—so I was asleep when he came in the door and yelled, 'Throw the sailors out, I'm home!'"

The former Harvey Girl and the Santa Fe Railway worker remained in Los Angeles. They missed their beloved Grand Canyon, but as Betty pointed out, "most of our friends had left, too." Many of their friends also had relocated to Los Angeles, so it was not too difficult a choice to stay. And though the canyon was a thousand miles away, its grandeur and memories of good times dwelled in their hearts. "To go back would not have been the same," Betty added. "We were at the Grand Canyon at the good time. Everything has changed now."

Betty Kent Meyer died in 1999. She never returned to the Grand Canyon. She would not recognize her home. The little village once home to Harvey Girls and railroad workers is now a town of approximately 2,000 people, no longer isolated from the world. Getting milk, butter, and eggs requires a simple trip to the grocery, and water, though still scarce, is a matter of turning a faucet. The lodges and shops serve millions of visitors each year. Although the lodges are operated by a large concessioner these days, the Fred Harvey legacy continues. As for the Harvey Girls, they have long vanished from the canyon, along with their "frontier" smiles and starched uniforms. Still, their spirit is present in the eyes and exuberance of present-day employees who are just as excited to be where they are as any Harvey Girl ever was.

CHAPTER FIVE

A Face in the Rain

THE FATE OF BESSIE HALEY HYDE
(1905—1928)

No one would have imagined the turn Bessie Haley's life would take after her successful high school years in Parkersburg, West Virginia. A model student, the diminutive Bessie—just five feet tall and ninety pounds in weight—participated in the Debating Club, wrote for the school newspaper, acted in plays, drew sketches for advertisements in the school yearbook, and showed promise as an artist and writer. Indeed, that was her ambition. When Bessie graduated second out of seventy-eight students in the 1924 class, her school yearbook predicted "a great future" for her, a future that would include glamorous travel "accompanied by a dark-haired man." Neither Bessie nor her classmates knew then that she would one day set out to be the first woman to travel the length of the Colorado River through the Grand Canyon.

In 1926 she and her high school sweetheart, the "dark-haired" Earle Helmick, married secretly while attending Marshall College in Huntington, West Virginia. Just why they kept their marriage a secret and never lived together is not known. Whatever the reason, the youthful romance would not survive the pressures of adulthood. Only a few months after their clandestine marriage, Bessie left alone for San Francisco to study at the California School of Fine Arts. In a collection of unpublished poems she titled *Wandering Leaves*, Bessie alludes to a possible reason for her leaving. In "A Visitor" she wrote:

This soft bundle
so close to me,
Is yours and mine
Come, love, and see.
I'm glad the stork,
In hurried flight,
Took time to stop
In here tonight.

If Bessie had a child, what happened? "Mermaid Doll" may reveal a startling, possible reality:

Oh! mamma dear, please come!
My dolly must be drowned,
When I put her on the creek,
She sank without a sound.
Wee Betty's eyes filled with tears.
Where could poor dolly be?
Perhaps she's turned into a mermaid,
And drifted out to sea.

Whatever purpose compelled her, Bessie fled marriage and the responsibilities that accompanied it—though if her poetry is any indication, she apparently did so reluctantly and with great sadness. Whether it was marriage, motherhood, or "the dark-haired man" that caused her to flee remains as mysterious as the unfolding of her fate.

She met her fate when she met Glen Hyde in San Francisco that same year. He was an intense, driven man—also dark-haired—whose charismatic charm attracted Bessie like a magnet, helping her to abandon whatever feelings she may have had for Earle.

Glen was a tall, muscular man who helped his widowed father, R. C. Hyde, run their ranch southeast of Twin Falls, Idaho, but craved a level of adventure and danger that living on a ranch did not provide. Glen escaped the humdrum of the ranch whenever he could to run rivers. He'd rafted the Peace and Fraser Rivers in British Columbia when the family lived in Canada, and after moving to Idaho, he and his sister Jeanne spent ten days in the fall of 1926 traveling down the Salmon and Snake Rivers. By the time he and Bessie met, Glen was talking about running the Colorado River.

Glen looked older and seemed wiser than his twenty-eight years. He was poised, opinionated, and astonishingly self-assured. His six-foot stance all but consumed Bessie's petite frame, and the two undoubtedly made a striking pair. Glen knew he wanted tiny Bessie to run the Colorado with him as his wife. After an embattled, drawn-out fight with Earle, Bessie and Glen finally married on April 12, 1928, the day after her divorce was final.

Glen persuaded Bessie to accompany him on a honeymoon trip down the Colorado, and they spent their first summer together, in between chores at the Idaho ranch, planning and preparing for it. He hoped the trip would ensure their fame as the first couple to run the Colorado River through the Grand Canyon. Bessie would be the prime attraction in a lecture tour as the first woman to make the trip. Rekindling interests in her earlier ambitions, Bessie planned to write and illustrate a book about the trip. Their future together did indeed look "great."

That October, with fall chores finished on the ranch, Bessie and Glen traveled to Green River, Utah, where Glen built their on-river home, a flat-bottomed scow twenty feet long, five feet wide, and three feet deep with long sweep oars at the bow and stern that Glen controlled from the middle of the boat.

Harry Howland, an experienced riverman, watched Glen building the scow at Green River. He told his friend Bill Reeder, who had rafted through Cataract Canyon in 1914, "Looks like he's building himself a coffin. Maybe you can tell the kid something." Reeder tried to convince Hyde to take life preservers, but he shrugged off the idea. Glen's sister Jeanne later recalled that Glen considered life preservers "sissy."

Glen finished the craft in good time, and together he and Bessie loaded the scow with food, tools, utensils, a set of bed springs, a mattress, and a small stove. They would take as their only guide a copy of *Through the Grand Canyon from Wyoming to Mexico*, Ellsworth Kolb's account of his 1911 trip with brother, Emery.

October 20, 1928, was a crisp autumn day in Green River, Utah. With puffy white clouds billowing into the blue sky, Bessie and Glen launched their scow onto the Green River and began the journey of their lives. From here, the two would join the Colorado and "float" 660 miles over some forty-nine days, with plans to reach Needles, California, on December 9. Glen's father would be waiting for them.

But did the couple realize what lay ahead of them? In those 660 miles, the Colorado ran across perilous rapids and through an unforgiving Grand Canyon whose waters did not differentiate between a tree pulled violently from its roots or a body jostled over the safe edge of its craft. A few people among the small crowd that had gathered to see the couple off might have suspected they were ill-prepared for the waters they would meet.

The Hydes' trip began peacefully enough. The Green is a patient and kind river, and it carried them through Labyrinth and Stillwater Canyons without incident. Past the confluence with the Colorado, however, lay their first real challenge: Cataract Canyon, curling forty long miles through narrow walls and across twenty-seven furious rapids.

At that time—the late 1920s—the section of the Colorado that ran through Cataract Canyon was fierce and wild. It harbored treacherous whirlpools, deep holes, and huge, obtrusive rocks that could wrap a boat like a sheet of paper; its waves could reach as high as fifteen feet. Working a scow through such water was an enormous challenge and required a vast reservoir of strength. The canyon's rapids are as relentless as they are unpredictable, and the river afforded no one time to study its water or line a boat through an especially treacherous section. Once you began the run, there was no turning back.

With the raging water roaring in their ears, Glen shouted orders at Bessie that she could barely hear. The flat-bottomed scow rocked and jerked across the rapids as red canyon walls rose to dizzying heights above them, denying an alternative passage. The sky narrowed to a blue strip high above, and trees clung precariously to the banks. Rocks and shrubs along the water's edge seemed to dip and bob with the churning of the boat. Whirling, turning, lunging, twisting—a roller-coaster ride—running through an egg beater would produce a more pleasant ride than did Cataract Canyon! Glen maneuvered the oars in frantic sweeps to avoid crashing into boulders. Bessie held tight, helping to push or pull the oars when she could, checking often to see that their gear was secure. Each rapid sucked them into a headlong dip and sent them plunging, blue sky disappearing above and muddy water opening up below, a gaping mouth ready to swallow them whole. Water washed across the bow in torrents, leaving them fully soaked. Then, just as suddenly as they were sucked in, the rapid spit them out like a wad of tired gum, advancing them toward the next raging dip. After each rapid, they were allowed only a few moments' rest before the next one was upon them.

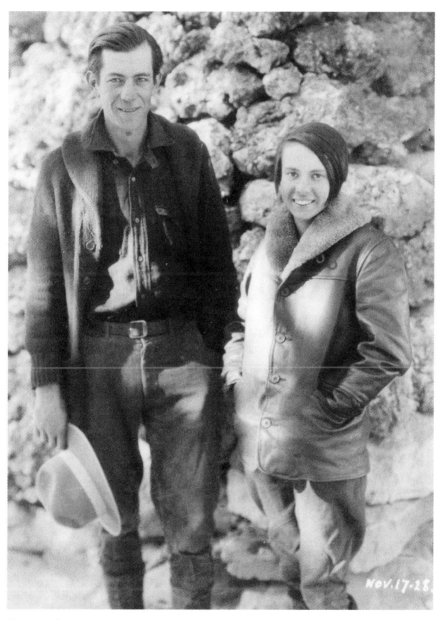

Glen and Bessie Hyde, Grand Canyon, Arizona, November 1928. *Photograph by Emery Kolb, courtesy of the Kolb Collection, Cline Library, Special Collections and Archives, Northern Arizona University. NAU.PH.568.4035.*

For forty grueling miles, the spray lashing them in the face like a driving rain, their muscles aching with fatigue, the Hydes fought the river—and conquered it. Exhausted, cold, and soaked to the bone, the two exited the canyon as victors. Bessie was the first woman to run Cataract Canyon. Exhilarated by their tremendous feat, the Hydes pushed on toward fame.

The next several days brought a welcome respite from Cataract as the couple floated peacefully through beautiful Glen Canyon. They then stopped at Lees Ferry, Arizona. Owen Clark, the man in charge of keeping flow records at the Lees Ferry river-gauging station, advised Glen not to "put all his eggs in one basket" and suggested he take a second boat along for safety. But with the victory of Cataract Canyon fresh under their belts, Glen said they could conquer anything now. It seemed to Clark that Bessie also was enthusiastic about the trip.

Sockdolager, the first major rapid in Grand Canyon's Upper Granite Gorge, lived up to its reputation. The men of John Wesley Powell's second expedition (1871-1872) had called this furious rapid a "sockdolager," a nineteenth-century slang term meaning "knockout blow." As Glen tried to hold the boat in the middle of the channel, the handle of a sweep hit him under the chin, knocking him overboard. Tiny Bessie grabbed both sweeps, threw Glen a rope, and managed to keep the scow going straight ahead. Glen caught the rope and made it back to the craft. It was a close call.

On November 15, twenty-six days and 424 miles past their put-in on the Green River, they stopped where Bright Angel Creek empties into the Colorado River. Here they planned to order additional supplies, traveling on foot up to the Grand Canyon's South Rim. They spent the night at Phantom Ranch, the tourist camp one mile up Bright Angel Creek, signing the register "going down the Colorado in a flat-bottomed boat." There they met Adolph G. Sutro, a San Francisco businessman and adventurer, also staying at the ranch. He arranged to accompany them downstream to Hermit Camp when they returned from the South Rim.

The next morning, Glen and Bessie hiked up the steep nine-mile Bright Angel Trail to the South Rim. A tired Bessie, happy to be sleeping in a real bed, wrote to her parents, "I just had a nice hot bath and am pretty sleepy 'cause this has been a long day." The next morning she talked to a reporter from the *Denver Post*, saying, "Our main object in this trip was to give me a thrill. It's surely been successful so far. I have been thoroughly drenched a dozen times and I'm enjoying every minute."

Glen spent most of his time at the Kolb Studio on the South Rim, talking with Emery Kolb, noted photographer and river runner. Impressed with their success but concerned that they had no life preservers, Kolb urged Glen to take a life jacket or at least to buy inner tubes from the Fred Harvey garage to use for flotation. Glen *pshawed* the advice as he had the first time it was offered, justifying his decision by telling Kolb he and Bessie were good swimmers, then quickly changing the subject. He ordered two mule loads of supplies to meet them at the foot of Hermit Trail.

As they left, Emery, with his wife Blanche and daughter Edith, accompanied them to the head of Bright Angel Trail. Bessie looked at Edith's new dress shoes and remarked, "I wonder if I shall ever wear pretty shoes again." Despite all her outward enthusiasm and comments to the press, Kolb sensed that Bessie was ready to quit.

The Hydes hiked back down the Bright Angel Trail and met up with Adolph Sutro as planned; he joined them for the overnight ride to Hermit Trail, where supplies would be waiting. The trip had barely gotten underway when Sutro fully realized Bessie's fears as she hung onto the side of the scow. Amazed at Glen's carelessness and lack of precaution, Sutro couldn't understand how they had come that far. "It was the most inadequately equipped outfit I'd ever seen," he said later.

Although Glen talked excitedly of vaudeville lecture tours around the campfire that evening, Sutro noted Bessie's lack of enthusiasm. The next day they met the supply mules at the foot of Hermit Trail, and Sutro was glad he'd completed his journey safely. As he climbed on one of the mules for the ride out, he waved good-bye and wondered if anyone would ever see the Hydes again. The day was November 18.

On December 9, 240 miles below Hermit Trail, Glen's father waited for the couple at Needles, California. The day came and went, and the couple did not show. They had sent no word ahead, and no one had seen them since they pushed off from Hermit Trail. The senior Hyde naturally grew concerned as the next few days passed, fearing that his only son and Bessie were in trouble. He envisioned them trapped on a sandbar or hanging on the side of a cliff, waiting for help. Convinced they'd met trouble, Hyde took action. He telephoned the governor of Idaho, urging him to call army headquarters in Washington and ask for search planes to be dispatched from the nearest base in California or Arizona. He then boarded a train for the Grand Canyon.

The army's response was immediate as they launched the first air search in Grand Canyon history. Two Douglas O-2 airplanes from March Field, California, landed at Red Butte Airport near the South Rim of the Grand Canyon on December 18. That day's *Prescott Evening Courier* announced, "Army plane is ordered to scan Grand Canyon for two lost thrill seekers." The story also reported that R. C. Hyde was offering a $1,000 reward for locating the missing couple.

Preston P. Patraw, assistant superintendent of Grand Canyon National Park, and Bob Francy, supervisor of trail rides for the Fred Harvey Company, accompanied the army pilots, Lieutenants L. G. Plummer and H. G. Adams, for an early morning search. In a hair-raising flight between narrow Grand Canyon walls scarcely seventy-five feet above the river, they spotted the empty scow floating in a quiet pool eleven miles below the mouth of Diamond Creek, 138 miles from Bright Angel Creek. There was no sign of Glen or Bessie.

Glen's father believed that Glen and Bessie were alive. Diamond Creek offered one of the few access points in western Grand Canyon to the river. A drilling crew testing the rock foundations for a possible dam had established a temporary camp there a few years before. Hyde planned to use the abandoned camp as a base for a ground search.

He asked Emery Kolb for help. Kolb flew above the site and returned to suggest that a small party take oars and camping equipment to the old drilling campsite. There they would build a boat and float down to the scow. Kolb telegraphed his brother Ellsworth, then living in Los Angeles, to join them for the search.

Hyde agreed with this plan but also wanted someone searching above Diamond Creek. He offered Bob Francy and Jack Harbin, owner of Rowe's Well, a tourist camp on the South Rim, $1,000 to conduct the search. The men hiked down Bright Angel Trail to the river, and using an old boat left by the trail, floated downstream. Temperatures plunged as a cold front moved across the canyon, and the searchers donned several layers of clothing and sheepskin coats to stay warm. Unless Bessie and Glen had thought to bring warm clothes, the possibility of their survival looked grim.

The search caught the attention of the media, which was, then as now, eager for any gory details that might surface. On December 20, Kolb received a telegram from Paramount News: "Have you any movies airplane search, Colorado River. Advise Collect." A week later, the Associated Press wired Kolb, saying the news organization "Will be glad to pay you liberally for any pictures from Hyde films

Petite Bessie Hyde showing off the scow. *Photograph taken by Glen Hyde, courtesy of the Hyde Collection, Cline Library, Special Collections and Archives, Northern Arizona University. NAU.PH.2001.11.6.26.*

found in scow. Appreciate having some negatives rushed here if good. Advise us collect." Though this was not the means by which they meant to achieve it, Glen and Bessie were indeed becoming famous.

While Francy and Harbin continued to search for the couple between Bright Angel Creek and Diamond Creek, the Kolb brothers, Mr. Hyde, and Park Ranger Jim Brooks repaired an old, flat-bottomed boat they'd found at the drilling camp. The finished boat would hold only three men, so the two Kolb brothers and Brooks headed downstream on Christmas Day, hoping to spot the couple marooned along the way. It had been close to a month since they were last seen by Adolph Sutro.

At Mile 232 the current crashed against a low cliff as high waves swirled over submerged rocks. The men decided the rapid was too dangerous to run and began lining their boat along the shore opposite the cliff. While lining, it occurred to Emery that the couple might have met their fate at this same rapid.

Anyone looking upon this rapid could imagine what might have happened to the Hydes: A weary couple halts their scow to survey the next of what have become countless rapids on their journey. Bessie is exhausted from the trip but she takes her husband's orders to "hold the line" while he walks downstream to study the

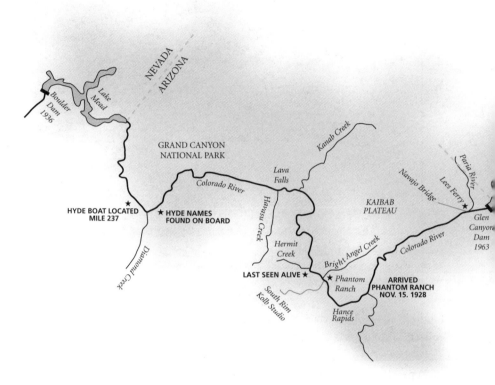

swirling water for the best route. A fierce wind blows through the Grand Canyon, spitting freezing rain into their faces, whipping the sweeps, and jerking the boat to and fro. It is all tiny Bessie can do to keep the boat from breaking loose in the raging current. Her eyes watering, her face stinging in the biting wind, she wraps the rope around her waist. The rope rocks and tugs at her and she digs her heels deeper into the soft bank. Her arms are weak, she can no longer feel her fingers. Tug, jerk. Bessie's knees wobble and her thighs burn as she fights to steady the boat. Glen surveys the water, his hand to his chin, looking this way and that. He seems suddenly very far away and Bessie tightens her grip on the rope. Without warning, the angry breath of winter issues a ferocious gust. It catches the scow and jerks it into the open jaws of the current.

Glen turns to the direction of his wife's scream in time to see her disappear in the muddy Colorado, tethered to the scow that has freed itself. Glen dives toward

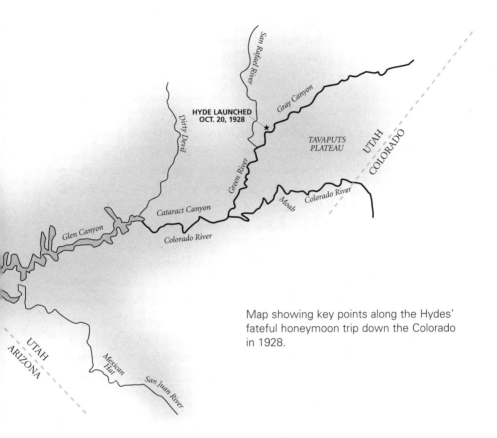

Map showing key points along the Hydes' fateful honeymoon trip down the Colorado in 1928.

the scream, the blast of cold water heightening his panic, and searches across rocks and current for his wife. "Bessie!" he screams. He sees the boat has jerked its way farther downstream, such a distance, too far to swim. The water is so cold as he is pulled back into dark swirling silence and feels his body slam against the rocks. Then his world turns black. . . .

No matter what their imaginations might have conjured, the only hard evidence the searchers had was the scow, which they found floating peacefully at Mile 237. There was some water in it, but the mattress, stove, camping gear, and the pair's personal possessions were not disturbed. The boat had not capsized. The searchers retrieved Bessie's diary, box camera, heavy clothing, camping gear, and boots. Regretfully, Bessie's diary revealed little. Apart from a series of circles and dashes—circles for easy rapids, and upright slashes for difficult ones—the diary contained few remarks. On November 20, sickness had kept her in camp all day.

On November 22 the boat got caught in an eddy, and Glen stayed up all night holding the boat in case the eddy broke. The next day they laid over at Bedrock Rapids while Glen repaired a broken plank in the scow. In the only sign of humor in the diary, Bessie noted that on November 24 they launched "Rain in the Face," her name for the boat. On November 27 she did laundry in a hot spring, probably near Lava Falls. The next day was windy. On Thanksgiving Day they saw a deer. The brevity of the entries was puzzling. There were no comments on her reaction to the Grand Canyon, no record of events, no reflections on the experience she was having with her husband, no hint about whether she was enjoying the adventure, no illustrations. In short, the diary contained nothing that would help her write a book. The searchers surmised from the diary and from the forty-two notches Glen had etched on the gunwale that the couple had disappeared on December 1.

Glen's father found a glimmer of hope in the diary. The last entry, dated November 30, noted bad rapids but did not mention their location. Convinced that Glen and Bessie could not have taken their clumsy scow on low water against headwinds the forty-six miles from Lava Falls to Diamond Creek during that short interval, Hyde decided the accident must have occurred above Diamond Creek and not at Mile 232 as the Kolbs and Brooks believed. This meant that Bessie and Glen might still be alive and waiting for help. Perhaps they had even hiked out of the canyon. Growing more desperate, he hired Hualapai Indian trackers to cover the reservation south of the stretch of Grand Canyon between Lava Falls and Diamond Creek for any signs of the couple, and cowboys to search the desolate north side of the Grand Canyon. Both searches were fruitless. Hyde himself backpacked into the gorge below Lava Falls but found nothing.

The first week of January, Peach Springs Deputy Sheriff John Nelson and Jack Spencer found what they believed to be the Hydes' last camp near Mile 210. They found women's footprints leading away from the campfire and the dim imprint of men's sneaker footprints on the beach. Lima beans were scattered on the ground near the remains of a campfire. Hyde recognized the label on the opened can of beans as the same brand his son had purchased for the trip.

R. C. Hyde could not give up the search for his only son. In a letter to Emery Kolb dated January 1, 1929, he wrote, "I have come here to St. George and am organizing a pack team to search this country between here and this river. I realize that this is likely of no avail but I wish to have nothing undone that can be done." February 28 of the same year, he wrote, "I am planning to return to the river, sometime, to search and see if I cannot find the bodies. I do not know when would be the best time. What do you advise?"

Hyde at least had the advantage of doing something. Bessie's family, however, were left to wring their hands with concern, the distance making the loss of their Bessie that much more mysterious, that much more unbelievable. Glen's sister, Jeanne, corresponded often with Bessie's mother and made efforts to comfort them. On January 8, 1929, she wrote, "We may have them back yet, Mrs. Haley, and if we don't, at least they have dared life and death, taken the sporting chance, and gotten as much out of life as any two people could." Later that year, responding to a letter from Mrs. Haley concerning the possibility of the pair being held hostage by hostile Indians, Jeanne explained that now all the Indians lived on reservations and were peaceful, adding, "I cannot see any slight hope of their being alive." A full year and a half later, Bessie's father joined R. C. Hyde in a seventeen-day search of the canyon in a final unsuccessful attempt to find an answer.

April 1931 brought the only subsequent clue to what might have happened to the couple. Glen and Bessie's names were found written on a board inside the blacksmith shop at the old drilling camp at Diamond Creek. They had reached Diamond Creek after all, making it almost certain that the accident had occurred at Mile 232. Although both families finally accepted the couple's death, questions about how they died and where they died would haunt them for the rest of their lives.

Over the years the legend of Glen and Bessie Hyde grew as river running became a popular commercial enterprise, and river guides recounted the story of the couple's disappearance around campfires. On one such occasion in October 1971, a passenger on a Grand Canyon Expedition twenty-day oar trip—Elizabeth "Liz" Cutler, a sixty-one-year-old retired schoolteacher from Pomeroy, Ohio—claimed that she was really Bessie Hyde. She told how she and Glen argued, and that to protect herself she stabbed him and hiked out of the canyon.

This account remained the province of river guides for fourteen years, gaining momentum and credibility when writer Scott Thybony suggested in an October 1985 *Outside Magazine* article that Bessie was indeed alive and well. This generated the interest of NBC's *Unsolved Mysteries*. A segment on the November 29, 1987, program called "Honeymoon Bones" shows Bessie reaching for a five-inch hunter's dagger and left the impression that Bessie was living in Ohio.

The story remained "true" until Martin J. Anderson, a river historian, undertook to answer the question: was Liz Cutler really Bessie Hyde? The answer: no. Liz was born Mary Elizabeth Arnold on December 2, 1909, in Pomeroy, Ohio. Bessie was born Bessie Haley on December 29, 1905, in Washington, D.C. Liz grew up and lived in Pomeroy most of her life. The local paper has her attending several Arnold family reunions in the late 1920s, at the same time Bessie would have been attending art school in California.

Still, if Bessie isn't Liz, she could be someone else. Usually, the Colorado River gives up its victims eventually, but neither her body, nor Glen's, ever surfaced. Did Bessie Haley Hyde's "bright future" end in the cold waters of the Colorado River? Or, did she in fact hike out to safety, to live out her life in obscurity?

CHAPTER SIX

A Ranger in Riding Habit

PAULINE MEAD PATRAW
(1904—2001)

auline "Polly" Mead first laid eyes on the Grand Canyon in 1927, when she was twenty-three years old. Raised among columbines and daisies on a Colorado ranch, Polly was studying botany at the University of Chicago when she had the opportunity to see the Grand Canyon and several other national parks during a summer-long field trip in the West. The trip was organized and directed by one of her professors, Dr. Henry Chandler Cowles.

"We went to Logan, Utah," Polly explained, "and then to several national parks—Yellowstone, Zion, Bryce, and the North Rim of the Grand Canyon. First we went to Zion, and I was so thrilled about Zion. I had never seen country like that. I thought, 'Wouldn't it be wonderful to live in a place like that?' never knowing that one day I would. At Bryce, Dr. Cowles had us hold hands and close our eyes as he led us to the lookout. What a thrill when we opened our eyes!"

With visions of Zion, Bryce, and Yellowstone fresh in their minds, the group of young botanists arrived at the Grand Canyon, a fitting place to end a brilliant summer. They had seen the vastness of landscape and a range of ecosystems so delicately balanced it made the students marvel anew at all they had learned in the confines of a classroom. For Polly Mead, the trip was life-defining.

"Why can't you see the Grand Canyon?" Polly Mead inquired as they set up camp along the canyon's rim. "Something as big as that, you should be able to see it."

"Take a walk down that little path," Dr. Cowles said to his dubious student. After meeting the graces of Zion and Bryce, little amazement was left for her mind to imagine. Could any sight compare with the awe and wonder of those two places? Polly ventured the few hundred yards to the overlook. "I walked down the path and discovered the Grand Canyon. A most emotional experience," she said. "It was so wonderful."

The moment she broached the canyon's edge, Polly was overcome by the power of nature. She looked upon a canyon spread as wide as the horizon, burnt as red as an earthen clay pot, carved as deep as the sky is high. Pine trees competed with patches of aspen for space along the rim, and as the canyon fell away, scrub oak,

Polly Mead in her improvised ranger uniform. *Photograph courtesy of Polly Mead Patraw.*

mountain mahogany, and New Mexican locust trees clung to the steep sides. In the slight breeze that wafted from inside the canyon she detected the essence of the West. The canyon has been here forever, and yet it was created over time, by time. Whether one is conscious of it or not, the canyon reminds each visitor that "I am evidence and proof of history, of yesterday, of change. I was here before you; I will be here long after you are gone."

Later, as the group drove along the Kaibab Plateau leaving the North Rim, Professor Cowles asked his students if they had noticed how the trees came right to the edge of the meadow and just stopped. "That would make an interesting study, to see why the tree line just stops suddenly at the meadow," Polly thought. Suddenly she had an idea. "That's the subject for my master's thesis."

With this first visit to the canyon, Polly, a petite young woman with a broad smile and an enthusiastic nature, had found a place she would return to again and again. "When I graduated, my aunt and benefactor said, 'I'd like to give you a gift of a trip to Europe or a trip to the Grand Canyon to do your research.' I'd never been to Europe, but I knew what I wanted to do."

A young woman of Polly's upbringing would be expected to choose the European tour, but a determined Polly Mead pursued her interests and spent the summers of 1928 and 1929 doing research for her master's thesis near the North Rim of the Grand Canyon. Polly expanded her thesis topic from the narrow approach of determining the cause for the sharp division between the meadows and the forest to encompass a complete study of plant life on the Kaibab Plateau. Hers would be the first such study and would provide the basis for all further studies on the North Rim.

Polly lived at the V. T. Lodge, about twenty miles north of the North Rim, while doing her research. The 350-square-mile Kaibab Plateau boasts virgin stands of yellow pine, Engelmann spruce, Douglas and white fir, and wide mountain meadows where deer graze. Summer daytime temperatures average 70 degrees Fahrenheit. By late October heavy snow blankets the plateau, making travel virtually impossible.

For her research, Polly used C. Hart Merriam's theory of life zones to draw a map of the Kaibab Plateau defining each zone: the Upper Sonoran Zone ranged from 5,000 to 7,000 feet elevation; the Transition Zone from 7,000 to 8,200 feet; and the Canadian Zone from 8,200 to 9,200 feet. The meadows, which intrigued Polly, were in the lower depressions of the Canadian Zone. She carefully identified and catalogued the plant life in each zone.

"I had a plant press on my back, and I'd go out and collect specimens. Sometimes I'd stay overnight. All I'd need would be a canteen and a bedroll," Polly explained. She also took a little pistol with her on these overnight trips, thinking that as a woman out alone, "I might need it if a drunken man or wild animal approached me. One time I was in my bedroll asleep and I was awakened by footsteps going around me. I put my hand on the pistol, but nothing happened. The next morning I saw deer prints all around my bedroll."

Polly used a vasculum, a can with moist paper in it, to store the plants she gathered for identification. "You have to have fresh plants to work on, so I would keep the fresh plant for a day or two and then find another one just like it to be put in the plant press." She sent her pressed specimens back to the National Museum in Washington to confirm their identification.

To study climatic conditions in each zone, Polly rode on horseback to set up weather stations. First she placed a maximum-minimum thermometer inside a wooden box with an opening on one side; she would then position the box with the open side shaded from the direct rays of the sun and mount it on a post thirty-six inches above the ground. She'd place Livingston atmometer cups for measuring evaporation and rainfall near the thermometer and surround both instruments with a wire fence for protection from animals. She also would don climbing spikes and climb the tall pines to install and check on instruments, and she took soil samples to determine the percentage of water content present along the plateau. These she sent to the Desert Botanical Laboratory in Tucson, Arizona, for determination.

Because Polly's advisor was a geologist as well as a botanist, he insisted that all papers contain information about the study area's geology. She decided to consult with Edwin (Eddie) McKee, Grand Canyon National Park naturalist stationed on the South Rim, whose specialty was geology. She had met him on the field trip the previous summer and knew he worked on the South Rim. "I decided to walk across the canyon and meet with him."

At the time, Polly did not realize a "walk" across the canyon was in reality a grueling twenty-three-mile hike. In addition to the nearly 5,000- to 6,000-foot elevation loss and gain, Polly also contended with temperatures hovering near 100 degrees, wading Bright Angel Creek several times, and in boots that didn't fit.

"Nobody knows how big the Grand Canyon is unless they have walked it every step of the way," Polly said. She spent the night at Phantom Ranch and then continued her climb up to the South Rim. "I crossed the bridge across the Colorado River with stiff boots and blistered feet. I went up the Bright Angel Trail. Some kind person poured a pail of water over me, and I made it. I was so tired I couldn't sleep," she recalled.

Polly spent several days meeting with McKee before hiking back to the North Rim. "I made a deal with him. I would work on a plant list of the Grand Canyon, and he would give me geologic material for my thesis."

One late afternoon, Polly returned to V. T. Lodge from a day in the field to find the owners quite excited. Stephen Mather, head of the National Park Service, had been looking for Polly. He left a note inviting her to be his guest at the dedication of the North Rim lodge. As life's fortune would have it, Mr. Mather was the father of Polly's old school chum, Becky Mather. He had learned from his daughter that Polly was living at the North Rim.

"I went down to the bottom of my trunk and pulled out a dress and got a ride down to the North Rim lodge. I was the only woman present at the dedication." Seated with Polly and Mr. Mather were Carl Gray, president of the Union Pacific

Ranger Polly Patraw giving an interpretive talk ca. 1930. *Photograph courtesy of National Park Service.*

Railroad, and Heber J. Grant, president of the Mormon Church. Making their acquaintance would later prove beneficial to Polly.

She finished her research on schedule, at the end of her second summer on the North Rim. Her resulting thesis provided a complete study of the Kaibab Plateau. Polly concluded that a difference in the lime content of the meadows accounted for the sharp demarcation of the tree line. Trees do not flourish in soils with high lime content.

Following graduation, Polly decided she wanted to remain at the canyon. She applied to the Forest Service to work as a ranger-naturalist but was told they did not hire women. She then applied for the position of ranger-naturalist with the National Park Service on the South Rim. "On my application someone had written a note: 'It will be remembered that Miss Mead was Stephen Mather's guest at the dedication of the North Rim Lodge.'" Although this no doubt helped her application receive some special attention, Polly believed she got the job because of her knowledge of the canyon and because she wanted it so badly. She was sworn into office on August 1, 1930, by the park's Assistant Superintendent Preston Patraw and became the first woman ranger-naturalist at the Grand Canyon—and the second in the entire National Park Service.

Because an official female park service uniform did not then exist, Superintendent M. R. Tillotson decided that Polly should wear a riding habit. "I had rather light britches and hip boots. He wanted me to wear a hat like the courier girls for the Fred Harvey tours wore. He just liked that hat."

"I loved that job!" Polly enthused. "I worked at Yavapai and gave campfire lectures in the evening." She also did the auto caravan tours, talking about plants and geology, and she occasionally led nature hikes.

Her favorite assignment was to stand at the edge of the canyon and give talks. "I loved to talk when I was standing on the edge of the canyon because I could talk about the canyon and not be self-conscious at all." Who, after all, could be self-conscious with such a backdrop? "One time I had a large bus tour listening to my lecture. I wanted to get them interested in the canyon, so I talked about the age of the rocks . . . and how it took a hundred million years for the canyon to be carved." She had the group's undivided attention. When she finished they seemed eager for more information, so she asked, "Are there any questions?" Polly was shocked when a man asked, "'And how old are you?'" I told him, 'twenty-five!'" The group was apparently as intrigued with their ranger as they were with the Grand Canyon.

Polly prepared her own talks. "I found that if you're interested, people will be interested. If you enjoy it yourself, the first thing you know, people will be interested." Polly particularly enjoyed talking about the yucca plant, which shares a unique, symbiotic relationship with the penumbra moth. The two rely on each other for survival: If one were to perish, so would the other. "The relationship between the two is fascinating," Polly exclaimed. "The penumbra moth fertilizes the flower and starts the seeds, so there's interdependency between the moth and the yucca. I would tell about the Indians using the yucca fiber for material and soap from the root to wash their hair. It made an especially nice soap for the hair."

Her love of flowers led her to attempt planting wildflower gardens at the Grand Canyon. In preparation for this, she began an elaborate experiment to determine which wildflowers would grow from gathered seed. "Wildflowers are very difficult to transplant," she explained. Polly searched for wildflower seeds in the fall of 1930, and she wrote about her project in the December 1930 *Nature Notes*, a mimeographed booklet published monthly by the Naturalist Department of Grand Canyon National Park. She had gathered nineteen varieties of wildflowers, including cliffrose, Apache plume, globe mallow, and pink penstemon. Polly planted one hundred seeds of each variety in a hothouse under various soil and moisture conditions. In her meticulous manner, she carefully noted the percentage of seeds that germinated. She was most successful with the bluebonnet (lupine), with a 75 percent germination rate, and least successful with the Indian paintbrush and cranesbill, with no germination at all.

Polly continued her wildflower project throughout the winter. In the January 1931 *Nature Notes*, she excitedly reported that the Indian paintbrush had germinated after all: on January 18 she discovered eighteen seedlings. Her goal, as stated in the article, was to "shed light on the behavior of wildflower seeds" and to "assist in the eventual replacement of exotic plants by native wild plants in landscaping within the national parks."

Despite her many projects, Polly found time for fun. She lived in the midst of one of the most beautiful places on earth, with brilliant moons, the milky flowering of the yucca, and the smell of hard-baked rock. The magic of the Grand Canyon is irresistible. As for the yucca and the penumbra moth, certain things attract there: water to dry earth, animals to plants, even man to woman. For Polly, that man was Preston Patraw, the park's assistant superintendent, who had sworn her in to the National Park Service a year earlier. Patraw was intrigued with the petite ranger in the jaunty hat and invited her to hike with him up Red Butte.

Before long, they were dating often, usually enjoying the attractions of the canyon after work hours. Preston, a tall, handsome man with a reticent manner, asked Polly to marry him in March 1931 during a drive around the canyon's rim. Few things are more magical than a sunset drive along the rim of the Grand Canyon: the shadows deepen, and the orange-red colors of the setting sun light up the sky. Preston stopped the car just west of El Tovar and walked with Polly to Hopi Point. She agreed to be his wife. "He wanted to get me a Navajo rug for an engagement present, but he wanted me to pick it out, so we stopped at Hopi House on the way back," Polly recalled.

They were married May 1 of that year in the home of Polly's aunt in Phoenix, Arizona. Polly thought she would continue with her job, which she loved, but

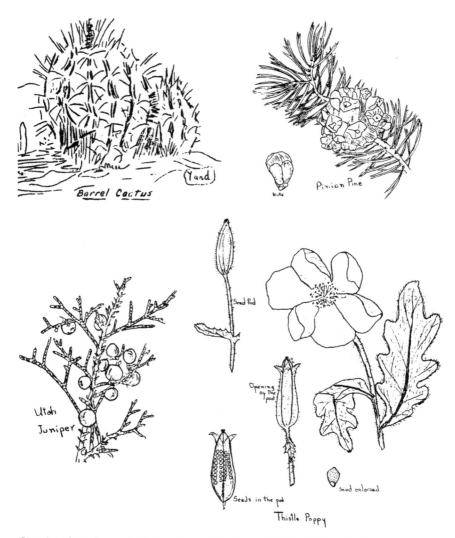

Sketches from Patraw's *Nature Notes. Courtesy of National Park Service.*

Preston did not want her to work. "I just said, 'Yes, dear,' as we did in those days!" Polly laughed. Her life shifted from botanist to wife overnight.

"As a bride at the canyon I got up and built a wood fire to make breakfast. We had an icebox and running water," Polly said, but the canyon offered few other amenities in 1931. Because of Preston's rank as assistant superintendent, he and

Polly were fortunate to live in a house in Grand Canyon Village. Many lower-level employees lived in tent houses.

Although Polly no longer was employed with the park service, she continued to study botany and write articles in *Nature Notes*, now with the byline Pauline Mead Patraw. In the May 1931 issue, she excitedly reported on finding a broomrape, a small parasitic flower rarely found outside of Utah and Nevada. Upon finding the flower, Polly had at first misidentified it. "At first sight I thought recklessly, 'a member of the Indian pipe family,'" she explained. After further digging, literally and figuratively, she determined that it was *Orobanche multiflora* (broomrape). "This is the first record of broomrape at the Grand Canyon and the only member of this family found here thus far," she wrote. Polly sketched the plant and explained in detail that it was a parasite, living on the roots of other plants without damaging the host plant.

Polly's knowledge of plants at the canyon introduced her to architect Mary Elizabeth Jane Colter, a woman she came to admire. "She was a fascinating person. I helped her with plants at the Watchtower. She wanted some Apache plume plants," Polly said, adding that it is sometimes hard to tell the difference between a cliffrose and an Apache plume since they are both in the same family. "Cliffrose has a pungent odor, and the flowers are very different. Apache plume is more delicate. The cliffrose flowers grow close together, and the Apache plume is more spread out."

Polly and Preston started a family, and soon after their second child was born, Preston was made superintendent at Zion National Park in southwestern Utah. The Patraws left the Grand Canyon in 1932. Polly made the transition easily, for Zion, at least, was in her beloved West. The rich red tones of Zion's earth resembled that at the Grand Canyon and kept her from missing it too badly. Polly made sure she and her family fit into the landscape. "The houses at Zion were built of red sandstone. You know how we like to have everything fit in with the scenery? I was a good park service wife: both of our children, George and Betsy, had red hair and fit in with the scenery," Polly laughed.

Preston went on to become superintendent at nearby Bryce Canyon National Park, followed soon after by Cedar Breaks National Monument and Capitol Reef National Park, all in Utah, and Polly's least favorite, a short stint in Hot Springs, Arkansas. "I preferred being in the West, climbing mountains," she explained. Polly got her wish in 1947 when Preston was named associate director of the National Park Service's southwest regional office in Santa Fe, New Mexico.

After moving to Santa Fe, Polly worked on a book titled *Flowers of the Southwest Mesas*, one of a series of flower books about the Southwest. She took nearly four years to accumulate material for the book. Five thousand copies were printed when it was first published in 1952 by the Southwest Parks and Monuments Association (now Western National Parks Association). In all, there were six printings and close to sixty-five thousand copies sold.

Polly's life came full circle in 1954 when Preston became superintendent of Grand Canyon National Park. Returning to the canyon, she noticed a significant change: "There were a lot more people," Polly recalled. "I remember one day my husband came home from the office and said, 'We had a thousand visitors this month.'" The increase in numbers of tourists led the National Park Service to discussions about providing entertainment for the visitors. This baffled Polly. "Isn't it enough enjoyment just to look at it? Why do you provide for anything except comfort? You don't need entertainment or anything of that kind when you've got the Grand Canyon to look at. I was talking to a woman from Phoenix who complained about taking visitors to see the canyon because there wasn't anything to do there. I don't feel that way at all."

Polly enjoyed her role as wife of the superintendent of Grand Canyon National Park, entertaining dignitaries and making new employees feel welcome. When Preston retired in 1955, the couple moved back to their Santa Fe home.

Polly died in 2001. Her legacy as ranger-naturalist continues at the canyon. In numbers that long ago put an end to any curiosity about them, women rangers give talks, lead nature hikes, assist visitors, and conduct scientific studies much in the same way Pauline Mead Patraw did so many years ago.

CHAPTER SEVEN

Race to Shiva Temple

RUTH STEPHENS BAKER
(1918—2006)

Having a canyon, train, hotels, tourists, cowboys, and mules near her home seemed perfectly normal to Ruth Stephens Baker. She grew up at the Grand Canyon, and it was as familiar to her as her own backyard. Yet, for all its familiarity, the canyon held mysterious worlds she yearned to explore. Worlds that towered above the canyon floor with intriguing names like Isis, Wotan's Throne, Zoroaster, and Shiva Temple.

Ruth was only two years old when her parents left San Diego, California, in the summer of 1920 for the Grand Canyon, where her father, an accountant, had accepted a three-month job with the Fred Harvey Company to balance the books. He stayed forty years. "Mom had acrophobia, so it was amazing for her to live at the canyon," Ruth said. "She couldn't look over the rim!"

When they arrived at the canyon, the Stephens family was shown to their new home . . . a tent house. Ruth remembered it well. "Our tent house had three rooms with a board floor, board siding, and board struts. Everything else was canvas, the sides and everything. There was a wood fence around it, and just outside the fence, out back, was the outhouse. Exterior plumbing!" she quipped.

"Mom made the tent house a real home," Ruth recalled. "We had a proper dining room with an oak table. The kitchen had a coal range and a table, chairs, and sink. Out back was a big old tub where mother did all the washing. We brought it inside and took our baths in it too." Ruth slept in a single bed, and her parents had a Murphy bed. "My mother was a perfectionist and a proper Main-Line Philadelphian. It

69

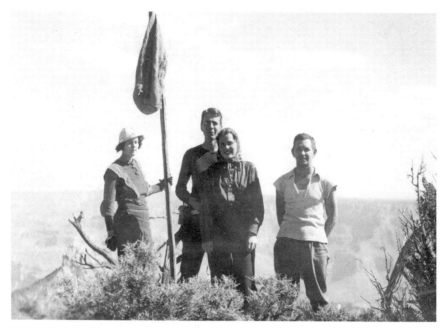

Edith Kolb Lehnert, Gordon Berger, Ruth Stephens, and Ralph White "lay claim" to Shiva Temple. *Photograph courtesy of the Emery Kolb Collection, Cline Library, Northern Arizona University, NAU.PH.568.512.*

was a chore for her to live in a tent. Cleaning house was a full time job. The roads weren't paved, and there was lots of dust!"

A childhood at the Grand Canyon was like no other. "A big 'do' for us kids was watching the Santa Fe train leave at night," Ruth said. "Also, I learned my alphabet by Pullman cars and my arithmetic by the freight cars." Thanks to the train and her father, Ruth was reading before she entered first grade in the two-room log school at the canyon. "Dad use to read me the comics, but he would not read me *The Katzenjammer Kids* because they used the word 'ain't' which was not supposed to be in my vocabulary. I learned to read so I could read *The Katzenjammer Kids!*" Ruth laughed.

"We played house in the caves under the rim," she remembered. "We used embossed wallpaper to make elaborate dresses for paper dolls and then wrote great stories about them. We put on plays for our parents in the neighbor's yard. We wrote the plays and made our own costumes. Then we sold them hot dogs and drinks our parents had made and charged them ten cents to get in!"

There was no charge to watch the sunsets! "If Dad saw that the sunset was going to be good, he'd tell my mother, 'OK, Lil, forget about dinner and let's go.' And we'd forget about dinner and go to Hopi Point and watch the sunset. Dad and I had fun looking at the clouds and seeing animals and objects in the clouds. We'd start talking about the cloud shapes, and pretty soon we'd have the dudes (tourists) doing it."

After eight years of living in the tent house, the family moved into one of the new homes built on Avenue A (now Apache Street in the South Rim housing area). Just two years after moving into the new house, Ruth graduated from the eighth grade. There was no high school at the Grand Canyon so Ruth spent her high school and college years in San Diego. She looked forward to the end of each term so that she could return to the canyon and home.

"Summers at the Grand Canyon were wonderful," Ruth said. "Every night during the summer we had a dance at Bright Angel Lodge. This was essentially for the tourists, but we joined in and danced with the dudes and each other. It was one big party. There was a program before the dance, about an hour's entertainment, cowboy songs and jokes."

Aside from the fun, there was plenty of work to be done; for Ruth that meant the Kolb Studio. Emery Kolb had come to the Grand Canyon in 1902, and by the time the Stephens family arrived, he was well established as a photographer and considered an expert on the canyon. In his studio, built at the head of the Bright Angel Trail, Emery sold photos and gift items and gave daily lectures. Ruth knew Emery well. At age ten she babysat his grandson, Emery "Sonny" Lehnert, and at sixteen she began working in Kolb's darkroom. Emery took pictures of all the people who went down Bright Angel Trail on mule trips and had them developed and ready for sale when the riders returned.

Emery promoted Ruth upstairs to the studio, where for twenty-five cents an hour she did whatever needed doing—waiting on customers, washing windows, dusting, cleaning drapes, setting up chairs for the lectures, and recruiting people to attend Emery's lectures where he showed films and slides of his river trips and his hikes in the canyon. "I became a regular barker," Ruth admitted. "I'd show them the telescope and get them to buy a book and come to a lecture. I had the spiel down pat. I was very shy, but I became a hard-sell barker."

Ruth's favorite time in the studio was during the four o'clock to nine o'clock shift. "Nobody would be in there around six in the evening, and that was the most beautiful time and I had the whole canyon to myself," she explained. It was a peaceful interlude—except when a late afternoon storm swept across the canyon, lightning streaking across the sky and reaching down to strike a pillar of rock or an isolated tree. "I was scared to death of the lightning," Ruth said. "One time the lightning came right through the studio. It traveled right across the room. I happened to have the window open in the studio and on the porch where they had the telescope, so it was natural for the lightning to come through. I never made that mistake again."

After a storm, the canyon would look spectacular as the sunlight broke through the clouds. "It was like a stage, and sometimes there would be spotlights when the sun would highlight Isis, Wotan's Throne, Zoroaster, and Shiva Temple. That's when I began to dream of climbing the mysterious worlds of the canyon, never knowing that I would get that chance."

Her chance came in the summer of 1937. Dr. Harold E. Anthony of the American Museum of Natural History in New York City planned to scale Shiva Temple that September and set foot where he believed no man had ever been before. Shiva Temple rises 7,570 feet above the canyon floor and is connected to the North Rim by a narrow land bridge. The press loved the story, and articles appeared in the *New York Times* calling Shiva Temple a "lost world" and speculating that dinosaurs might still roam in the isolated forest. Emery Kolb, whose reputation as an explorer of the Grand Canyon was well known, offered to guide the expedition but was rejected by Dr. Anthony and the park service.

Kolb was furious. When the park service refused to even to let him come along on the museum's expedition, he decided to beat them to Shiva Temple. He made a preliminary climb in mid-summer and then began to assemble his crew. Because much talk was being made of a woman going on the museum's expedition, Kolb invited his daughter, Edith, and Ruth to accompany him. Ruth's dream of climbing a part of the mysterious world of the Grand Canyon came true at age nineteen.

It was essential that Kolb's trip be kept secret. His relationship with the park service was contentious at best, and he feared he might be banned from the canyon at any time. The approach to Shiva Temple is from the North Rim, a 200-mile drive from the South Rim. So to save time, Emery arranged for the group to be flown across the canyon.

"We flew over to the North Rim one evening and spent the night on Point Sublime," Ruth explained. "We got our gear together and started our descent about 6 A.M., just about daybreak." The climb of Shiva Temple actually begins as a steep descent to a saddle. "We got down easily; it was not bad climbing at all, except in one little part where I twisted my knees, but I didn't pay any attention to it. When we got down to the saddle, there were pools of water. It had rained the night before. We got down there about 10:00 A.M. and here were all these great puddles of water, so we designated one puddle for drinking water, one for washing faces, one for washing feet, and one for washing socks. We left clean socks and some crackers there."

Kolb worried that someone looking through the telescope on his studio porch might see them, so, although the chances that they would be seen were remote, he decided to climb the north side of Shiva Temple. "The climb was a bit more difficult an ascent than we had anticipated. We did use ropes once. We topped out just before noon, and they let me be the first person to be on top of Shiva Temple," Ruth recalled, her eyes sparkling at the memory. "I remember that the noon whistle was blowing on the South Rim. I was wearing this bright red shirt. We had decided that somebody would wear something bright when the plane flew over so we could be spotted." The pilot flew over around noon, and on spotting the climbers, tossed the parachutes out the window. "They landed in a tree, and Mr. Kolb had to climb up and get them. We had tomatoes and water and crackers for lunch."

Although Emery Kolb did not want the park service to know he had climbed Shiva Temple, he did want Dr. Anthony and his museum expedition to know that someone had been on Shiva Temple. "We went over to a point we knew we could see from the studio, and we found an agave stalk and put a burlap bag on the stalk that would blend in nicely, but if we wanted to look at it, we could see it through the telescope. That was our flag," Ruth said. But a burlap bag was not enough. "Just because we were feeling a little rambunctious and did want people to know that other people had been there and it wasn't such a great thing after all, we left a few boxes of Kodak film, obviously made since 2,000 years ago. Also, I had heard that there was going to be a female on the expedition, so I had some lipstick and some tissues and left it on a few bushes so it couldn't be missed," she remembered. "We found that the deer had made a trail to the top of the landform and we found horns, antlers locked. We found some interesting fossils, and we took a couple things back as specimens. We took pictures."

By now it was late afternoon, and the group hurried to make their way down to the saddle by nightfall. "We spent the night in a kind of overhanging cave so that we could build a fire and nobody could see it. We could hear noises from the North Rim and could see the lights of the South Rim. It was the most fabulous feeling to think there was all that civilization over there and here we were where nobody had ever been before. It was the most fantastic experience." The group arrived back at the North Rim about 10:00 A.M. the next morning and flew back to the South Rim. "I was sworn to secrecy. Absolute secrecy. Nobody could say anything because of the fact that we had done it surreptitiously, and Mr. Kolb was not to be gotten into trouble. I didn't see the pictures for twenty years. It was the thrill of a lifetime. No one told for years, but the word eventually leaked out it was Emery Kolb who had scaled Shiva first," said Ruth.

The following month, the museum expedition arrived at the North Rim. With great fanfare and movie cameras rolling, the group—Dr. Anthony; noted mountain climbers Mr. and Mrs. Walter E. Wood Jr.; Wood's assistant, Elliott H. Humphery; naturalist and photographer James B. Shackelton; and George B. Andrews of the museum staff—started up Shiva Temple guided by Edwin McKee, chief naturalist of the Grand Canyon National Park, and M.R. Tillotson, park superintendent. They were supported by two private aircraft and six strong young men to carry their gear.

The September 17, 1937, *New York Times* reported that a party of scientists "tied together like beads on a string" disappeared over the rim of the Grand Canyon headed for Shiva Temple. Later articles told of finding perfect arrowheads, indicating that man had once been on the plateau. Dr. Anthony remained on the plateau for ten days collecting small animals and plant life.

The October 4, 1937, issue of *Time* magazine called the expedition to "treasureless island" a "scientific joke". In a long account of the expedition in the October 16, 1937, *Science News Letter*, Dr. Anthony attempted to justify the expedition, although his findings must have been a disappointment to him. He alluded to finding "convincing evidence . . . that someone else had tried to jump the gun and beat us to the summit of Shiva." He referred to finding a coil of rope, a small camera, and a hooked climbing staff at the base of a steep slope on the approach to the top of Shiva Temple, and called it "mute evidence that at this point the adventurer had lost his nerve." No mention of Kodak film canisters, lipstick smudged tissues, or a burlap bag on an agave stalk. The Kolb expedition got a real chuckle out of this account.

Ruth's time at the Grand Canyon ended soon after her climb to the top of Shiva Temple. In the summer of 1938, she met the man who would become her husband, Albert Baker Jr. "He was what we called a 'ninety-day wonder', a three-month temporary ranger who came out for the summer," she said. Four years after they had

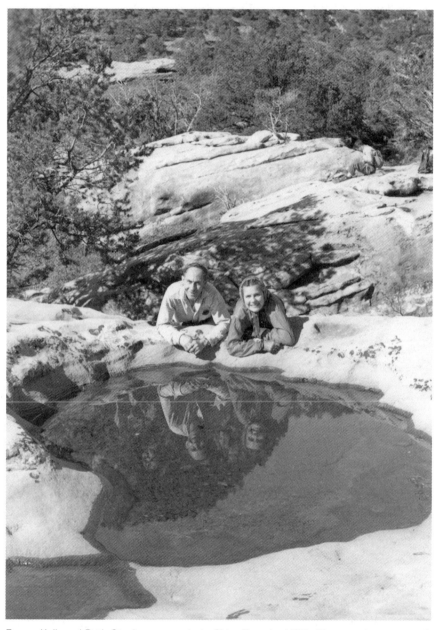

Emery Kolb and Ruth Stephens enroute to Shiva Temple, 1937. *Photograph courtesy of the Emery Kolb Collection, Cline Library, Northern Arizona University, NAU.PH. 568.508.*

met, Ruth was teaching in the three-room schoolhouse in Warner Springs, California, when she received a telegram from him. Albert was in the Air Corps and was being sent to Riverside, California, only sixty miles from her teaching assignment. They married on February 7, 1942, and subsequently lived all over the United States. Their three children were born in the East, but all since moved West.

"To me the Grand Canyon is still home," Ruth Stephens Baker said. "I never think of any other place but this as home. It was a closeness. I don't think we ever thought of it as anything really special. It was just a part of where we grew up."

CHAPTER EIGHT

Two Women, Three Boats, and a Plant Press

ELZADA CLOVER (1897—1980)
LOIS JOTTER (1914—2013)

Late in the summer of 1937, Elzada Clover relaxed over dinner in the Mexican Hat Lodge in southern Utah. After having spent a hot day in the surrounding desert collecting cacti, she was discussing a possible trip into the Grand Canyon with Norm Nevills, thirty-two-year-old son of the lodge's owners. It was a discussion they had had before. Elzada, botany instructor and assistant curator of the botanical gardens at the University of Michigan, had spent most of that summer collecting specimens for the university's collection. Elzada believed the Grand Canyon would hold a host of different or related species that would round out the collection, and she considered it a shame to miss the opportunity to explore it. She planned to go into the canyon by pack mule. Norm thought a boat trip would be better.

Norm Nevills eventually won out. A frequent "runner" on the nearby San Juan and Green Rivers, Norm now wanted to try his hand at the Colorado. He proposed a boat trip the following summer from Green River, Utah, to Lake Mead, on the Arizona-Nevada border—a distance of 660 miles. The cost of the boats—which Norm would build—equipment, and food would be shared equally by all members of the expedition. If the trip were successful, Norm planned to launch a commercial river running venture. Elzada hoped the expedition would advance her academic

The "crew" poses against a magnificent backdrop. Left to right, Bill Gibson, Lois Jotter, Lorin Bell, Elzada Clover, Emery Kolb, and Norm Nevills. *Photograph courtesy of the Belknap Collection, Cline Library, Special Collections and Archives, Northern Arizona University. NAU.PH.568.1137.*

career. She would be the first botanist to catalog plants along the Colorado River through the Grand Canyon.

Elzada left Mexican Hat in time for the fall semester and began making arrangements for the Grand Canyon trip, securing university approval and financial support for the venture and selecting her companions. She invited twenty-four-year-old Lois Jotter, a graduate student in botany, and Eugene (Gene) Atkinson, a zoology major then working as a graduate assistant in the botany department. Both were serious students and enjoyed the outdoors. Lois, a tall, athletic woman, loved hiking and camping. Gene was an avid canoeist.

As word of the upcoming trip spread, the botanists became local celebrities. The campus newspaper, the *Michigan Daily*, headlined on Sunday, June 5, 1938, "Faculty Women to Face Danger on Stormy Colorado for Science." The women, according to the article, would traverse "650 turbulent rapids-filled miles of Colorado River—a feat never before accomplished by a member of their sex." At the botany department's spring picnic, the threesome endured unmerciful kidding about being, as the newspaper account said, "intrepid explorers."

On the afternoon of June 7, 1938, Elzada, Lois, and Gene left Michigan for the long drive to Mexican Hat. They arrived there on June 14, at what was then little more than a crossroads beside the San Juan River. Named for a huge hat-shaped rock formation, the dusty "town" consisted of the Nevills' H-shaped lodge built of native red sandstone and a few other buildings. Their departure on the Green River was planned for June 20.

Norm took them immediately to see the boats. Extremely well built, the boats were constructed using a new marine plywood called Super Harbord with oak framework. Each boat was sixteen feet long, four feet across the stern, five feet amidship, and tapered to a pointed bow. Two thousand brass screws held them together.

Painted in large green letters against their gleaming white exteriors was NEVILLS EXPEDITION. Individually, the boats were named the *Wen*, Norm's father's initials; the *Botany*, in honor of the purpose of the expedition; and the *Mexican Hat*, after the rock formation near the Nevills' lodge.

During the few days before departure, the Michiganites met the other adventurers who would accompany them. Bill Gibson, a soft-spoken commercial artist and industrial designer from the San Francisco Bay area, joined the trip primarily to further his photography career. He hoped to capture the adventure with his new movie camera. Norm's right-hand man, Don Harris, was a resident engineer for the United States Geological Survey (USGS). He rented a bunkhouse from the Nevills and often rafted on the San Juan with Norm. Don had helped to build the boats in his spare time, and in return Norm offered to give him one of the boats following the expedition.

By 1938, several men already had ridden the Colorado River through the Grand Canyon, but the only woman to attempt the trip until that time had been Bessie Hyde, who disappeared, presumably drowned (see chapter five). An Associated Press reporter from Salt Lake City asked Elzada and Lois what they thought of river veteran Buzz Holmstrom's statement that the river was no place for a woman. Lois replied, "Just because the only other woman who ever attempted this trip was drowned is no reason women have any more to fear than men." Overall, the news accounts recording the group's departure emphasized the "flora-minded women" and the "treacherous rapids" the party would surely encounter.

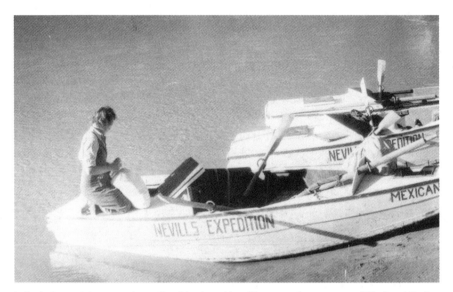

Lois Jotter getting gear from the *Mexican Hat*. *Photograph courtesy of National Park Service.*

At 9:00 A.M. on June 20, the party started down the Green River, which had been flooded by unexpectedly late snowmelt. Family members and a small crowd of onlookers gathered to see them leave. Elzada later wrote in her diary, "The natives of Green River and Moab looked at us as if they would ne'er see us [any]more." Norm and Elzada went first in the *Wen*, Lois and Don followed in the *Mexican Hat*, and Bill and Gene came last in the *Botany*. They planned to arrive on Lake Mead by the end of July.

Despite a strong upstream wind that made rowing difficult, the first day was uneventful. They camped the first evening on a sandbar near Labyrinth Canyon at Mile 84. As it was inconceivable in 1938 that a man would cook if a woman were available, Elzada and Lois became the expedition cooks. For the first evening's meal, they grilled fresh steaks.

Their few days on the Green River were peaceful. Except for contending with mosquitoes and sunburn, the members voiced little complaint. Elzada and Lois took turns collecting plants, usually in the morning and evening. In the evenings around the campfire Elzada and Don played their harmonicas while the others sang.

The evening before they would meet the Colorado River, Norm grew serious.

He gave the group a lecture on running rapids, beginning with a description of "holes." Water pours over an obstruction in a rapid and comes down with such force that it makes a hole in the river. The hydraulic forces in such a hole are unpredictable and exceedingly dangerous. To a group of novices, the description of this phenomenon was frightening. Norm cautioned them to avoid holes if possible, but if they couldn't be avoided, to hit them stern first. If you are thrown into the water, Norm continued, hang onto the rope on the side of the boat.

During breakfast the next morning, Norm reiterated his instructions. Nervous tension mounted among the group during the day, and remarks such as "What kind of flowers would you like?" and "It's been nice knowing you!" flew between the boats. That afternoon, at 2:30 P.M., Norm stood on the forward deck of the *Wen* as they approached the Colorado and shouted, "There she is! She's a big 'un and she's a bad 'un!" The Green meets the Colorado near Mile 216, three miles upstream from Cataract Canyon, so named because of its twenty-seven rapids in thirteen miles.

The confluence of these two rivers is impressive. Suddenly, the calm of the Green is overcome by the frenzied rush of the Colorado's muddy waters. Lois wrote, "The character of the river changed, and slowly we realized the power of the Colorado." Norm signaled the boats to pull in at a sandbar. While Elzada and Lois took pictures, the men walked down to survey the first rapid. It appeared to be about fifteen feet high, followed immediately by a second rapid with a large mushroom-shaped wave. As the men were inspecting the rapids, Bill happened to look back upriver. "My God!" he yelled. "There's the *Mexican Hat*!" Lois and Don's boat had broken loose and was riding the crest of the first wave, stern first.

Norm shouted to Don to run upstream and get the *Wen*. Don ran, motioning to Lois to follow. They threw on their life preservers and shoved off in the *Wen*. Meanwhile, Norm, Gene, and Bill scrambled over the rocks to the end of the rapid just in time to see the empty *Mexican Hat* disappear in the next rapid. Norm sent Bill and Gene back to get the *Botany* and bring it down to the head of the second rapid, adding that the women should walk along the shore and catch up to them.

Bill and Gene had just set off when the *Wen*, with Don at the oars and Lois waving, passed. Aghast, Norm ran down to meet the boat as it swept into the second rapid.

"With a sinking feeling, I ran on as fast as I could. Not far to the reportedly bad [rapid] number 4 and worse than a greenhorn at the oars! Words can't tell the all-gone feeling I experienced," Norm later wrote in his journal. Norm ran along the shore, trying to catch up with Don and Lois. He watched the *Wen* careen down the river, rocking like a carnival ride gone bad.

Don and Lois had a wild ride through seven rapids, finally stopping in a back eddy. Elated to be stopped and safe, they tied the *Wen* securely and walked along the shore. Lois thought she saw oars sticking up ahead. They ran, and there, floating peacefully in an eddy, was the *Mexican Hat*. Leaving Lois in sight of the two boats, Don walked upstream to let the others know they were safe.

Believing that Don and Lois were sure to capsize and drown and that the *Mexican Hat* and the *Wen* were lost, Norm had turned back at Rapid Four. Above Rapid Two he joined Elzada, Bill, and Gene, sitting dejectedly with the *Botany* tied nearby, eating dinner from cans without utensils, which were on the other boats.

As Norm sat down to eat, Don yelled from the opposite bank. Relieved that at least Don was safe, the four piled into the *Botany* and crossed the river in the strong current. "I never saw a better fight in my life than to see Norm crossing almost straight in that rough water," Elzada said. Norm estimated the current at twenty miles per hour.

Now five members of the expedition were together, and they learned that Lois was safe, though alone. Don and Gene set out to rejoin Lois, but approaching darkness and the treacherous terrain prevented them from reaching her. They spent a miserable night on a large rock. Elzada, Norm, and Bill endured a cold, uncomfortable night without dry clothing or bedding. "All in all, it was a most unusual horrid night," Elzada later remarked in her journal.

Though alone, Lois fared better than her companions. She had the bedding and plenty of food. She built a large fire, ate some toast and jam, and slept near the fire. Rising water forced her to move and build a new fire during the night, but as she later wrote to her mother, "Aside from a few ants, the rustling of packrats in the bushes, and the lapping and sucking of the waves, I had a lovely time."

At first light, Don and Gene worked their way downstream to Lois' camp, finding her safe and comfortable. Norm brought the *Wen* through the rapids with Elzada and Gene aboard. The group, intact and safe, celebrated with a breakfast of venison steaks. They had survived their first test, but much awaited them. "This river's really showing its teeth," Elzada wrote in her journal that night.

On their seventh day out, still in Cataract Canyon, they camped above a series of four rapids. Norm, Don, and Bill looked the rapids over and decided they could run the first two but would have to portage (physically carry the boats and gear) around the latter two. The group, already fatigued, ran the first rapid and managed to get the *Wen* and the *Botany* through the second rapid, but the *Mexican Hat* had to be lined (guided with ropes) through the second rapid. They lined the *Botany* around the third rapid before, weary and exhausted, they stopped on a steep slope for the night.

Norm had trouble sleeping, worrying about the next day's efforts. He confided in his diary that the women were doing too much work whereas Gene didn't know how to work. Portaging required tremendous effort. Tomorrow, all three boats would have to be completely unloaded and carried around the rapid. Then they would return for the supplies. It was tortuous work in difficult terrain under a hot June sun.

By this time, as will happen with small groups in trying situations, ten-

Haldene "Buzz" Holmstrom gives a souvenir to Lois Jotter on Navajo Bridge—his waterproof matchcase with a compass. *Photograph courtesy of the Lois Jotter Cutter Collection, Cline Library, Special Collections and Archives, Northern Arizona University. NAU.PH.95.3.27.*

sions were developing. Don and Gene thought Norm too cautious, that he was insisting they line rapids they could easily run. In her journal, Elzada noted that "Gene is inclined to be a little cynical of Norm's handling of lining, etc."

In the morning the tired crew began unloading the boats and dragging them to the top of the slope above the rapid. This was by far the hardest day yet. Lois noted in her journal, "Painful as heck and hot. All of us pretty low, and Don feeling sick." In fact, everyone but Norm and Elzada had been sick, probably from drinking river water without letting it settle, thereby irritating their digestive tracts. That evening before dinner Norm gave everyone a half-jigger of whiskey.

After a fitful night's sleep, they finished the portaging and by late afternoon were back on the river again. Spirits rose. They camped on a sandy beach, built

Elzada Clover (center) and Lois Jotter looking no worse for wear at the end of their 1938 river trip. *Photograph courtesy of the Belknap Collection, Cline Library, Special Collections and Archives, Northern Arizona University. NAU.PH.96.4.114.3.*

a big campfire, and cooked a hearty meal. A light rain began to fall, and the men made a makeshift shelter. The group talked and laughed, listening to Norm's stories of his river-running escapades. When the rain turned into a downpour, they crawled into their bedrolls—but inside their flimsy shelter, they all got good and soaked.

They spent most of the next morning drying their clothes and gear. The river looked smooth as Norm headed for Gypsum Canyon, and he decided to forgo his customary scouting. He and Elzada led the way, running several rapids easily. At the mouth of Gypsum Canyon, a steep drop appeared out of nowhere. It was too late to pull for shore. Norm and Elzada hung on and miraculously stayed upright, but they looked back and saw the *Botany* flipped, tossing Gene and Bill into the river. Gene hung onto the *Botany*, but Bill was nowhere in sight. Don and Lois made it through the drop, spotted Bill trying to swim to shore, and pulled him into the *Mexican Hat*. Norm managed to row to the capsized *Botany*. Elzada caught the bow line and pulled Gene into the *Wen*. Norm grabbed the stern rope, jumped out of the boat, and swam to shore, intending to tie the *Botany* and *Wen* together. "Got to shore as rope began to pull through my fingers. Couldn't hold it," Norm wrote. The *Wen* swept out into the swift current. Gene negotiated eight rapids in the *Wen* while Elzada hung onto the bow rope of the *Botany*. Finally, five miles from where the *Botany* first flipped, Gene and Elzada pulled into an eddy, exhausted, but with both boats safe.

Norm ran, but unable to catch the boats, he signaled Bill, Don, and Lois to pick him up below the next rapid. The four—Norm, Bill, Don, and Lois—crowded into the *Mexican Hat*. "The worry," he wrote later, "just about shot my nerves. One boat and four passengers!" Norm feared that Elzada and Gene had drowned and lost both boats. How would he get the four of them through the Grand Canyon? He said aloud, "This is the end of my career as a riverman."

Norm insisted on lining a small rapid in Clearwater Canyon even though Don argued that it was unnecessary. It took thirty minutes to line the rapid. A half mile downstream, they rounded the bend to the welcome sight of Elzada, Gene, and the boats, all safe. "The relief," Norm wrote later, "was more than words can describe."

They made camp, Lois cooked supper, and they played a game of Hearts around the campfire before collapsing into their private thoughts. The series of mishaps had put the trip behind schedule. Norm now believed that their arrival at Boulder Dam (now Hoover Dam) would be between August 10 and 20, not the end of July as originally planned. Still, Norm refused to rush the trip and eliminate planned side trips.

On July 3, they pulled into the right bank above Trachyte Creek and walked to the Chaffin ranch, owned by a Mormon couple who had lived in the Grand Canyon for several years. The Chaffins served the river runners a feast: homemade bread and cheese, home-canned beef, fresh vegetables, and lots of coffee. Elzada recalled, "We all ate until we were nearly helpless." Lois said, "We fell to like harvest hands and had a wonderful time."

They left in the late afternoon and drifted into Glen Canyon. This beautiful respite between Cataract Canyon and Grand Canyon enchanted all who entered with its exquisite narrow side canyons, grottoes of hanging ferns, and tiny waterfalls. Today, Glen Canyon lies buried in the waters of Lake Powell, but for weary travelers in the 1930s, it meant smooth, comfortable river running. There were no major rapids for the next 149 miles, until Lees Ferry. The canyon itself was peaceful, but discontent stirred among the group. The younger members, Lois, Gene, Bill,

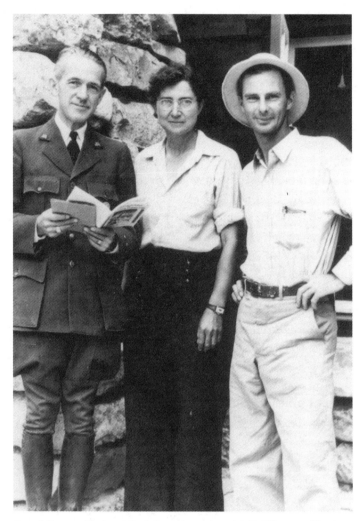

Grand Canyon National Park Superintendent M. R. Tillotson, Elzada Clover, and Norm Nevills. *Photograph courtesy of National Park Service.*

and Don, began to float behind Norm and Elzada, comparing grievances, particularly about Norm, whom they found too high-handed and authoritarian.

Their estimated date of arrival at Lees Ferry had been July 4. The July 5 *Los Angeles Evening Herald and Express* headlined "Planes Seek Six Explorers" and announced that four daily Trans World Airline (TWA) flights would deviate from their routes while pilots looked for the missing Nevills party.

Unaware that they were "missing," the group took time on July 6 to hike to Rainbow Bridge, the world's largest stone arch, standing 290 feet high and spanning 275 feet. Elzada commented in her journal that the bridge was "a breathtaking thing." They all signed the visitor book kept in a galvanized box and then walked to Rainbow Camp, where people who came to see the bridge by the land route often stayed. The director of the camp had previously told Norm to use the food cache. Elzada made fifty biscuits in a Dutch oven and opened several cans of food to make a delicious stew for lunch. They spent the afternoon climbing on the bridge and taking photos, and unable to resist, returned to the food cache and made more biscuits for dinner. It was dark before they made their way back to their own camp.

The next evening, July 7, as Lois cooked dinner, a small plane flew over them, circled once, and began dropping notes. One fell directly in camp. It read, "We are the U. S. Coast Guard plane searching for a party of six U. of Michigan geologists reportedly late at Lee's Ferry. If you are they, lie down all in a row, and then stand up. If in need of food, sit up. If members of party are all OK, extend arms horizontally. It is imperative that we know who you are, so identify yourself by first signal first." Lois and Gene, the only ones in camp, had fun answering the instructions and waved as the pilot dipped his wings in acknowledgment.

After supper, now anxious to reach Lees Ferry, they floated on in the moonlight a few miles before setting up camp. Elzada and Don played their harmonicas as the others sang, "When It's Moonlight on the Colorado."

In the morning Don built a roaring campfire, and when everyone was up, announced that he would leave the trip at Lees Ferry. He worried that if he stayed with the trip he would not make his new job assignment in Salt Lake City on time. The group changed into clean clothes for their arrival at Lees Ferry and broke camp. Just before 10:00 a.m., they floated single file to the landing.

Reporters were sleeping and lying about in the sun. Norm shouted, "Church is out, we're here," and they scrambled awake, persuading Norm to restage their entry, which they did. The reporters then served the crew watermelon, which they ate sitting on a log, responding to questions between bites.

A flurry of activity took place during the brief layover, and the weary crew relished the chance to be landlubbers for the first time in three weeks. Bill, Gene, and Lois stayed at the Marble Canyon Lodge near Lees Ferry, and Norm and Elzada drove to Mexican Hat. Norm was anxious to see his wife, Doris, and young daughter. En route, they stopped at the Tuba City Trading Post to order more supplies. Upon learning that the trader's twenty-four-year-old cousin, Lorin Bell, had recently returned from a trip to the South Seas, Norm convinced him to join the expedition in Don's place. At Mexican Hat, Norm also convinced Del Reid, an acquaintance of the Nevills family then prospecting in the vicinity, to join the crew.

Back at Marble Canyon Lodge, Bill, Gene, and Lois were surprised when Buzz Holmstrom, whose comment about women on the river had been widely reported, came to meet the expedition members. The three expeditioners shared their complaints about the trip with Buzz over dinner. Before leaving, as they walked out on Navajo Bridge, Buzz gave Lois a present, the waterproof matchcase with a compass that he had carried on his solo trip through the Grand Canyon the previous year.

When he returned to Lees Ferry on July 13, Norm decided to meet the tensions head on. Believing that Gene was the major cause of the discontent, he told him he had to leave the group. A heated discussion followed, and finally Elzada convinced Gene that it was in his best interests to return to Michigan. That matter settled and new supplies loaded, the reorganized party left shortly after noon to begin the second leg of their trip. As they passed under Navajo Bridge, 467 feet above, a large crowd gathered to watch the now-famous group of river runners depart.

With Gene gone, tensions dissipated. Norm wrote in his journal that evening, "This is a swell gang and we're going to town." Elzada commented, "The morale of the crowd is good," and later, "I'm glad Gene is gone. We have a fine bunch now."

On July 16 they pulled into Vasey's Paradise near lunchtime. This garden paradise could well have served as a set for the movie *Jurassic Park*. Water jets out of the canyon wall 125 feet above the river, providing life for an abundance of plants. Elzada and Lois rushed to collect the red monkey flowers, paintbrush, and even the most abundant plant, poison ivy.

While they worked, the men grew impatient and hungry. Elzada remarked in her journal that the boys "wanted lunch, although it was not twelve o'clock. Finally, I suggested that they get out the lunch things. The four of them managed to round

Elzada Clover studies a cactus at the Grand Canyon. *Photograph courtesy of National Park Service.*

up bag number 2, but they were sitting bug-eyed and expectant under a rock when we came to them. They had not mixed the malt or anything. We have spoiled them completely."

The next day they would arrive at Bright Angel Creek, but several major rapids lay in their way: 75-Mile Rapid (called Nevills Rapid since 1966), Hance, Sock-dolager, and Grapevine Rapids. This was the first real test with the new crew, but despite Norm's anxieties, all went well. At about 5:00 P.M. on July 19 the three boats rounded a curve to the left and saw the river gauging station and, sixty feet above the river, the Kaibab Suspension Bridge. Three newsmen on the bridge yelled, "Wave at us, look as if you were glad you're landing!"

They camped that night on the beach near Bright Angel Creek. The next morn-ing, everyone but Del hiked up the Bright Angel Trail to the South Rim. They started the eleven-mile, 5,000-foot climb at dawn in an attempt to get near the top before the intense summer sun hit the canyon. The trail tops out at Emery Kolb's home and studio. Blanche Kolb met them with pitchers of iced tea and invited them to lunch. She offered the women hot baths, and Emery directed the men to the showers. Norm invited Emery to join them for the rest of the trip, and he accepted. Emery, already a well-known photographer and canyon legend, had run the Colorado in 1911–1912 with his brother Ellsworth. His experience would be invaluable to the expedition.

Although it was a treat to sleep in a real bed, Lois and Elzada soon tired of all the attention. Wherever they went in Grand Canyon Village, they were besieged by autograph hunters. At 5:15 P.M. on July 21, after dinner and singing around the Kolbs' piano, the group started back down the Bright Angel Trail and into the canyon.

The next morning, boats were loaded and a false start staged so Emery could take movies. They had 247 miles to go before pulling into Lake Mead, the end of their journey. Norm estimated that it would take two more weeks, allowing time for plant gathering. They ran or lined several major rapids—Horn Creek, Granite, Hermit, and Serpentine. Lois and Elzada found an abundance of cacti in this section of the river, including many large barrel cacti. Elzada noted in her journal, "Must go now and collect plants. You've no idea how difficult it is to keep the mind on mere plants when the river is roaring and the boats are struggling to get through."

Emery Kolb was a great addition to the trip. In addition to being a skilled river runner, he played the harmonica and told stories. Elzada wrote in her journal, "You should see Mr. Kolb standing up on the stern holding to ropes, riding the waves in his BVD's, shirttail out, life preserver on, and a red hankie of mine fixed into a knotted affair on his head. He just loves this life."

Their final challenge would be the thirty-seven-foot drop at Lava Falls. The group pulled in for lunch just ahead of the rapid, and the more Norm studied it, the more he thought he could do it; but he believed the chances of capsizing were great and so decided to line it. After an extremely difficult day, all three boats were lined through Lava Falls. That night everyone was tired, but the worst was over. Norm predicted they would arrive at Lake Mead in three days.

The last days were anticlimactic. On July 29 after breakfast, Emery officiated over the River Rat Initiation Ceremony, initiating Norm, who then initiated the others. Each novice, on hands and knees, heads deeply bowed, repeated after Norm, as he had done after Emery, "I know I'm weak, I know I'm blind, I swear that I extend behind." As the word "behind" was uttered, Norm gave them each a resounding swat with a life preserver.

The next day, July 30, at 5:11 P.M., Norm wrote, "We're on the LAKE." They were eighty miles from the dock at Boulder Dam, completed only a few years earlier and backing up Lake Mead. With no current, unless someone came to tow them in it would be a long, hot row. The "intrepid explorers" rose at 4:00 A.M. on August 1 and rowed four hours before pulling into a side canyon for lunch and a nap. While eating, they thought they heard a motor, and everyone ran out to the point to yell and wave. The boat turned and roared into the side canyon. It was Buzz Holmstrom at the wheel of the *Navajo*, a twenty-foot powerboat. Their rowing hours ended as the three boats were tied to the powerboat. What a relief! Civilization was never a more welcome sight. Buzz wrote on Lois' helmet, "To the girl who proved me badly mistaken." Women, he'd decided, did belong on the river after all!

In all, the trip took forty-three days. Elzada and Lois claimed the distinction of being the first women to raft the Colorado River successfully through the Grand Canyon. Trip over, the group went to Boulder Dam Hotel to enjoy the comforts of a hot shower and soft bed. The next day, their history making adventure over, the group split up, returning to their normal pursuits.

This would be Elzada Clover's only trip through the Grand Canyon. She often gave talks about her adventure and always informed her botany classes that she was the first woman to run the Grand Canyon. A complete report of her and Lois's botanical findings appeared in the November 1944 *American Midland Naturalist* under the title "Floristic Studies in the Grand Canyon of the Colorado River and Tributaries." Following her retirement in 1967, Elzada Clover, by then a full professor, moved to the Rio Grande Valley in Texas to be near one of her sisters. She led an active life until her death in 1980 at the age of eighty-three.

Lois Jotter returned to Michigan to complete work for her Ph.D. She married Victor Cutter Jr. in 1942 and finished her doctoral dissertation while her husband was teaching at Cornell University. In 1947 they moved to Connecticut, where he taught at Yale for five years; they next moved to Greensboro, North Carolina, where he became chairman of the Department of Biology at the University of North Carolina. Lois devoted her time to raising their two children, Ann and Victor III. In 1963, following her husband's death, Lois joined the faculty at the University of North Carolina as assistant professor of botany. She retired in 1984.

Lois returned to the Colorado River in September 1994 to join the Legends Trip, a group of "old-timers" whose purpose was to compare river conditions before and after the construction of Glen Canyon Dam. At the Grand Canyon River Guides

Training Seminar in late March 1995, Lois, a tall, distinguished woman with a friendly smile, braved a harsh spring storm to tell stories and share experiences with fellow river rats. She still had the waterproof matchcase and compass given to her by Buzz Holmstrom on Navajo Bridge.

When I spoke with her in the summer of 2003, Lois had just returned from a trip down the Amazon River! Ten years later, in 2013, Lois Jotter Cutter passed away at her home in Greensboro, North Carolina, at the age of ninety-nine.

CHAPTER NINE

A Grand Canyon Trailblazer

GALE BURAK
(1917—2011)

Gale Gardner Burak was twenty-four when she first saw the Grand Canyon in May 1942. Like the blink of an eye where strangers fall instantly in love, she knew with her first breath of canyon air that it had become part of her and she had become part of it. Through the dissolution of one marriage and the embrace of the next, across the births of three children, moves from place to place, and management of a business, Gale would return again and again to the canyon like a homing pigeon. She would live, hike, visit, and work there in the course of her life; its expanse gave her the greatest gifts her independent nature craved: solitude and freedom in a setting of stupendous beauty.

"Everyone thought I was crazy," Gale said of her earliest days in the canyon. "After all, I was one of the few nuts, male or female, who hiked in the '40s. Everyone rode a mule in those days. Hiking! Imagine!" And hike she did, usually alone, across more trails and to more remote places in the Grand Canyon than any other woman. The Grand Canyon became, as her daughter Pam would say years later, "Mom's backyard."

Gale was born, she said, "with wanderlust in my blood." She learned about seeing new places early in life as her father, who worked for a large chemical company headquartered in Boston, helped start up new plants. "Each time he was sent to a new city, we went too. I'd moved ten times by age twelve," Gale explained, "but mostly I grew up in the suburbs of Boston." She loved the outdoors and as

93

a teenager joined the Appalachian Mountain Club, where she was introduced to hiking, white water canoeing, skiing, and rock climbing in the White Mountains north of Boston.

"By the time I graduated from high school, I really had itchy feet and was ready to move," Gale said. But she married Reuel "Mac" McLaughlin instead, a man much older than she was. "I shouldn't have. It wasn't a very happy marriage. Mac contracted tuberculosis and had to be in a sanitarium for a year and then needed another year of convalescence. The doctor advised us to go out West."

Gale contacted a married school friend who lived on a ranch east of Springerville, Arizona, and made arrangements for them to live there

Gale Burak and her Grand Canyon.
Photograph courtesy of Gale Burak.

for a few months, helping with the chores, while they decided where to settle. "It was wonderful," Gale said. "I hiked from one end of the Penasco Valley to the other. . . . [There was] such beauty to this barren country that it just was immediately home. When we left the ranch we decided to take a look at the Grand Canyon before settling down. I was overwhelmed. I telephoned my mother and said, 'Send me my clothes and my bicycle, I've found Utopia.'" Gale wanted the bicycle for exploring around the South Rim of the canyon.

Gale and Mac, who was by now well again, both enjoyed the canyon and wanted more time to explore. They found jobs at the Fred Harvey Motor Lodge—Gale as a waitress, and Mac as a maintenance man. The nation was in the midst of World War II, and most business at the canyon involved soldiers on "R and R"—rest and relaxation. "The army had a big mechanized unit outside of Kingman, Arizona, and the men were brought up to the canyon for R and R," Gale explained. "The Motor Lodge was one of the places they came because they didn't have much money. I got a lot of proposals of one kind and another," she laughed.

The Air Force came to the canyon, too. "In the morning we would hear a rumble to the south, and it would be pursuit planes from the Phoenix bases," Gale recalled. "They would come in formation, a few at a time. They would aim for the flagpole by the El Tovar Hotel and dive-bomb down just above it, then just keep going on down into the canyon, zooming out north, east, or west, once they got down. A normal sound in the canyon is amplified, whether it's a voice, a bird, or the roar of a river. When you add mechanical noise, it is certainly not conducive to serenity in the canyon!"

But the serenity of the canyon did not help Gale's relationship with Mac, and a few months after getting jobs at the canyon, they agreed to divorce. "He took the car, and I kept my bicycle and the canyon. I got the better deal for sure," Gale said.

After Mac left, Gale usually ate dinner with the Fred Harvey wranglers who took "dudes" (eastern tourists) into the canyon. The wranglers gave her the nickname "Pigtails" in reference to her preferred hairstyle. "It was fun to have dinner at the transportation dining room in the back of El Tovar," Gale said. "I used to listen to them try to outdo each other with 'trail tales.' I enjoyed these stories, and the men were good to me. I never really minded when they called me 'that doggone crazy Pigtails.'"

During this time Gale became friends with Emery Kolb, the famous photographer and canyon explorer who had been living at the canyon since 1902, and his family. In his younger days, Emery had hiked all over the Grand Canyon, so he was a wellspring of information about areas Gale could explore. In return, she would visit Emery after her trips and share stories about what she did and what she saw. Unable to explore the canyon as deeply and fully as he once could, Emery relished the opportunity to compare notes with this intrepid, pigtailed explorer. "He hiked vicariously through me," Gale explained.

She arranged her work schedule so she'd have a few days off in a row. "Sometimes I'd pop down to Phantom Ranch after work for an exploring trip up Phantom Creek, up to Utah Flats, over to Clear Creek, or to the North Rim for a few days," she said. Gale especially enjoyed moonlight hikes where she felt herself float down the thin, white thread of trail into a breathless shimmering void. "I can still feel the thrill of those night hikes. Cliff walls dipped away in successive waves of looming then lessening glow and shadow, indistinctly softening into nothingness behind me."

Midnight might find her taking a quick swim in the Phantom Ranch swimming pool before going to bed in the little stone cabin that her friends Phil and Em

Poquette, ranch managers, kept open for her. "It was bliss just to stretch out and breathe in the canyon night as sleep gradually stole over me. There'll never be better nights than those; never be times of feeling so sublimely alone yet so completely part of that wonderful world."

Come daylight, Gale would head out with some leftover hotcakes, a chunk of cheese, and an apple or two that Em or Phil gave her. When she got out of sight of Phantom Ranch, off came most of her clothes. "I am, I must admit, by nature a nudist, and even though the theory is to be sure to cover and conserve the moisture of your body, I am much happier when I'm freer," Gale said.

Gale would pull off her hiking boots along Bright Angel Creek, for in the 1940s there were no bridges in The Box, and she had to wade. "Eventually my feet got so tough that I'd go barefoot between crossings. I had the canyon to myself. It was bliss."

Gale often hiked from the South Rim to the North Rim and back, seeing no one save an occasional fisherman in Bright Angel Creek and the staff at Phantom Ranch. "I'm so sorry that people can't experience that today," she said. With more than four million visitors a year to the canyon, of which perhaps a quarter are either day or backpacking hikers, it is quite impossible for one to find such solitude there now.

When time permitted, Gale headed out for several days of more distant backpacking. "At first, I had a heavy wooden pack that I'd made myself. Then I started using a blanket roll. I put my food, spare socks, a long-sleeved shirt, and a canteen in the center of the blanket. I'd tie it on [to myself] different ways, either over one shoulder like the doughboys used to do in World War I or else I had it around my shoulders and dangling in front of me, and then I tied it to my waist. I would just decide which direction I was going in and I would tell either a friend or a ranger on the rim or Phil and Em where I was headed. I would establish a base camp and hike out from the camp." These were days and nights of pure solitude. Time was limitless, and Gale would spend hours exploring side canyons for hidden waterfalls or Indian ruins. At night she'd watch millions of stars ignite the sky as she fell asleep atop her bedroll.

Gale's initial time at the canyon was too short. She was transferred to Fred Harvey's Escalante Hotel thirty miles south of the canyon in Ash Fork, Arizona, at the end of the summer tourist season. She worked there until the following spring, when she quit to hike down Havasu Canyon to Supai, a village in the western end of the Grand Canyon that was home to three hundred Havasupai Indians. Havasu Canyon is an oasis in the desert—striking blue-green waterfalls tumble through red sandstone cliffs to form deep blue bathtub-like pools. Over a mile below the village, Havasu Falls cascades about ninety feet, and a mile farther down the canyon, spectacular Mooney Falls drops nearly two hundred feet, forming a large pool at its base.

Unlike today, when helicopters fly daily into the canyon and electricity and satellite dishes connect the Havasupai with the outside world, in 1943 they lived an isolated life deep in the canyon. Although some of the tribe worked at the South Rim, most remained on the reservation, growing their own food and eking out a meager existence, either by farming or working for the small lead and zinc mine halfway between Havasu and Mooney Falls. They were well known for their peach orchards and each fall celebrated the harvest with a rodeo and Peach Festival. Although many visitors came each year for the festival, few tourists came at other times during the year.

Burak at Havasu Falls, ca. 1943.
Photograph courtesy of Gale Burak.

Anyone going down to Supai then caught a ride with Foster Marshall from the South Rim post office out to Topocoba Hilltop. Marshall hauled the mail and other supplies to the hilltop every two weeks, meeting a Havasupai packer, Lorenzo Sinyella, and his strings of horses there. As Gale climbed in the back of Marshall's pickup and found a seat on a mail sack, she met two women who were also traveling into Havasu Canyon. Gladys Broderson and Sonia Buchholz had already explored Supai on horseback on several previous trips. The three women got acquainted during the bouncy thirty-mile ride to Topocoba, where the two women mounted horses for the trip, while Gale set off gaily on foot down to the village. They spent the late afternoons together that week comparing their separate adventures, Gale on foot and Gladys and Sonia on horseback, as they swam and relaxed in the pools below Havasu Falls.

Later in the week, the mine owner, Mr. Sanderson, came up to the village frantically looking for a new cook. His cook, seriously ill, was leaving for medical care. Never shy in the face of opportunity, Gale agreed to take the job for one week. "I had never done any cooking for other than my immediate family in my lifetime. But I figured, 'Well, he'll have pans and he'll have food and if they don't like it, I am just as happy not to be doing it anyway.'" The week lasted three months.

Gale's new living quarters lacked amenities. At first she slept in the cook shack beside the table; that ended when mice started falling out between the overlapping corrugated roofing and landing with a thump beside her. "I had visions of them falling in my open mouth," she laughed. "One night I caught a little spotted skunk in one of my mouse traps, and that settled it! I slept out under the cottonwoods from then on."

The cooking conditions would have challenged even the most experienced cook. Only someone like Gale—flexible and resourceful—could have managed so well. The tiny shack had a kitchen area on the left with a counter and some cupboards. At the end was a small woodstove vented through the roof. The stove had no oven, so Gale was unable to make bread. "I made spider bread," she explained. "That is, corn bread made in a 'spider': an old-fashioned heavy skillet." The heat in Supai in the summer is intense, and Gale had no refrigerator, but she did have an old-fashioned double soapstone tub. "I put water in the tubs and kept vegetables in there. At the spring I had a little frame box with netting—a refrigerator-type frame box on legs. It had netting on all four sides and hemp sacks hanging down all around, letting water from a pan on top drip down with the wind blowing through to keep food fairly cool. There was an old prospector's dugout I used for a cold cellar. A big bull snake lived in there and kept the mice down."

The men she cooked for worked hard and ate heartily. They wanted three square meals a day and always insisted on onions. "Onions three times a day proved a little difficult until I realized that I could pickle them and keep them on the table," she said. "The noon meal would usually be a beef stew or sow belly and beans and was the main meal of the day."

Havasupai packers carried out the lead ore five days a week to Hualapai Hilltop. They also hauled down mine supplies and food for the camp. Gale made a list once a week and sent it to be filled at the grocery in Seligman and packed for horse transport. Gale ordered enough meat for fifteen men: a case of eggs, several heads of cabbage, bunches of carrots, many pounds of potatoes and onions, apples and oranges, rice, and oatmeal. "I'd always get candy for the village children, and ribbons, rickrack, sugar, and other notions for the mamas, not to mention the latest newspapers for the miners. It took quite a few horses to lug it all down each week!" Gale said.

All was not work. With a day off each week she found much exploratory fun up side canyons or on the Redwall rim about the creek. On workdays, Gale took time in the afternoons, usually from 2:00 to 4:00 o'clock, to go down to the creek to enjoy the combination of the sun, heat, and cool water in the pool below Havasu Falls. She became friends with several of the Havasupai women, most of whom spoke English. "I couldn't figure out why the children were such good swimmers and their mothers would never get in the water," Gale said. "I would lie in the creek nearly every afternoon and read and write letters, and Effie Hanna, who became a good friend, would come down to the bank to talk and giggle, but she wouldn't take off her Mother Hubbard dress and enjoy the sun as I was doing. She wouldn't even go in the water."

In the evenings everyone in camp sat under the cottonwood trees. "I enjoyed listening to the stories of these fellows and the jokes, which would be a bit off-color sometimes but never really raunchy. The stories usually involved either narrow escapes in the mine, some drinking escapade, or some other tales that made good listening. But you knew there was a borderline of truth and fancy in the stories." Being the only woman did not present a problem because, as Gale said, "I wasn't the sweet, helpless little doll-baby that perhaps they might have had different ideas about."

After she'd been a cook three months, Gale had a disagreement with Sanderson. She agreed to stay one more week, until he got a new cook. When word of her impending departure spread, many of the Supai, especially the women and children, expressed their sorrow that she was leaving. They had grown to love this unusual young woman who clearly enjoyed being with them and their canyon. Effie invited her to take a sweat bath with the women before she left. This was an unusual honor and one that Gale could not refuse.

A Havasupai sweat lodge is a small igloo-shaped hut formed with bent willow branches and covered with green hides, built beside a creek to allow for quick cooling off afterwards. Rocks are placed on hot coals in a pit in the center. Pouring water over the rocks creates intense steam. "There were four of us using this particular lodge, and I was nearest the door. You had to crouch in the fetal position around the edge of it with your head well down because it was so low and rounded that there was no chance to sit straight up," Gale explained. "When you figure the condition of the old hides as affected by the heat, plus the accumulation of both smoke and strong perspiration odor, the effect of it all was pretty strong.

"In about fifteen minutes I was praying silently but very fervently, 'Please Lord, don't let me faint because I'll fall flat on my face on these hot rocks and scar myself for life.' Between the heat, the humidity, and the 'fragrance,' it was just more than I could stand for a longer period than that. And so I just got out and jumped in the creek, which is cold and deep. The shock is tremendous, and you do feel like a million after that, but once was enough."

On the day Gale left, Jim Crook, the Supai village minister, sent his favorite horse down to the mining camp for her to ride out to the hilltop. "As I went up past the village, past the homes and fields and gardens, past the [Indian Affairs] agency and rodeo grounds, everyone, even the kids, was out. They all said, 'Good-bye, good-bye,' and it was really very traumatic for me. I felt happy that they felt that way."

Though her time there was short, Gale's experience at Supai and the mining camp was meaningful. The openness of the Havasupai people and their acceptance of her despite their differences lent a human edge to the canyon walls and water she loved so well. She had become a richer person for having been there.

Gale was again struck by the familiar pangs of wanderlust, and she set out to explore more of the West. Living the carefree life of a vagabond, Gale spent the next couple years of her life hitchhiking to Los Angeles, Reno, and Yosemite, visiting old friends and making new ones, exploring the countryside and mountains. She worked odd jobs as needed to get from one place to the next, often hitchhiking along lonely stretches. "I looked like a fellow," Gale laughed. "I had a slim body. I had Levis on, I had a big pack and a cowboy hat on. My braids were tucked up under the hat, and invariably when someone stopped, they said, 'My God, it's a woman!'"

During the summers of 1944 and 1945 Gale worked in Yosemite National Park for the Yosemite Park and Curry Company, the park concessioner; and as she had done at the Grand Canyon, she spent her days off hiking in the high country. When the summer season of 1945 came to a close, Gale decided to take one last backpacking trip. "I headed up out of Yosemite Valley to Merced Lake, where the cook was closing up camp for the season. He gave me a big piece of hot apple pie, and I went on up the trail with it in my hand covered with a napkin."

Just before the junction with the Half Dome turnoff, she came across a fellow bent over, drinking from a brook. "He looked up and grinned, and, oh, what a grin!" The grin was on the face of Ted Burak, a Rhode Island man who'd gone west in an old jalopy in the late 1930s. He'd worked in Yosemite Valley until he was drafted into the army and sent to Alaska, where he worked on the construction of the Alaska Highway. When his term with the army was over, he returned to Yosemite to visit friends. "We climbed up the trail to Vogelsang Camp, where he polished off most of

Gale Burak with her good friend Emery Kolb, ca. 1976. *Photograph courtesy of Gale Burak.*

the food I'd planned to use for several days." This meant that they both had to return the next day to the valley; Ted treated Gale to a sumptuous home-cooked dinner in his small, rented cabin. That's when they really got acquainted.

With a mutual love of mountains and hiking as a start, the two soon married and settled in Sonora, California, where Ted opened a service station. Their three children, Lance, Susan, and Pam, were born there.

In 1955, when Gale developed an acute allergy to poison oak, and Ted's service station fell victim to an interstate, the couple decided to move to New England to be nearer both families. They settled in Lincoln, New Hampshire, in the White Mountains, where Ted ran a service station and Gale managed a grocery and gift shop, cabin rentals, and campground. Over the next eighteen years they carried their beloved West deep in their hearts as they led a very busy life, working seven days a week during the tourist season, which began with fishing in April and didn't end until after the fall foliage faded in early October. It was not until 1973, when the children were grown and on their own, that Ted and Gale consolidated their holdings and sold all but their home and garage. Although Ted still had to tend the garage, Gale was now free to return to the West to work.

While on a hiking trip in Utah's Capitol Reef National Park, Gale, then fifty-five, met an older woman behind the visitor center's information desk and learned that she was a Volunteer in the Park (VIP). She thought, "If she could do it, I jolly well could too!" She contacted the personnel director at the Grand Canyon about the program and, as fate would have it, was hired for the following season as a VIP in the backcountry office.

Gale and other qualified volunteers received a small stipend for expenses and an RV campsite with hookups as accommodations during the summer tourist season. That fall, with Gale's service at the canyon complete until the next spring, Ted turned the supervision of his garage over to his manager and headed west for a "honeymoon" winter with Gale, roaming the deserts of Mexico and the Southwest. For the next several years, Gale spent long summers at the Grand Canyon as ranger in charge of inner canyon campgrounds, and she and Ted were reunited each winter for their travels around the West.

These later years at the canyon had brought Gale full circle. Some thirty years after she'd first laid eyes on it, she was back again, working as she had before—but this time for the National Park Service. She worked three seasons as a VIP and then spent most of the next eight years employed as an inner canyon seasonal ranger, working six to seven months of the year. Still slim, fit, and, eager to explore, Gale spent her off-duty time hiking in the canyon.

Once, on a return hike from the Inner Gorge near the lone pine overlooking Horn Rapids, Gale noticed an elaborate spider web and pulled aside a small bush to get a better look at the web. There, behind the bush, lay the corrugated, coiled base of an earthenware jug. "What a thrill!" she said. "Normally, something like this should not be touched, but right along the bench below the cliff, I had seen the recent tracks of man-sized boots, traipsing along. They served to remind me that others go far off the beaten trails now too. I didn't dare leave this bit of history." Gale carefully drew the pot out and examined the treasure. It was whole and in perfect condition except for a small hole on its down side with a ring of caliche stain around it. The jug was empty with no evidence of a lid, pollen, grain, or charcoal, and no black widow spider either!

Finding the heavy pot was one thing, but getting it safely up to Indian Garden was another matter. "I had a long-sleeved cotton shirt in my daypack," the ever resourceful Gale recalled, "and by tying opposite tails and sleeves together I made a fine sling to carry it. It was tricky, swinging it carefully from arm to arm as I scrambled hand and foot up the slickrock gully to the plateau, but at that point I'd rather have broken an arm than that pot." Luckily, she met Ranger Wayne Paya, who carried the pot on horseback to Indian Garden. From there it was helicoptered to the South Rim.

Robert Euler, then National Park Service archeologist, told Gale that her find was a utility jug, probably a thousand years old, and had most likely been used as a water storage pot for hunters who had hidden among the boulders waiting for bighorn sheep to come down for water in a tinaja (small rock pool). Today the pot is in the museum collection at Grand Canyon National Park.

Gale found the pot while on a hike that her longtime friend Emery Kolb had suggested. Emery, by then an ailing ninety-five years old, had lost both his wife, Blanche, and brother Ellsworth in 1960 and was alone in his studio and home on the edge of the Grand Canyon. Gale stayed with Emery in the summer of 1976, sleeping in the same bed that Theodore Roosevelt once used. "Emery needed somebody who could supplement his lack of sight, lack of hearing, and a pair of hands as well," she explained.

Leaving the National Park Service temporarily, Gale worked for Emery for five months, May through September, helping him sort through his memorabilia and photographic collections. "He was such a packrat!" Gale said. She would describe an item, and he would say, "Yes, that's something I want to save," or "This is something that is nobody's business. I want you to destroy it." Gale sorted papers according to subject matter and date and put them in boxes. She found piles of photos garnered from every shelf, closet, and drawer. "There were hundreds of duplicates," Gale exclaimed. "I saved the best for Emery's files and then sent the rest up to the studio to be sold at many times their original price. This pleased Emery to no end!" She felt her work was a labor of love. "It was of great importance for Emery as well as to me, and one of the most exciting times of my life," Gale said.

Kolb died that December, only two months after Gale had left for her winter trip with Ted. They were in Tucson for Christmas with friends when Gale received the phone call about Emery's death. Because she had so recently acted as his secretary, housekeeper, chauffeur, and companion and knew not only about his affairs but of his wishes concerning certain matters, she was asked to return to the canyon for a few days to help sort out his estate. "It proved to be a fitting farewell to Emery, in a way, as there were many things he and I had discussed which put a bearing on decisions. I was glad to do it," she said.

Gale helped pave the way for women rangers to work in the inner canyon posts—stations that were traditionally given to men—when in the spring of 1978, she became the second woman ever stationed in the canyon, replacing the supervising ranger at Phantom Ranch. The following summer she was stationed at Hermit Camp, a popular wilderness camping area at the foot of the Hermit Trail, but it was Cottonwood Campground that Gale came to call home.

She spent four seasons (1980 to 1983) as the ranger in residence in the tiny cabin in the shade of the tall cottonwoods along the North Kaibab Trail. She was responsible for all maintenance, law enforcement, and minor medical work, as well as assisting hikers and campers, checking permits, patrolling the North Kaibab Trail, and answering questions. She especially enjoyed giving interpretive talks in the early evening. She liked to let hikers headed for the North Rim know what to expect.

"Near the end of the talk, I emphasized to everybody that if they were going to the North Rim they'd best get started by 4:00 or 5:00 A.M. I would stand right beside a big rock in the group campsite where I could look up Transept Canyon and see the Grand Canyon Lodge while lecturing. I would keep my eye on it, and as soon as the light came on up in the lobby, I'd say, 'I see that the eye of the North Rim is on us, so it's time to get to bed.' They'd look up too, and the light looked almost straight overhead. Shocked, they would say, 'My God, you mean we have to go up there?'" The North Rim was a seven-mile hike away, and nearly a 5,000-foot climb!

Gale often stopped hikers she thought were headed to the North Rim too late in the day. Late one afternoon, she stopped two men to warn them they didn't have enough daylight left to reach the top. As it turned out, they were only going another three miles, to Roaring Springs, where they planned to turn around and go back to Bright Angel Campground. One of the men, Abdoul Balsharoff, told her he had decided he would like to spend more time in the canyon, and Gale arranged by radio for him to spend two nights at Indian Garden on his way out to the South Rim. While they were talking, Gale commented that they had on identical hiking shoes: men's size 8 Nikes of the same color. Even the canyon has room for small coincidences. The three finished their conversation, and Abdoul, his friend, and Gale went their separate ways.

Glad to have met and helped the young men, Gale's attention turned to her

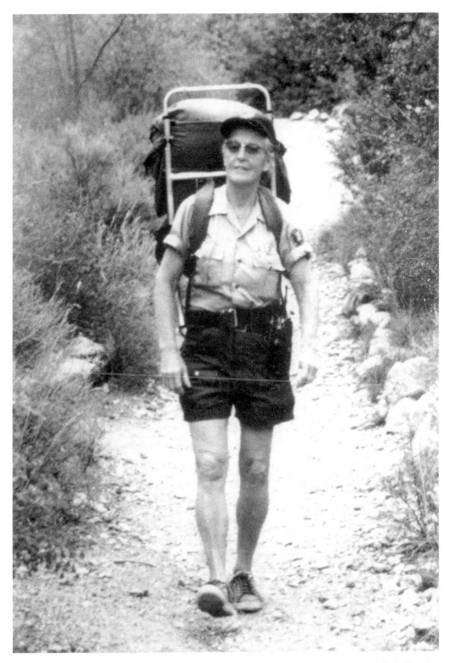

The intrepid ranger near Cottonwood Campground. *Photograph courtesy of Gale Burak.*

upcoming hike to Phantom Ranch, where she would meet Ted after their long summer apart. They would hike the canyon together for a week before closing Cottonwood Campground for the season. When she arrived at Phantom Ranch, she found a scene of unusual excitement. Before even saying hello, Dave Bucchello, head ranger for Bright Angel and the Colorado River, asked Gale if she planned to stay at Phantom.

"Yes, tonight and tomorrow night," Gale replied. "Why?"

"We're getting ready for a manhunt. It's a kid that was supposed to get up to Indian Garden last night and didn't get there," Dave explained.

"Anybody I should know?" Gale queried.

"He went up the canyon a couple of days ago, Abdoul Balsharoff," Dave said.

"Oh my Lord!" Gale exclaimed. "I'm the one that gave him his permit to go to the Gardens." Gale described Balsharoff, including what he was wearing, and the size and style of his shoes. Gale maintained the base at Phantom Ranch during the search, handling the helicopter traffic, answering the radio, and providing any information she could, such as the various trails she had recommended to him.

Two days after he disappeared, searchers found a footprint from a size 8, Nike-type sole near the mouth of Clear Creek, headed downstream. This led the rangers to speculate that Balsharoff had gotten disoriented and tried to follow the river back to Phantom Ranch. A Huey helicopter with sophisticated infrared equipment came in from an airbase in California and searched the river and side canyons for two days but found no sign of him. The search was called off, and he was never found. Gale could not help but wonder what had happened to Balsharoff. She knew full well the dangers that await even experienced hikers like herself.

In 1983 Gale left her work in the canyon to spend more time with Ted. He sold the business in New Hampshire, and they bought a house in Moab, Utah, to be close to the canyon country they both loved. Gale worked as a VIP interpretive guide at Arches National Park while Ted golfed. A year after making Moab their home, Ted was diagnosed with cancer. They returned to the East so that he could spend his remaining time near their family. He died in 1987. Gale returned to Moab for one more year before moving back to New Hampshire.

She came back to the Grand Canyon again to work the winter season of 1991–1992 as a VIP interpretive ranger at Phantom Ranch. She would hike in and work ten days on with four days off, staying at the Phantom Ranch Ranger Station along with two other employees.

"The first thing I did in the morning was to call dispatch and get the weather forecast. I had to write up copies of this for the various display cases, including two at Phantom, one down at the lower bridge over Bright Angel Creek near the river, and one in the campground. I also put up the title of that evening's talk and a notice of the 4:00 P.M. informal gathering under the cottonwoods by the dining hall, both of which I would give."

Burak at home in the White Mountains of New Hampshire, fall 1995. *Photograph by Betty Leavengood.*

Once again Gale especially enjoyed delivering the afternoon talks. She prepared and presented a variety of programs about Grand Canyon history, including accounts of the Civilian Conservation Corps building the River Trail during the Great Depression, early days at Phantom Ranch, or evidence of prehistoric Indians that lived in the canyon. Each group of visitors had questions. "They'd invariably start by saying, 'Do you mind if I ask you a personal question?' and I'd know what was coming. 'How old are you? How did you get down here? Did you get flown in?' I'd say, 'I'm seventy-four, I hiked in, and I'm hiking out,' and then get on with the program."

Gale had completed that winter at Phantom Ranch in early March and set out on her hike back up the Bright Angel Trail. She was to meet her friend Myla at the top, and the two would spend a few days together on the South Rim. The weather looked forbidding that day. "I shouldn't have tried to go out," Gale later reflected, "but I thought that the next day might be worse. It was raining down at Phantom, and by the time I got to [Indian] Garden it had turned to slush. In the Redwall [section] the slush turned to ice." As any true Grand Canyon hiker, Gale measured her progress in terms of geologic layers. The steep cliff of Redwall, about five trail miles up from the Colorado River, is one of the more difficult sections. It is hard enough when the trail is dry, but on rainy days—and, especially, snowy days—the trail is treacherous.

"My feet were wet, and by the time I got up to somewhere in the upper Hermit layer, it was snow. Just when I got to the tunnel in the Coconino layer I heard way up above, 'Gale! Gale!' and I didn't have enough wind to answer. By the time I got to Kolb's Corner, I could tell whose voice it was; it was my friend Myla. She was up there in the snow waiting to give me a ride home. When I hadn't shown up earlier, she had called down to the Gardens and knew that I was on the way. Here I was hiking out of the canyon, snow swirling around me, ice and slush on the trail, with no one else around, and I wondered if I would ever be doing this again."

Gale never did get to the bottom of the canyon again. Though she did return to visit friends and take walks part way down, her home was in North Woodstock, New Hampshire.

In June 1996 at the Grand Canyon Pioneers annual picnic, Gale stood on the rim of the canyon at Shoshone Point side by side with Harvey Butchart, a legendary Grand Canyon hiker. No one yet has come close to hiking the canyon as much as these "pioneers." The two, one nearing eighty and the other ninety, talked animatedly of their experiences in the Grand Canyon, laughing, remembering, and wishing they could do it all over again. Harvey Butchart died in 2002 at the age of ninety-five. Gale Burak died in 2011 at the age of ninety-three.

CHAPTER TEN

Woman of the River

GEORGIE WHITE CLARK
(1910—1992)

When Georgie White Clark first saw the Colorado River in 1945, she said, "I'd always been restless, but when I saw the Grand, I knew I was home. It had everything I wanted. It was beautiful beyond words, like nothing I'd ever dreamed of, and it was wild, and at the same time you had the parts that were peaceful."

Born Bessie DeRoss in Guthrie, Oklahoma, on November 13, 1910, she quickly acquired the nickname "Georgie," probably after her father, George DeRoss, a sometime miner and general n'er-do-well who abandoned the family when Georgie was very young.

Georgie grew up too fast. At age sixteen she married Harold Clark, an all-American-looking six-foot blonde, and gave birth to her only child, Sommona Rose, a year later. Unprepared for the responsibilities of parenthood, Georgie and Harold left their daughter with Georgie's mother and moved to New York City. There Georgie worked as a comptometer operator (a pre-calculator device used to tally receipts and keep books), and Harold took on part-time jobs; together they did their best to make ends meet during the Depression.

Partial to open spaces, Georgie didn't like New York. She thought the city to be too expensive and far too crowded. The turning point in her life came when she met some professional bicycle racers training in Central Park. Intrigued by their unusual lifestyle, she learned to ride a bike and decided to cycle to California. In August 1936, a determined Georgie quit her job and announced to Harold that they were going to ride bicycles to the West Coast. Now twenty-six, Georgie had a

Georgie White in action. *Photograph courtesy of the Delphine Gallagher Collection, Cline Library, Special Collections and Archives, Northern Arizona University. NAU. PH.93.5.120.*

fierce, independent nature. She rarely let anything or anyone stand in her way—not even her husband. When he hesitated, Georgie informed him that she would leave without him. Unwilling to let her go alone, Harold agreed, and they started across the country. They ate at farmhouses along the way and picked up odd jobs where they could. When the couple reached the West Coast they flipped their last quarter to decide whether to go to Los Angeles or San Francisco. Los Angeles won. They spent the quarter on waffles and syrup, then set off to pawn Georgie's diamond wedding ring for seventy-five dollars.

Georgie found a job again operating a comptometer. She convinced her mother to move from Oklahoma to Los Angeles, bringing her son Paul, her daughter Marie, and granddaughter Sommona Rose along. Older, wiser, and more interested in mothering, Georgie now found time for her daughter. Sommona Rose, at twelve, had taffy-colored hair and blue eyes and the same fearlessness and love for adventure that drove Georgie. They were kindred spirits, "peas in a pod," as Georgie said. Georgie and Sommona Rose climbed nearby mountains, skied in the winter, and rode their bikes along the coast to Santa Barbara. As Georgie and Sommona Rose grew closer, Georgie and Harold drifted apart. They were divorced "by reason of his absence" in May 1941.

Georgie did not remain single long. On February 6, 1942, she married a man eleven years her senior, James Ray White, a driver of oil tankers. Friends warned her that he had a drinking problem, but Georgie insisted that the jovial "Whitey" was only a social drinker. Before their marriage, Georgie told him that she would not be a dutiful wife: if she wanted to go on skiing trips or long bike rides, she would do it. And this would prove true. In return, Whitey would disappear for lengthy periods, and increasingly Georgie seemed to prefer it that way.

Soon after she and Whitey married, Georgie learned about the Ferry Command, a group of female pilots who delivered planes to airbases around the world during World War II. With Sommona Rose in tow, she went to a training facility in Quartzite, Arizona, to learn to fly. Sommona Rose flew with Georgie on several occasions and once landed the plane while sitting on Georgie's lap. Georgie completed her training with the 318th AAF Flying Training Detachment in Sweetwater, Texas, on February 12, 1944, but the war ended before she received an assignment to deliver a plane.

Disappointed, Georgie and Sommona Rose returned to Los Angeles and Georgie began working as a real estate agent, again spending her free time with her daughter. On a June afternoon in 1944, the two were biking on Highway 101 to Santa Barbara when a drunk driver hit Sommona Rose. "She was singing a song, and it quit right there," Georgie said.

Georgie remembered vividly and painfully the events of that day, the sound of screeching brakes and the dull silence of her daughter's body. She had memorized the license number of the car that hit her daughter. The driver, a U.S. Coast Guardsman stationed at Santa Barbara, was later arrested, but Georgie chose not to press charges against him, saying, "It wouldn't bring her back." But Sommona Rose's death affected Georgie profoundly. Not only had she lost her daughter—an inexpressible grief for any mother—but she had also lost her best friend. The two had become inseparable companions and, as true kindred spirits, shared a particular understanding of life and of each other. Georgie was rudderless without her daughter. Any sense of purpose or direction she may have had bled from her with Sommona Rose's passing. She had lost interest in her own existence.

Trying both to console her and to reawaken some interest in her life, her friends brought Georgie to a Sierra Club meeting. There, she met Harry Aleson. It was he who would help her get back on her feet—quite literally, in fact. Aleson was scheduled to lead a Sierra Club trip to the Grand Canyon where participants would hike from the canyon floor to the top of Mt. Dellenbaugh, a 7,072-foot peak on the Shivwits Plateau. Georgie signed on. Along with Aleson's only other recruit, Gerhard Bakker, a biology instructor from Los Angeles City College, they left Boulder City, Nevada, on August 20, 1944, and crossed Lake Mead by powerboat. They continued up the Colorado River to Quartermaster Canyon, where Aleson had a camp he called "My Home." Now on foot, they began the long, treacherous climb out of the Grand Canyon. They went up Burnt Springs Canyon and then turned up into Twin Springs Canyon, which turned out to be a dead end. They retraced their steps back to Burnt Springs Canyon, eventually pulling out on the North Rim and heading toward the town of St. George, Utah. Their blisters festering, they decided not to take the extra day to climb Mt. Dellenbaugh.

Georgie and Aleson became close friends. They hiked together in canyon country several more times. In her book Georgie writes that the strenuous hikes were good for her. Indeed, they provided a unique kind of therapy that was just the right ointment for her grief.

"Much of the time right after my daughter's death, I hardly knew where I was or what I was doing. Thoughts of Sommona completely occupied my mind. All I

The celebrated "G-Rig." *Photograph courtesy of National Park Service.*

knew out there on those desert trails was that I had to keep putting one foot in front of the other," Georgie explained. "Looking back now, I know that the best thing I could have done at the time was to take those long hikes with Harry. While they did not take my mind off of Sommona, they acted as therapy to cleanse and renew me."

Some people criticized Georgie, a married woman, for spending so much time alone with another man. Georgie explained that there was never a romantic attachment between her and Harry. "I became determined to explore the desert and canyon country," she said, "and Harry was the only person who would go with me." Whitey, she said, understood her need for these trips.

During her trips to Aleson's camp, Georgie enjoyed swimming in the Colorado River; in fact, she loved being in the water and became determined to raft the river. "I knew nothing about the deep canyon country, the sheer walls, the turbulent water, or the tremendous power of the rapids," she said. She and Harry discussed all the possible problems they might meet, including what would happen if their boat capsized and fell apart. Could they swim out with their life preservers? And then there was the problem of securing a boat, which neither could afford. Finally one day Georgie said, "Harry, instead of waiting to save the money to buy a raft, why don't we swim the lower canyon in our life preservers?"

A year after Sommona Rose died, in June 1945, Georgie and Harry decided to do just that. They drove to Boulder City, took a bus east to Peach Springs, Arizona, stripped down to swimsuits, tennis shoes, light jackets, and their life preservers, and hiked twenty miles to the Colorado River. Once on the river, they gasped in disbelief at the raging water swelled by above-average spring runoff. They had originally planned to take the river by sections—swim a bit, then rest, and swim again. But looking at the river, they realized it would be impossible to stop once they got in the swift current. They stood a few minutes and stared into the rushing, roaring water. The river's voice was deafening; yet, if it was shouting "turn back, fools," it did not shout loud enough. The two swimmers looked at each other and exchanged a sly grin.

Harry waded in first. Without a moment's pause, the current caught him from behind and pulled him out of sight. Georgie stepped in next. "The current grabbed me and swept me downstream at breakneck speed," she said. "What a helpless feeling! As I shot along I had the feeling that I had passed Harry in the current, but I wasn't positive." When the current finally swung her toward the shore, Georgie climbed out and waited. No sign of Harry. She thought he had drowned, and then she heard him shout from downriver.

They decided it would be better if they stayed together in the river, and so they spent twenty minutes devising a wrist lock. "We stepped into the river then. The current caught us and shot us downstream," Georgie said. For six hours, Georgie and Harry were carried through rapids and bounced around like two bobbing corks. "It was like riding a roller coaster made of water. But the wrist grip really worked, and we stayed together as if locked in a vice. Time after time, Harry and I tried to make the bank, but the raging water kept forcing us downstream."

At one point they were sucked into a whirlpool. "Round and round we went. All afternoon that wrist lock worked well. But now it proved to be a terrible handicap. The whirlpool plunged me under head first, dragging Harry feet first. Then it threw me out and pulled Harry under head first." Georgie thought she would die. "The whirlpool caught both of us and threw us violently against a rock wall. I grabbed the rock desperately and held on." She and Harry eventually pulled themselves up on the rock and onto a narrow ledge. "It was turning dark fast. I knew we couldn't get back in the river again because we had no way to know when we could crawl back out again. Besides that, I didn't even know that we could swim through the whirlpool." Wet, hungry, and alone in the Grand Canyon, the two spent a cold night on the ledge, unable to build a fire, unable to sleep, and unable to keep from worrying about the whirlpool that awaited them at daybreak.

At dawn, they locked wrists and prepared to go into the whirlpool. It was gone. The whirlpool had vanished in the night. "Later I learned that this happens frequently on the river," Georgie said. "A whirlpool will form right under you, then travel to high water or disappear completely." The rest of the trip seemed uneventful after that, even though the water remained as fast and furiously unpredictable.

Arriving at Pierce Ferry on Lake Mead, they found themselves completely alone, seventy miles down a rough dirt road from the main highway. They came upon a recluse living in a shack nearby, but he had no transportation. As the likelihood of anyone coming in the next few days was remote, they resigned to walk to the highway. With some food given to them by the recluse, they hiked for three days across the desert to the highway, where they flagged a bus for Boulder City.

Back in Los Angeles, Georgie and Harry assured each other that they would never swim the Colorado again. But as time went on, the bad parts faded into memory's black hole, especially for Georgie. She began to wonder what it would be like to cover twice the distance. "Finally, I made up my mind that I wanted to try swimming again," Georgie said. Harry at first refused, but Georgie kept mentioning it on their hikes in and around Grand Canyon. Finally Georgie told Harry, "Okay, I'll go by myself. I can find my way down to the river." Harry responded, "Okay, Georgie, you win. We'll try the river again."

This time they planned what they called a "raft-drift." They would build a raft of driftwood and, if that didn't work, use the one-man collapsible rubber air float designed for rescue at sea, which they purchased at an army-navy surplus shop. The shop also provided United States Navy kapok vests, Army Air Corps Mae West life preservers, and backpacks to carry equipment and food.

Two summers after Sommona Rose died and one summer after their first "expedition," the two met in St. George, Utah, in mid-June. The next day a friend drove them the 100 miles from St. George to the 6,000-foot-high Shivwits Plateau, where they strapped on their supplies and set out through a vast, roadless, unmapped land to where Parashant Wash empties into the Colorado River. Four days into the trek, their canteens were empty. Georgie remembered that the barrel cactus contains water. "I cut one open and started to chew," she said. "I made a big mistake.

It tasted like a mouthful of hemp, and I spit it out immediately." Finally, Harry spotted a few yellow jackets buzzing around a pothole in the limestone. An hour's digging produced a little muddy water, enough to get them down Parashant Wash to the Colorado.

Once there, Georgie and Harry built a makeshift raft using driftwood and old timbers, only to have it capsize after four hours. They inflated the air float, which barely held both of them. It capsized in an hour, tossing them into the river. And so they struggled for seventy-six miles, one person using the float, and the other swimming. Often, they thought the river would win. Swirling rapids sucked them under, tossed them out, then pulled them under again. After six days on the river they arrived on Lake Mead. Harry wrote in his report in the Sierra Club newsletter, "Under no condition must others plan a similar raft drift, unless it be to save your, or other's, life."

"Harry told me if I wanted to go again I had to go alone," Georgie said. "People often ask me how I could have done something so foolish. Actually, those two swims proved invaluable. I learned more about water and the Colorado River on those two trips than I could probably have learned in ten years any other way. I came to understand how the currents acted both on and below the surface. I saw firsthand how rocks affect the water, and I learned some important lessons about controlling myself in high water."

The hours and days Georgie spent swirling about the waters of the Colorado did more than teach her about its rocks and currents. The river got under her skin and into her veins, coursing through her body like her own blood. It became part of her. Whether she knew it or not, the river had become inextricably linked to her life. Her longing to be near it, on it, in it, meant the difference between simply existing or utterly living life. She would return to it again and again, until she found a way to make it her life.

At this point, however, she needed only to find a way to convince Harry to return with her; whenever she would mention the Colorado River to him, he would say, "Don't you ever say 'swim' to me again, because I'm not going! I'm going to shoot you if you mention it!" Georgie then suggested they get a larger raft, one large enough to carry both of them and their supplies. Army surplus stores in Los Angeles carried all sizes of rafts, so Georgie purchased a ten-man raft, and Harry bought a seven-man raft.

In early November 1946, when Georgie's real estate business was at a seasonal low, the adventurers headed again for the Colorado River. Georgie took a bus from

Orville Miller and Georgie White induct Delphine Mohrline Gallagher (center) to the Royal River Rats with the traditional shot of blackberry brandy. *Photograph courtesy of the Delphine Gallagher Collection, Cline Library, Special Collections and Archives, Northern Arizona University. NAU.PH.93.5.173.*

Los Angeles and met Harry in Richfield, Utah, where together they caught another bus to Green River, Utah. "I can still see the look on that driver's face when he saw Harry's seven-man, 250-pound raft sitting there on the sidewalk," Georgie said. They convinced the driver to put the raft in the baggage compartment and hurriedly boarded before he had a chance to change his mind. This time they planned to launch on the Green River, join the Colorado, run Cataract Canyon, and take out at Hite, Utah, a distance of 150 river miles.

Neither had been to the high desert in November, and they were sorely unprepared for the cold. Harry wanted to turn back, but Georgie said, "No way, I've come this far. I'm going the rest of the way." Reluctant to leave her alone, Harry went against his instincts, and the two pushed the raft into the Green River. For three days they drifted in the swift water, suffering from the cold, with snow and wind swirling about their heads. When they joined the Colorado, the nature of the trip changed.

The steep, narrow walls of Cataract Canyon channeled the Colorado through narrow chutes and over huge boulders. "We shot suddenly through one of these chutes, banging against the rocks as water pounded us from all sides. We were now literally bouncing from rock to rock. The raft suddenly flipped upside-down and, with Harry and me hanging on, banged through the rest of the rapid," Georgie recalled. They managed to work their way to shore, climb out, and build a small fire to ward off the miserable cold. For two more days they ran the rapids of Cataract Canyon—Satan's Gut, Dirty Devil, Dark Canyon—before reaching the tiny town of Hite.

There they caught a ride to the highway from an older couple who'd walked down to the river to watch them land. Nineteen miles north of Hite, the car stalled; the battery was dead. Although they were tempted to leave the couple and walk on to the highway, Georgie and Harry headed back to Hite, retrieved a new battery from the couple's shed, and walked back to the car. With the car working again, they reached the highway and caught a bus home.

The cold temperatures, freezing water, treacherous rapids, and nearly forty-mile hike of this trip were enough for Harry. Although he and Georgie remained friends and he described her as "a most courageous person, a woman without fear," Harry refused to run the Colorado with Georgie again. Perhaps he secretly feared they might not survive another trip. Georgie had no such fears. "If you believe in yourself and you know what you can do and can't. . . . I wasn't foolhardy. I figured I could hike out of the canyon because I had really good legs. And I felt positive about my swimming."

Georgie returned to the Colorado alone for the next three summers, experimenting with her own ten-man raft. In 1950 she worked for a Mexican Hat river running expedition as chaperone for five young starlets being featured in a Capitol Enterprises feature film, *Six Girls Against the Colorado*. Georgie had to keep running the same "riffle" below Lees Ferry. They would ride down the rapid and then helicopter the girls back to the beginning.

Following the filming, Georgie decided that if she could take care of those "ding-a-lings" (her word for the young ladies in her charge), she could lead anyone through the canyon. In 1952, she took her first passenger, Elgin Pierce, on a raft trip. They put in at Lees Ferry in midsummer with Georgie's trusted ten-man army-navy surplus raft. She managed to get through Badger Creek, Houserock, and other rapids with little trouble, but on her third day out, she hit Hance.

"The water, frothing and white, rolled in full boil, with huge waves crashing sideways into the big rocks. The holes that day were the wickedest I think I've ever seen," she recalled. "Suddenly a huge hole loomed directly in front of us. I couldn't possibly avoid it . . . whoosh . . . the front end of the raft dipped, a giant wave loomed above us, and all at once the raft tilted sickeningly and hung there suspended!" Elgin panicked and jumped from the boat. Georgie saw him out of the corner of her eye, climbing onto the shore. "A swift back current caught the raft, taking me forcefully toward a rock wall," she said. The raft flipped upside down, but Georgie managed to hang onto the rope running around the raft and get a grip on a rock. Elgin rushed to help her, and together they tied the boat to the rock. This was the first of several upsets, but they made it successfully to Lake Mead. The trip gave Georgie the confidence she needed to run river trips.

Georgie's long-gone husband, Whitey, reentered her life about this time. Possibly deciding that if he were ever to see Georgie again he would have to join her on the river, he agreed to drive a truck loaded with rafts to Lees Ferry, where she and a group of customers set out; he then met them at the end of the trip. He learned to handle a raft and occasionally joined Georgie on the river. The rest of Georgie's family also got involved in the business. Her brother, Paul, became an expert boatman, and sister Marie did the bookkeeping, logistics, food purchases, and even the laundry after trips.

In 1953 Georgie led her first "Share the Expense" trip on the Colorado. At a time when other outfitters were charging from $850 to $1,000 a trip, Georgie charged $300. Many men, including her longtime friend Harry Aleson, were outraged at a woman guiding trips on the Colorado. Georgie was far more interested in refining her skills than responding to such unfounded criticism. And she had plenty of customers, to boot—both women and men. The trip was exciting except for the required portaging at major rapids, done to ensure the safety of novice river runners. Hating the tiring process of carrying boats and supplies around the rapids, Georgie began thinking of ways to make portaging unnecessary.

Halfway through a trip in 1954 she got the idea to lash three ten-man rafts together, side by side. A ten-man navy life raft is seventeen feet long, eight feet wide, black in color, and shaped like a paper clip. If one section got into trouble, she reasoned, the other two would pull it along. It worked. After Georgie lashed the boats together, she ran every rapid but the dreaded Lava Falls, a thirty-seven-foot drop that roared like a freight train as the rafts approached.

Georgie had stumbled onto something workable, but she wanted to run all the rapids this new way, even the notorious Lava Falls. Plus, she wanted a craft safe enough to carry small children and elderly people. She reasoned that if the seventeen-foot rafts would work, larger ones would do even better. Georgie purchased three, twenty-seven-foot bridge pontoons and lashed them side by side. Each pontoon had a Johnson outboard motor, but she used only the middle motor, saving the others for emergencies and spare parts. After further experimentation, she placed inflated rubber tubing in the oval center of each pontoon, giving the passengers a convenient back rest and eliminating much of the bailing because there wasn't room for as much water to stand. The contraption became known as the G-Rig—or Georgie Rig—by other boatmen.

It had only one limitation. It was so large that occasionally the leading raft folded and flipped over onto the rest of the rafts, making what came to be called a Georgie Sandwich. Georgie explained that people just think it is a sandwich, but it really isn't. "When you go up on a wave, because they're so high they're looking down on the other people who are down in this trough . . . so they think it's coming on them; it isn't." There were many who disagreed with Georgie's analysis.

Her 1955 trip carried the largest group of people ever down the Colorado: twenty-eight. The entourage included Whitey and her brother Paul. Also on the trip was Park Ranger Dan Davis, the first river ranger in the Grand Canyon, whom Georgie had invited. "I almost quit the park service and began working as a boatman," Davis said. "It was the greatest trip. Georgie was the toughest woman I have ever seen. She could pick up two Johnson outboard motors as if they were nothing." Georgie enthralled Davis with stories about swimming the Colorado, climbing sheer canyon walls, and cycling across the country. "She kept us spellbound," he said, "but I sometimes questioned the details."

The big boat exceeded Georgie's expectations; she had found her mode of operation. For nearly forty years Georgie's big boat was on the river. For fifteen of those years Whitey helped sporadically as a driver and guide, but his drinking worsened over the years. By 1971, Georgie could no longer tolerate his excesses, and they divorced.

Georgie's true love was the river, and she conveyed that love to the people who accompanied her on her river trips. A "Georgie trip" started with a list of instructions mailed well in advance of the event. Bring an air mattress with three compartments, a rain suit, colorful clothes for pictures, bathing suits, a plastic bowl, a plastic cup, two stainless steel spoons, and two can openers.

Canned food was a vital part of Georgie's food supply. "Every night we had a slightly different version of 'Georgie Stew,'" explained Delphine Gallagher, a Georgie regular. "All kinds of canned vegetables were dumped in a big kettle and heated. Then we each received a small can of some kind of meat, which we mixed into our bowl of stew. So our dinner would be Georgie stew with meatballs, or Georgie stew with chicken, or Georgie stew with ham."

Georgie's river runners also knew to expect boiled eggs every morning. Delphine recalled Georgie putting thirty eggs in a large kettle to boil for breakfast. "Shortly she would yell, 'Anyone who wants soft-boiled eggs, come and get 'em.' A little later, 'Anyone who wants medium eggs, come and get 'em.' Still later, 'Anyone who wants hard boiled eggs, come and get 'em.'"

Her trips put in at Lees Ferry. Loading seemed chaotic but was actually highly organized. Two Los Angeles firemen once joined her on a trip, and Georgie told them how her boatmen often argued with each other. The firemen suggested she should use firemen because they worked together as a team. Word spread among Los Angeles firemen that Georgie needed boatmen, and for years many of them spent part of their summer vacations on the river with Georgie.

Loading complete, Georgie would launch the boats, dressed in a leopard-skin bathing suit and flying a leopard skin flag from the big boat. A mile or so below Lees Ferry, when the raft would bounce over a ripple and invariably a newcomer would say, "Is this a rapid?" Georgie would laugh and say, "That? That's a miscellaneous!" In Georgie talk, this could be interpreted as "You ain't seen nothin' yet!"

First-timers soon learned that whatever they were in life—doctor, company president, lawyer, bus driver—on the river they were all equal. Georgie had no use for pretentious people. The only people that weren't allowed along were sourpusses. "One sourpuss can ruin an entire trip," she said. Nor could she tolerate whiners. When she asked a passenger how things were going, she expected them to answer, "Everything is just the way we like it!"

That response was critical in the initiation that took place near the end of each run. Georgie decided that if you made it through Grand Canyon, you should be dubbed not simply a River Rat but a Royal River Rat. The initiation ceremony was held after dinner, as the sun left the Grand Canyon. The new "rats" were blindfolded, led to a beach, and seated in a circle. "Then we'd throw some cold water on them and tell them that's just to clear their memory," Georgie laughed. "Then we would say that this was an educational experience and that if they got the correct

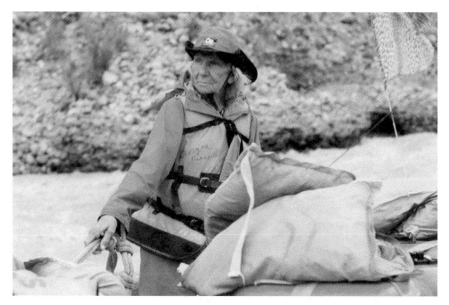

Georgie White on the Colorado in her later years. *Photograph by Rosalyn Jirge, courtesy of Cline Library, Special Collections and Archives, Northern Arizona University. NAU. PH.2006.46.463.*

answer, they didn't get a bucket of water thrown on them; but if they were wrong or answered out of turn, they would get a bucket. We'd ask all sorts of questions about the geology and where we camped. Then we'd crack an egg over the person's head, give them a crown, and tell them they were going to take an oath."

Those who passed the test (everyone passed) were brought over to Georgie, where they kneeled down, still blindfolded, to listen to Georgie's speech. "On the river, you know, by this time, that no matter what happens to you, the main thing that you must learn is a slogan that everything is just the way you like it." She then asked, "How is the trip?" to which a chorus of would-be Royal River Rats replied, "Everything is just the way we like it!" They would get a whack with a paddle, then they would stand up, their blindfold removed, and they would receive the congratulations of all. They had become Royal River Rats. Doctors, lawyers, and professional men and women throughout America proudly displayed their Royal River Rat Certificate on their walls next to their degrees.

The morning after the initiation, headed downstream, the River Rats sang, "I'm a river rat, you're a river rat, we're all a river rat, and when we get together we like to sing our song." Then everyone would go "Yak, Yak, Yak" and clap their hands three times, and then repeat the verse as long as they wanted to and, when the song was finally over, give a loud yell, "Yah."

Georgie became as famous as John Wesley Powell, in part because she engineered that fame. She put modern-day public relations firms to shame. The well-known photographer Josef Muench went on fifteen trips with Georgie; his photos appeared in publications around the country, particularly *Arizona Highways Magazine*. And then there was *Call of the Grand Canyon*, a ninety-minute documentary filmed by Roger Bowling and narrated by Georgie, billed as "a dramatic, educational chronology of a twenty-one day expedition in rubber life rafts through 330 miles of the Eighth Wonder of the World." Thousands of viewers saw Georgie in action.

Georgie appeared on some of the most popular television shows of her time. When Art Linkletter of *House Party* asked her, "Aren't you afraid of anything?" she replied, "Oh you bet! I'm afraid of anybody driving me on the freeway!" To Groucho Marx, who said, "You know, Georgie, with all those horrible things that happen on the river, what you really need on trips is an undertaker," she quipped, "Oh no, you just take a shovel along and bury the bodies right there on the spot." This comment, a reference to the time Georgie found and buried a body along the river, left the audience in stitches.

On *To Tell the Truth*, where a panel of four celebrities had to guess who the real "Georgie" was, she fooled all but Bill Cullen, who pointed to her and said, "She has to be the real Georgie; she is the only one that came down the steps without looking or holding the handrail. I'm sure that's the kind of confidence it takes to run a raft through the rapids."

Georgie had her critics. Her boats were too big, she took too many people at once, she grabbed the best campsites and then left them littered with opened cans, there was too much horseplay, too much Coors, not enough attention to safety. In her long career, three people drowned on her trips. When Georgie didn't cry, people accused her of being heartless.

Still, Georgie made rafting the Colorado River affordable and safe for the ordinary passenger. The rafts she pioneered, at first ridiculed by boatmen, became an accepted mode of river travel. Although she hired only men for her crew, she led the way for women to work on the river. Her spirit was indomitable, and her love for the Colorado River of the Grand Canyon was fierce. People would ask her, "When are you going to retire?" and she would reply, "I'm retired to the river."

In November 1990 over two hundred people gathered at the Hatch Warehouse in Marble Canyon, Arizona, to celebrate Georgie's eightieth birthday. Georgie danced like a teenager that day, and it seemed like she could live forever, running the river. But a little over a year after the party, she was diagnosed with stomach cancer and became so weak she could barely walk. She longed to go back to the river. "How I wish I was running that river," she wrote to friends in April 1992. "I could be dressing to go put on coffee water for early coffee hounds before dawn. I used to love that early hour." Georgie died a few weeks after she wrote the letter, on May 12, 1992. One imagines that Georgie didn't mind dying so much. If she couldn't live on the river, she wouldn't want to live.

CHAPTER ELEVEN

Cataloging the Grand Canyon

LOUISE HINCHLIFFE
(1922—)

As a child growing up in Massachusetts, Louise Hinchliffe would stare longingly at the painting of the Grand Canyon hanging in her parents' living room. The painting depicted a landscape that was utterly unfamiliar to Louise. Layers of rocks plunged to hidden depths and she could only imagine what beauty lay beyond the painting's frame. She dreamed of one day stepping into that scene. The artist was her uncle, Hans Kleiber, a forest ranger in Wyoming.

"I'd look at that painting and think about going out West," Louise recalled, "but during the Depression, money was scarce, and I went to work right out of high school." Although she'd learned typing and shorthand, she found her first full-time employment with the American Optical Company, assembling eyeglass and goggle frames. She advanced steadily through the company over the next eight years. It was then that her mother suggested she take a vacation trip out West.

"In 1947 I went on a tour of several national parks, including Union Pacific's 'Utah Parks' tour, which branched out beyond Utah and gave me my first look at Grand Canyon from the North Rim," Louise remembered. The painting in her childhood home had not prepared her for the canyon's vast reality. Its beauty was immense, inarticulate; and its grandeur touched and quieted her soul. She knew she would return to this place some day.

Louise then took a "packaged tour" of Yellowstone National Park and went by bus and train to Dayton, Wyoming, to spend ten days with her Uncle Hans and the aunt she had never met. "Uncle Hans and his wife took me on a lot of 'local' trips, places like Sheridan and Custer battlefields, dude ranches, and up into the Bighorn Mountains," Louise recalled. She returned from the West with new confidence in herself. She obtained a promotion to assistant editor of American Optical Company's newsletters, a job she enjoyed for the next four years.

Still fascinated with the West, especially the Grand Canyon, Louise came back again and again. "I made another trip in 1949 through Zion and Bryce and to the North Rim again. Then, even though I couldn't afford it, I came back again in 1951." Louise began corresponding with people in the parks about finding a job. "I learned that there were openings for women in the National Park Service," she

Louise Hinchliffe in the library at Grand Canyon National Park. *Photograph courtesy of National Park Service.*

said, "and that was rather a revelation, because you didn't see very many women in those days employed at the national parks. You knew there were families living with the rangers, but you didn't find very many women actually working for the park service."

Louise passed the Civil Service examination and began receiving offers from various places, but none from the Grand Canyon. "Finally I wrote to Grand Canyon National Park Superintendent Harold C. Bryant, and I was very fortunate because my letter arrived just about the time the Naturalist Division was looking for a new secretary, so on the basis of the qualifications I described in my letter and my experience, they decided to take a chance on me."

Visiting the West was one thing, but the sudden prospect of moving there made the West seem remote and far away from Massachusetts. "My mother encouraged me to take the job. I'd always lived at home," Louise said. "It was the hardest decision I made in my life." Feeling very much alone, but determined, Louise boarded a train headed west and into a new life. "I was on the train headed for the Grand

Canyon on Thanksgiving Day, 1951, and it was the loneliest Thanksgiving of my life," she said. "I'd given up a pretty good job and a very good home. The only thing I regret is that my mother didn't tell me how ill she was. I never saw her again."

Louise arrived at the South Rim of the Grand Canyon the weekend after Thanksgiving. Although she had been to the North Rim several times, this was her first visit to the more populated South Rim. Her living quarters proved challenging. "They called it the 'stenographer's cabin.' It had two rooms—a living room–bedroom combination and a kitchen. There also was a three-foot by five-foot bathroom," she recalled.

Although Louise admitted she was a bit "let down," she understood the reasons for her meager quarters. "You had to work your way up the housing chain based on your pay rate, longevity, and size of family," she explained. She mustered her resolve and worked to make the house her home. "I saw it as a chance to 'make the best of it,' so I made curtains and slipcovers for the steno's cabin."

Her first year at the canyon was rough for Louise. Alone, really for the first time in her life, she grew homesick and a bit scared. The canyon can either amplify or mollify loneliness, depending on how one opens up to it. Louise was fortunate to take comfort in the canyon's grandeur, which softened her loneliness, and soon grew to love being at the canyon. "I didn't get tired of looking at the canyon. I think some people do. There were people who worked here, who lived here, who never went out of their way to go out and look at it. . . . I can't quite understand anybody having so little interest or curiosity about things right on their doorstep."

Louise lived in her tiny cabin nearly four years, until after her mother's death. "My father wanted to sell the house, and I wanted to keep some of my furniture, a bedroom set and a drop front desk, and some keepsakes of my mother's. I told the man in charge of housing assignments that I needed a bigger place to live in so I would have some place to put the furniture, and eventually I got an apartment in an old CCC barracks," Louise said. "The walls were like cardboard, but at least I could have my furniture. I stayed there for about three years, until the park service built some new apartments for single employees, and by then I had enough seniority that when the eight apartments became available, I had my choice."

As she grew used to living at the canyon, Louise looked increasingly forward to her time alone with the geologic wonder. "Weekends or whenever I could, I'd go out there," she recalled. "Some mornings I got up extra early and walked along the rim to come to work. . . . Simply because it was different every time. And it wasn't just the Grand Canyon. I mean, it wasn't just that big beautiful view out there. It was the little things that I'd notice along the way. I keep discovering something I hadn't noticed before about the way the pine trees grow or some flower that I hadn't seen before, or some bird comes along that I hadn't seen for a long time and I think, 'I used to remember what your name was.' It just continued to be exciting to me, and I kept discovering little places that I'd never walked before."

She also made friends in the small community. "That helped through the rough parts. There was a church group, and I met the wives of the men I'd worked with." She participated in community activities such as the Square Dance Club, picnics at Shoshone Point, and movies in the community building. Grand Canyon Village in 1951 had only 1,000 year-round residents, compared to approximately 2,500 in 2004.

Although many women lived at the canyon and several worked for the Fred Harvey Company, only three women worked for the National Park Service in 1951: Louise and two secretaries, one in the superintendent's office and the other in the engineer's office. "It was strictly a man's world," Louise commented. Even so, Louise enjoyed her job, which turned out to be much more than the "clerk-typist" designated on her employment form. She worked for Louis Schellbach, head of the Naturalist Division.

"When you think of Schellbach, think of a turtle who carries his shell on his back," Schellbach told Louise, and then he added a bit of advice. "When you think of the turtle, remember he never gets anywhere unless he sticks his neck out." Louise liked and respected "Louie," as everyone called him, and later, when she disapproved of some of the changes made at the canyon over the years, she would remember Louie saying, "Nothing is permanent except change." Schellbach would prove to be a tremendous influence on Louise. She would work for and with him over the next seven years. It was from him that she would gain a deeper understanding of the Grand Canyon's plants, animals, and geology.

Schellbach laid the foundation for much of the interpretive program in place at the canyon today. He wanted visitors not just to look at the canyon but to understand and appreciate it. Consequently, he built a large study collection and developed interpretive programs to teach people about the Grand Canyon. He believed that when people understood the canyon they were more likely to protect it.

Louise, Schellbach, and his assistant, Ernst Christensen, plus a few seasonal employees in the summer months, made up the Naturalist Division in 1951. Their office was in a three-room school building that had been earlier condemned before

Schellbach convinced the National Park Service to refurbish it. The study collection, an assortment of specimens from preserved animals to rocks to pressed plants, filled one room. The largest room, where Louise worked, contained a combination office, workshop, and library. "If somebody was running the power saw, you got sawdust all over your desk," Louise laughed, "but, at the same time, it was a very pleasant working arrangement in that everybody took part in everything that was happening. You felt very much a part of the team."

This little building comprised all the canyon had in the way of a visitor center in the early 1950s. "We were so much off the beaten track that most visitors weren't aware we existed," Louise said. "People would come around and knock on the back door. We'd greet them enthusiastically and show them around and, if they wanted to stay in the exhibit room for a while and look around, fine. If it was somebody that was quite interested, as often they were, we'd spend some time giving them a tour of the study collection. And if they were really interested, they got the rare treat of perhaps spending an hour listening to Louie." Schellbach was a riveting speaker, and his dedication to the canyon was clear. Louise said that listening to his enthusiastic talks helped her get through the early parts of the job. "When I was feeling pretty homesick, the realization that there were such dedicated, interesting people in the park service helped my determination to stay."

As the primary contacts with the public, the naturalists gave talks on various topics, including daily geology lectures at Yavapai Observation Station on Yavapai Point. Louise assisted with talks whenever one of the men was ill, on vacation, or too busy to appear that day. Before Louise was hired they had sometimes asked one of the rangers to fill in, she explained, "but there was always a friendly rivalry between the two groups; the rangers were the 'cops,' and in their view the naturalists were 'butterfly chasers' or 'fern feelers.' To avoid asking favors, my boss got the idea that I should do it."

Louise had been listening to the talks on her days off or by occasionally closing the office to attend. "Geology was my favorite, and often, when they did a nature walk, I would go along. My first talk was on geology, and it went pretty well. It was forty-five minutes long, and I'd prepared a few three-by-five-inch cards as reminders in case I forgot what came next. In the second talk, I unexpectedly had real stage fright for the first time, but after that I was okay. At first I didn't wear a uniform, but soon they decided that because I was before the public representing the park, I should obtain a uniform."

Louise gave talks when needed for about five years. "It was a challenge because I was shy and had a limited background. Occasionally we'd get a crank in the crowd, but I got so I could deal with them. Louie taught me how to handle the people who objected to the statement that the Colorado River made the Grand Canyon. When someone said, 'God made the Grand Canyon,' Louie would pull out his pencil and draw a line in his notebook. Then he would say to the group, 'Did this pencil make this line, or did I make this line?'"

Louise also helped design and build exhibits. "I learned how to mount plants and spread butterflies. I just did whatever needed doing. I even skinned birds for the study collections." Skinning birds was a complicated process that Louise learned by observing and using a handbook. "It's like taxidermy, except that you don't strive for a lifelike pose." Louise removed the perishable 'innards,' taking care not to injure the skin or feathers, then treated the cavity with preservatives to avoid insect infestations. She filled the cavity with cotton, sewed up the skin, smoothed the feathers into place, and after it had dried, placed the bird in a sealed cabinet.

Louise pitched in whenever she was asked, even if it meant hiking nine miles down the Bright Angel Trail in the heat of summer to repair damage done by vandals to the River House (a trail shelter near the Colorado River) exhibit. Louise designed the exhibit, organized the specimens and labels, and, with the help of two seasonal employees, hiked down the trail to install it. One of the panels Louise designed had a relief map of the river's course, another explained the geology of the canyon, and the third depicted exploration of the river. Exhibits today are made by professional artists, and though topnotch, they lack the personal feel of the early homemade designs.

Often Louise drew the morning chore of driving out to Yavapai Observation Station to "open the doors," which involved more than simply turning the key. "There wasn't any glass around the front of the building. It was an open porch out there. The binoculars had to have covers tied over them every night and taken off every morning to protect them from the weather," Louise explained. "Plus, the exhibits that explained the binoculars had tin lids over them that had to be placed each night and removed in the morning." The job proved more difficult in the wintertime. "If there had been some snow, you'd have to shovel the snow off the porch and fling it over the edge into the canyon. The oil stove had to have oil carried to it from a tank down by the parking lot."

All the talks, exhibit preparation, and snow shoveling came second to what would eventually be Louise's primary responsibility: managing the library that supported the Naturalist Division. When she arrived at the canyon, 2,320 entries were recorded in the library accession book. The library was in a little corner room, about ten feet square, and on some additional shelves in the workshop. "Part of my job was cataloging anything that came in, so I learned the Dewey Decimal System," Louise said. "We were a specialized library, and the Dewey system hadn't expanded to its later levels—it tended to lump together, under one number, every book about the Grand Canyon." Louise improvised a more detailed system that would let her categorize books about the canyon into specific subjects, so that as the collection grew, library users could find what they wanted more readily. As the Grand Canyon Natural History Association (now Grand Canyon Association) increased the library's budget, Louise bought books and subscribed to more periodicals.

In 1957 the National Park Service built a new visitor center near the entrance to the canyon. More emphasis was placed on visitor interpretation, and the name of the Naturalist Division was changed to Interpretive Division to better reflect its purpose. The "new" Interpretive Division, including the extensive study collection and the library, moved to the new center. Although Louise excelled at her job and adapted easily to her many unexpected duties, she had grown accustomed to her cozy office and the close working relationship with the small staff, and she had difficulty adjusting to the new visitor center. Moving the library proved especially frustrating.

"At the time that we were ready to move into the new building, the library shelves hadn't arrived yet, and all we had was a big, empty room. Fortunately it wasn't raining on moving day, since they sent an open, flat-bed truck," Louise explained.

Louise waited at the visitor center. It was her plan to direct placement of books on the floor by the windows so she would have an easier time shelving them in order. "When they arrived with the books, they didn't have enough manpower to carry them all in carefully. So, to cut down on the number of trips they had to make, somebody said, 'Let's pile them up in the wheelbarrow! We can carry more of them that way,'" Louise recalled. "So they came in with wheelbarrow loads, books just piled in, helter skelter. To make it worse, somebody had been mixing cement in the wheelbarrow, so it was a little bit gritty." The books were piled all over the floor in no particular order, and Louise faced the demoralizing task of having to reorganize and shelve the books when the shelves arrived, as well as cleaning bits of cement from many of the volumes.

Thankfully the move was easier for the study collection. "Everything had to be moved: the insect and butterfly specimens, geology samples, and archeology artifacts," Louise said. Because someone on the staff had to drive to the Yavapai Observation Station at least three times a day to open, give a talk, and close, Louie suggested that Louise utilize those trips to assure that the delicate butterflies and insects reached the new visitor center, which was midway on the route, safely. "We would put a few drawers in the car and drive very carefully. It took a lot of trips, but was worth it," she explained.

The move to the new visitor center brought added responsibilities to Louise's job description. The tiny department was now charged with staffing the information desk seven days a week, in addition to their other responsibilities. "It was a bit of a job to provide that much service with just three staff members," Louise said. "At first, there weren't too many visitors, so we kept a bell out front on the desk so that when somebody came and wanted something, they'd ring the bell and we'd go out."

The most difficult part of the move, however, was that it brought with it the retirement of Louie Schellbach. Louise feared that some of Schellbach's beloved study collections and exhibits would be dismantled once he was gone, but that was not to be the case. The new park naturalist, Paul Schulz, did attempt to upgrade the exhibits with mechanical devices: "There was a little map showing the trails, exhibits, and museums, and there was a light on each one." Louise recalled.

Needless to say, the once quiet, smooth workdays of the old Naturalist Division were gone forever, giving way to the increasing pressure of the growing attendance at the Grand Canyon. By 1960, half a million visitors were coming to the Grand Canyon annually, most of them making the new visitor center their first stop.

Louise now devoted most of her time to the library and study collection. She responded to the increase in visitors by offering tours of the study collection and an open day in the library. "Most tourists were content with a chance to just enter the library, hear a little of its history and purpose, and get back to more interesting activities, but the study collection tours were rather popular," she said. "I explained the purpose of study collections, some of the history of our collection, and why it smells so awful in here (it was the preservatives); and after some cautions about not handling anything unless I passed it around, we toured the whole room, exploring cupboards and drawers from anthropology to zoology, hummingbirds to eagles, skunks to skinks." Louise recognized that the nature of the canyon tourists was changing. No

A beloved Louise Hinchliffe (center front) is honored by colleagues and friends upon her retirement in September 1985. *Photograph courtesy of National Park Service.*

longer were the majority English speaking. "Sometime in the early 1960s we recognized the need to have a condensed version of the Yavapai geology talks translated into the most often requested languages. At first we mimeographed them—no photocopiers then—and did French, German, and Spanish. Japanese was a greater challenge; we had to have it printed in California." Today on the South Rim, the number of international visitors makes up nearly 50 percent of total visitorship, thanks in part to one-day flights from Las Vegas to the canyon that are a regular part of many foreign tour packages.

By 1975, as the staff of the Interpretive Division increased, Louise became full-time librarian. As such, she was often enlisted by writers doing research on the canyon. "I've worked with many authors who have come here to write books about the canyon," Louise admitted, "and while I don't mean that I've had any impact on what they've written . . . it has been an interesting opportunity to add to the accuracy of some of the books that were published by helping them with their research, by reviewing their manuscripts, and pointing out things that they really shouldn't say because they weren't accurate or they were misleading or they might cause people to get a wrong impression about what could be done here in the park." Many authors have mentioned Louise's invaluable assistance in their acknowledgments.

After nearly thirty-four years at the Grand Canyon, Louise retired in August 1985. At her retirement party that September, Superintendent Richard W. Marks renamed the park library in her honor. It is now the Louise Hinchliffe Library, a tribute to how she built the library's small holdings to a comprehensive 7,000-volume collection.

Why did she stay at the canyon so long? "People often ask me, 'Doesn't it get tiresome to see the same place and the same people and the same buildings for such a long time?' The answer to that is you don't see the same people. They are always coming and going. . . . You keep getting your batteries charged by meeting new people." Louise compared her long tenure at the canyon with being married to the same person for a long time. "It may not be quite as exciting as a lot of turnover in jobs or partners,

Louise Hinchliffe at home in Arizona, 1995. *Photograph by Betty Leavengood.*

but that doesn't mean there isn't any chance to grow and to develop and to have new experiences. . . . There's always been a challenge."

Part of the challenge for retired Grand Canyon National Park Service employees is giving up their canyon home. Many, as did Louise, stay nearby so they can return occasionally. At her home in Sedona, Arizona, looking at a dramatic view of the red rocks through her living room window, Louise offered a bit of advice: "I think maybe what I might say I've learned is that if you have a dream, for goodness sakes, do something about it. Don't say, 'That's impossible, that's too difficult or it involves too many changes, too many chances to take.' Follow it, because you only get one chance. You only get one life, and if you don't do those things that seemed a little bit out of reach, what was the point of living?"

CHAPTER TWELVE

My Heart Knows What the River Knows

KATIE LEE
(1919—)

My heart knows what the river knows
I gotta go where the river goes
Restless river, wild and free
The lonely ones are you and me

I magine a sunrise in the southwest section of the North American continent, sometime in the early twelfth century. The brilliant ball of fire rises slowly in the east, bringing the day. Its first light heightens and defines shadows. Before long, everything is bathed in a fiery red, and the baked stone of the earth begins heating. This is the light that funneled into Glen Canyon for millennia, lending depth and nuance to countless natural arches, river-carved walls, ledges and alcoves, and the yellow sand on the canyon floor. It is the light by which groups of people collected water, hunted and gathered, and carved their stories and histories into rock. The cycle of day is evident in the constancy of this place, a place so sublime that its existence is reliable, unequivocal.

Fast-forward now to the twentieth century, where the same sun rises upon a dramatically altered landscape. No natural disaster, no ice age, not even the hand of God turned this remarkable canyon into the underbelly of a deep artificial lake. This was the handiwork of the U.S. Bureau of Reclamation.

Katie Lee serenades a most special place. *Photograph by Frank Wright, courtesy of Katydid Books and Music.*

It was this, and a score of other unfathomables, that left folksinger Katie Lee aghast.

Katie Lee grew up in the desert east of Tucson, Arizona. She is an accomplished singer and songwriter, but she is more famous for her unyielding devotion to a certain river and its canyons. She turned her fame and talent to a worthy cause: saving Glen Canyon and the Colorado River.

She was introduced to the Colorado River in 1953, when she took her first trip down the Colorado through the Grand Canyon. The trip left her spellbound. "It was just the most awesome, magnificent thing," she recalled. "You could see the way the whole world's put together, by looking at how it's been cut away millennium after millennium, and then you'd feel just like what you really are a grain of sand in all this creation."

Katie returned to the Colorado River the next year, this time to Glen Canyon, 164 miles upriver from Lees Ferry. Her arrival there was preceded by many other visitors, one of whom was John Wesley Powell. Upon first seeing this canyon in 1869, he noted, "We have a curious ensemble of wonderful features. . . . Carved walls, royal arches, glens, alcove gulches, mounds, and monuments. From which of these features shall we select a name? We decide to call it Glen Canyon." Writing in his expedition logbook, Powell described "mounded billows of orange sandstone," "fern decked alcoves," and rocks that are "chiefly variegated shades of beautiful colors—creamy orange above, then bright vermilion, and below, purple chocolate beds, with green and yellow sands."

Like Powell, Katie was enchanted with Glen Canyon. "It was utterly the most beautiful place I've ever seen in my life," she said, "with its marvelous rock formations, gorgeous little canyons, and waterfalls, and every single one of them had water in them. Nooks and crannies and pools to swim in. It was inspiring, that's all." On that first trip in 1954, Katie and her fellow boaters heard about the proposed Glen Canyon Dam. "I didn't believe it. None of us did. We said, 'They'd never do that, they won't dam this.'"

But Katie and her friends were wrong. By the close of 1954, the idea to build dams in the West had been around a long time. President Theodore Roosevelt advocated "reclamation of the arid lands in the West" in his State of the Union message in 1901. He said, "The western half of the United States would sustain a population greater than that of our whole country today if the water that now runs to waste were saved and used for irrigation." In other words, developing ways to collect and store the West's water was critical to the region's settlement. In June 1902 the Reclamation Act created the Bureau of Reclamation. In 1916 and again in 1922, E. C. LaRue, chief hydrologist for the United States Geological Survey, proposed dams that would flood Glen Canyon, providing water for irrigation and hydroelectric power.

Just thirty-two years later, the bureau had built over fifty dams, including the spectacular Hoover Dam (originally named Boulder Dam, completed in 1935). In the spring of 1956, President Dwight D. Eisenhower signed into law the Colorado River Storage Project Act (CRSP), which authorized eleven irrigation projects, including the Glen Canyon Dam. Blasting would start in mid-October.

As the "Wreck-the-Nation" Bureau's designs on Glen Canyon deepened and solidified, so did Katie Lee's devotion to the river and the canyon. She worked out a deal with Mexican Hat Expeditions, a local river running company, to help keep her on the river. "I would take my guitar. . . . I sang on the beach every night for passengers, and that way I got my passage for nothing," she said. "What is greater than being on this river?" she wrote one evening, after playing her guitar and singing for the passengers. "To be able to sit and talk about things with the magic roar of the water in your ears and the smell and spell of the canyon all around you . . . the night a blanket of stars . . . oh, river . . . you put all problems to shame!"

The river became her refuge. It grounded her. "It was just necessary for me to get out with nature and be in this most beautiful place. It was just like having a soothing balm rubbed into me for two or three weeks or a month when I was there. And I would go back just completely cleansed and feel like a whole new human being." She was fortunate, for river runners who came after Katie did not and will not know the depth of soul to be found in Glen Canyon. "I know who I am now, and that river helped me find out—especially Glen Canyon helped me find out—so that there isn't any question about it."

For many, especially those who called the Colorado River and its canyons "home," the damming of Glen Canyon was unthinkable. The project grew more controversial as awareness increased. "I started fighting," Katie said. "At first, I did everything wrong. I got mad and angry and every time I opened my mouth, I insulted somebody. The only way I could get anything across was to shut my mouth and sing. People listened to music. I wrote songs, and I sang them everywhere I went, all over the country, singing in nightclubs."

By 1957 she'd written five songs of protest, including "The Wreck-the-Nation Bureau":

Three jeers for the Wreck-the-Nation Bureau!
Free loaders with souls so pure-o
Wiped out the good Lord's work in six short years.
They never saw the old Glen Canyon
Just dammed it up while they were standin'
At their drawing boards with cotton in their ears!

(Chorus) Oh, they're gonna dam the Frying Pan

You're next, old Roarin' Fork.
And when they built Glen Canyon dam
The San Juan got a cork!
No river's safe until these apes
Find something else to do
So have your fun in Cataract
'Cause after that, you're through!

Three beers for the Wreck-the-Nation Bureau
For them I know there is no cure-o
All the waters of the world they would impound.
I'll tell you now of their latest whimsey;
To fill Grand Canyon to the brimsey
While Rainbow Bridge comes crashing to the ground!

(Chorus) Oh, they've gone and dammed the Frying Pan
The Muddy and the Blue
If we'd left it to Half-Aspinall,
He'd got the Crystal River too!
These little hard hats with their toys
Of dynamite and drills,
Won't rest until each mighty gorge
Is choked with cement fills.

No fears have the Wreck-the-Nation Bureau,
In their ignorance secure-o,
What's a few more billion? . . . ain't that nice?
'Bridge Canyon for the Havasupai'
Dams and trams and tacky-poop, I
Wonder at my river's slow demise!

(Chorus) They've gone and dammed the Frying Pan
The Yampa, Green and Bass,
In Steiger's book a ripplin' brook
Was a place to drown your ass.

He'd rather shoot a burro
Than a rapid, anyway-
And leave a dam down in the Grand
To mark his cocky way!

No ears have the Wreck-the-Nation Bureau,
Blind as well you can be sure-o;
Domminy, old Floyd, was their head *fink*.
They'd drowned the wildlife of Alaska,
Build Rampart Dam, not even ask ya
If you want the world's most useless skating rink!

(Chorus) They've gone and dammed the Frying Pan
The Gunnison and the Snake.
For them, all rivers of the world
Have got to be a lake!
So busy with inundation
They can't unsalt the sea . . .
'Cause that would mean an end
To their Pork Barrel Revelry!

A pox on the Wreck-the-Nation Bureau
Down with the Wreck-the-Nation Bureau
Up the Wreck-the-Nation Bureau
And their little cousins,
Hard-hats by the dozens,
The stupid Army Corps of Engineers!

(© Katie Lee; reprinted by permission of Katydid Books & Music.)

Others joined in the fight, all believing that if people knew what was being destroyed, surely the dam would be stopped. Ken Sleight, a river runner, formed Friends of Glen Canyon, a loosely organized group of river runners who sought to educate the public about the beauty and historical significance of Glen Canyon. David Brower, executive director of a conservation group called the Sierra Club, started a campaign to save Glen Canyon. William L. Thompson, a member of the

National Parks Conservation Association, was quoted in the October-December 1955 issue of the *National Parks Magazine*, "There are others that are more grand and more violent, but none that is more beautiful."

Despite the growing protest, the public's eye was fixed fast on the benefits of the dam. Two powerful Arizona politicians, Stewart Udall and Barry Goldwater, argued in favor of building it; chambers of commerce in Utah, Arizona, and Colorado saw dollar signs. Boaters and fishermen wanted a lake in the desert, and even conservationists, who believed in maintaining a balance between reclamation and conservation, supported the project.

In October of 1956 the first blast of dynamite struck the canyon walls.

"When I think ahead," Katie wrote in her journal, "I begin to choke. . . . This will all be under water. Why? Why? I know why. Man's stupidity; his greed and thoughtlessness. The canyon I stand in now will be full of slime and stink from lack of free drainage, and the beauty and mystery of the incredible Glen will be gone forever." It was unthinkable, and Katie grappled with what she couldn't fathom.

"That mile through Labyrinth—it just isn't believable that there could be such a place! Six hundred feet high and an average of a foot or two wide, winding like a snake through solid rock! Oh, how I cry in anger against these imbeciles who will build a dam to cover this." Katie and some friends visited and boated down the canyon early in the construction of the dam. She noted: "At Sentinel Rock there is the horrible scar on the wall where the bloody business of beginning the dam is evident. They have white lead paint marks all over the walls for several miles upstream and below the site itself. A big gaudy sign, which is an infringement on the constitutional rights of American citizens (since this part is a navigable river) shakes its fist:"

WARNING
No travel beyond this point to Lees Ferry
Blasting on Canyon walls is dangerous to
boat travel.

Katie and her companions disregarded the sign and continued down the river. "A mile below, little men were crawling over the walls from the top in little rope chairs, all silent and busy, marking the wall for blasts. On Monday, President Eisenhower presses a button in Washington, and the first explosion begins construction officially. Back in the boat and down our river, I cannot hold back tears of anger and resentment against this wrongdoing."

Two days after she wrote these words, on October 15, 1956, President Eisenhower pressed a ceremonial key in Washington, DC, and a roar filled Glen Canyon, catapulting boulders into the air. As they tumbled into the river, a cloud of dust rose from the canyon. The Glen Canyon Dam project was a reality. It would be seven years before the dam was completed and the diversion tunnels closed.

The realization that Glen Canyon would soon be gone forever led many other people to flock to the area. River companies advertised, "Last chance to see Glen Canyon," and many people came on their own to wonder why such an exquisite place was being destroyed. Two well-known photographers, Philip Hyde and Eliot Porter, spent time capturing the images of Glen Canyon. Hyde's 1955 photographs became a fourteen-page photographic essay in the November 1958 Sierra Club *Newsletter*. Porter photographed Glen Canyon in 1960 and again in 1961. He brought his photographs to Sierra Club Director David Brower, and together they planned to publish a book.

Katie and her friends Frank Wright and Tad Nichols had their own private plan; they would explore the hidden canyons of the Glen. "We didn't set out particularly to name them, but we went down there so much that we needed to know where we were, and when we got off the river we would try and remember, 'Now was that Mile 64 or what?' That doesn't stay in your mind as long as a name, and, for our own reference, we started naming the canyons," Katie explained.

Their efforts brought forth names like Cathedral Canyon, Dangling Rope, Dungeon, and Wishbone, which made a wishbone before it emptied into the river (the United States Geological Survey called it Oak). Naming these special places helped Katie and her friends imprint them permanently on their minds. "There are twenty-five names left on the canyon by us; names that we gave them from 1955 to 1960. My last run was in 1962," Katie said. During construction of the dam, diversion tunnels carried the water of the Colorado past the site, allowing Katie and her friends the chance to do their work. In January 1963, the diversion tunnels were closed, and the Colorado River began to fill Lake Powell.

The extra trips to the canyon, protests, letters, articles, and Katie's songs did little to impede the inexorable progress of the dam. A town—Page, Arizona—was developed to house the workers. Millions of tons of concrete were poured into massive footers. Nothing—not a six-month strike by construction workers, not weather, not changes in administrations in Washington—stopped the steady rise of the dam.

Growing increasingly defeated, those opposed to the dam held out one last hope. "From the beginning we knew that Rainbow Bridge National Monument was supposed to be protected," Katie said, referring to a key sentence in Section One of the Colorado River Storage Project bill, which says, "No dam or reservoir constructed under the authorization of this Act shall be within any national park or monument." Section Three of the bill further stated that "the Secretary of the Interior shall take adequate protective measures to preclude impairment of the Rainbow Bridge National Monument." If they couldn't save Glen Canyon, perhaps they could save the monument. In legislation dating from 1910, 160 acres surrounding the stone arch were included in the designated monument area. However, if the new lake were backed up to its maximum height, an elevation of 3,711 feet above sea level, water would be fifteen feet deep beneath the bridge.

Katie's suggestion was simple: make the water level lower. Other suggestions included building barrier dams around the monument to protect it. In the summer of 1960, as the campaign to save Rainbow Bridge National Monument escalated, Stewart Udall, U.S. Representative for Arizona and member of the House Interior and Insular Affairs Committee, went to inspect the monument.

Frank Wright and Tad Nichols took Udall up Forbidding Canyon to Bridge Canyon and finally to Rainbow Bridge. He climbed on top, cooled his feet in the creek, and later met with the chief project engineer, Lem Wylie. Wylie said the monument could indeed be protected with two barrier dams, a pumping system, and at least fifteen miles of new roads.

Although Udall believed that the wording in the CRSP act called for protection of the monument, he came away convinced that the resulting construction would do more damage to the area than letting water intrude on the monument. If the barrier dams were built, Rainbow Bridge National Monument would be sitting in a box, its dramatic impact destroyed.

When in the spring of 1961 Congress again refused to allot money for the protection of Rainbow Bridge National Monument, the Sierra Club's David Brower called for construction on the Glen Canyon Dam to cease until funds were provided for its protection. His call fell on deaf ears.

Time grew short. Late in 1962 the National Parks Conservation Association filed suit in United States District Court on behalf of several conservation organizations against Udall, by then President John F. Kennedy's secretary of the interior, to prevent him from closing the dam's diversion tunnels until Rainbow Bridge National Monument was protected. The court ruled that the National Parks Conservation Association did not have the right to sue the government.

The final blow to the monument was struck on January 18, 1963, three days before the scheduled closing of the left-bank diversion tunnel. Interior Department lawyer Frank Barry reported to Udall, "the provisions originally included in the Colorado River Storage Project Act calling for protective measures at Rainbow Bridge National Monument have been suspended by the Congress and are no longer operative."

Brower flew to Washington in a last-minute effort to persuade Udall to change his mind. Udall wouldn't see him. He was holding a press conference to announce plans for two new dams downstream from Glen Canyon. Brower left in shock. They were going to dam the Grand Canyon!

On January 21, 1963, the tunnel was closed, and the reservoir began to fill. The battle for Glen Canyon and Rainbow Bridge National Monument was lost, but Brower vowed to save the Grand Canyon.

Katie's songs became a lament. In 1964, Folkway Records released her album *The Folk Songs and Poems of the Colorado River*, some collected from years on the river, many written by her in protest of the Glen Canyon Dam. In the liner notes, she wrote, "To those of us who love the river for what it is, who have found the Glen Canyon to be one of the most beautiful, unmolested, clean, fascinating areas in the country, packed with scientific information, with ancient history and ruins, and who have experienced adventure unparalleled amid its winding side canyons, the damming of its flow seems an appalling waste of everything."

Katie's liner notes warned about future dams proposed for the Grand Canyon. She asked, "Is it progress to destroy beauty, wildlife, ancient ruins, solitude? And now, though nobody will be able to tell you why, it is progress to destroy one of the wonders of the world—your Grand Canyon."

Eliot Porter's Glen Canyon pictures were collected in the book *The Place No One Knew*, edited by David Brower and published by the Sierra Club in 1963. Stewart Udall received an advance copy. Brower clearly blamed Udall for the destruction of Glen Canyon. In the introduction he wrote, "The man who theoretically had the power to save this place did not find a way to pick up the telephone and give the necessary order."

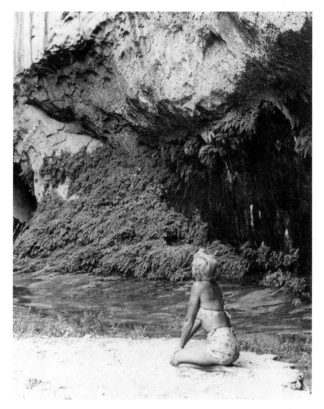

Katie Lee, 1956, in Grotto Canyon, a tributary of Glen Canyon, prior to the building of Glen Canyon Dam. *Photograph by Frank Wright, courtesy of Katydid Books and Music.*

Katie believed the title of the book explained why we lost Glen Canyon. "There weren't enough of us who knew anything about it. It really was the place no one knew." But she likened solving that problem to a snake eating its tail: "The more people you get to fight for the rivers, the more people you have to take to the rivers, thereby ruining them in order to save them from destruction. You get a lot more people on the rivers than many of the rivers can take. The river's a very delicate ecosystem. Those little canyons in the Glen, if there had been more than ten footprints in there a year—some of those hanging gardens—they'd have been gone."

Glen Canyon Dam marked the end of an era for the Bureau of Reclamation. Now people knew that dams destroyed. The Sierra Club took out full-page ads in the *New York Times, Washington Post, San Francisco Chronicle*, and *Los Angeles Times* stating, "This time it's the Grand Canyon they want to flood. The Grand Canyon." And later, "Should we also flood the Sistine Chapel so tourists can get nearer the ceiling?" The Sierra Club published a coffee table book, *Time and the River Flowing*, about the Grand Canyon. Hundreds of thousands of letters were sent to the Bureau of Reclamation, Congress, and the White House. All said in effect, "Keep out of the Grand Canyon." On July 31, 1968, House and Senate conferees specifically prohibited the future construction of dams on the Colorado River between the Glen Canyon and Hoover Dams. The Grand Canyon was saved.

Although there would be no more dams built in the Grand Canyon, the Glen Canyon Dam continued to fill the lake. Those who opposed the dam's creation stumbled on something they hadn't considered before. The river might save itself by destroying the dam. "Geologists said, 'This is not the place to build a dam. The sandstone is too porous,' but they went ahead. They work constantly on the right bank beside the dam to hold their cement plug in place, so it's going to go. It will happen," Katie believed.

And it almost did in 1983. Heavy snowstorms in May, followed by a sudden warming, swelled runoff to flood level. Lake Powell had not been drawn down enough to accommodate the unanticipated runoff. When operations manager Tom Gamble directed the east spillway gate to be opened, the river spewed house-size boulders. The tunnel ripped apart, and Gamble quickly ordered the spillway closed. Workers lowered into the tunnel the next morning found the concrete eaten away, and huge, gaping holes in the sandstone. The spillways could not be used. The dam's engineers would have to wait out the runoff.

When the crest reached 3,700 feet, however, the water would automatically spill over and into the damaged tunnels. Time was critical. Gamble installed temporary plywood flashboards on top of the gates to hold back the rising water. The water level in Lake Powell reached 3,708.4 feet on July 14 and then began to recede. Amazingly, the plywood held, and the dam was saved. Both spillway tunnels were repaired using new technology that would theoretically prevent the destruction from occurring again.

Glen Canyon Dam still stands. There are those who say we lost a beautiful canyon but gained a beautiful lake. And there are those who say we lost a beautiful canyon, period. But problems with the lake and dam continued. A November 19, 1995, headline in Tucson's *Arizona Daily Star* read, "Filth in Lakes Powell, Mead

Prompts Health Concerns." The accompanying article noted that "Water quality in spots along both lakes has tested dangerously high for fecal coliform bacteria associated with human wastes." Glen Canyon National Recreation Area (GCNRA) is the National Park Service's number one destination for overnight visitors. According to Stephanie Dubois, then-chief interpreter at GCNRA, there were 2.5 million visitors in 1997. Many lauded these statistics and pointed to the use of Lake Powell as justification for the building of Glen Canyon Dam.

Not Katie Lee. Her home in Jerome, Arizona, is filled with artifacts and photos from her days on the river and in Glen Canyon. Her personalized automobile license says "DAM DAM." There's no question where this outspoken defender of Glen Canyon has stood. Her book, *All My Rivers Are Gone* (1998), describes her experiences in Glen Canyon, her transformation into protest singer and environmentalist, and the failed movement that she helped lead against the building of the Glen Canyon Dam, an action she described as "trying to put out a wildfire with a teacup."

She took her boat, *Screwd-River*, on Lake Powell a few times. "I spent all my time crying and looking down into the water, trying to find the places that I knew were so beautiful." Instead, she found the lovely little side canyons once so enchanting to explore were choked with rotting logs, drift, orange peels, and floating beer cans and bottles.

Katie has never gone back. "And when I drive across the dam I put the blinders on so I can't see the reservoir. I can smell it; it doesn't smell like a river." She referred to the "poor, castrated thing down there called the Grand Canyon." She'll never see it again, either. "You couldn't pay me to go down in Grand Canyon now. . . . And I think that the blue, stinking, bloody cold, freezing ice water is an unnatural sickness, and all the long, clean beaches and bars that were down there are gone. The happiest day of my life will be when the 'Wreck-the-Nation' Bureau screws up one more time and the river cleans that place out again."

It's always hard to reconcile memory with change. But at least Katie has kept many memories of the sandy beaches in Glen Canyon. She recalled, "We would build a fire at night with driftwood. Where'd this one come from? Well, this piece of wood, this came from the Colorado. No, this one came from the Green. This is the tree that grows up on the Green. No, this is . . . you know, all these pieces of wood from all over, all washed down over the years. May take a tree two, three years to go down the river. Depending on what you knew about wood, you could

Katie Lee relaxing on one of her many trips down river. *Photograph by Frank Wright, courtesy of Katydid Books and Music.*

just about tell where it came from." Those days are gone, as is the driftwood. Gone too is the Driftwood Burners Society, whose claim to fame was lighting a driftwood bonfire with one match. The warm, red, silty Colorado—too thick to drink, too thin to plow—is gone, and with it, Glen Canyon.

Katie's anger, and that of others too, was encapsulated in the sentiments of her song "The River . . . to the Dam Builders":

You've silenced me! You've cut my chattering string!
Are you glad that I no longer sing?
Are you proud, now in my millionth year,
Proud to see my journey's end so near?
And when you've covered o'er my secret carvings back beyond,
Will you feel might at having laid my restless waters still?
I'm sure you will!
You never knew, nor took the time to find
What strange and wondrous scenes I left behind.

Nor felt the blanket pressure of the stars
Hold you against the warmth of my sandbars.
My deep and winding crevasses you've never climbed with
    pounding heart
To turn, and, down the fluted sides in wonder let tear fall
    through.
No! Not you!
You have no tears! You've dollar signs for eyes!
Not one of nature's wonders made you wise.
Your only thought was how to cloak the facts.
Which men can we buy? Who'll get the fat contracts?
I nearly flipped my stream that day I saw my face in *Life*
You had me growing corn on rock where even God had never
    tried!
Again, you lied!

Only a few who've stood with me alone
In the twilight bottom of a bowl of stone
Only those who've followed me in wild elation
Will feel each drowning inch with suffocation!
To them I leave a gift you dam builders will never own.
It can't be bought, or sold, nor spit upon, nor torn apart.
The music in my heart!

(© Katie Lee; reprinted by permission of Katydid Books & Music)

In November 1996, the Sierra Club board of directors, at the urging of eighty-four-year-old David Brower—who carried the destruction of Glen Canyon in his heart for forty years—voted unanimously to drain Lake Powell, to "pull the plug" and let the Colorado River run free through Glen Canyon once again. When Richard Ingebretsen, founder of the Glen Canyon Institute, called Katie to discuss the proposal, she said, "That call was the first glimmer of light at the end of an incredibly depressing tunnel."

The Glen Canyon Institute is a nonprofit organization that has battled to restore the natural ecosystem and beauty of the Glen Canyon, the Colorado, and its tributaries; Katie Lee has been a key player and advisory board member. Glen Canyon and Katie were featured in the PBS special *Cadillac Desert*, based on Mark Reisner's best-selling book. She also was quoted in a 1997 feature story on Glen Canyon in *National Geographic* magazine. In her book, *All My Rivers Are Gone*, Katie told the story of her "lost rivers," including the Colorado.

Congressional hearings, debates, and studies about the Colorado River and Glen Canyon Dam have continued. This time the question has been not "should a dam be built?" but "should a canyon be restored?" Who will win? Only time will tell.

Katie Lee still lives in Jerome, Arizona, and continues working to restore Glen Canyon. She has published another book, a collection of essays about her life titled *Sandstone Seduction*.

CHAPTER THIRTEEN

A Hopi Connection

PHYLLIS YOYETEWA KACHINHONGVA
(1959—)

Phyllis Yoyetewa Kachinhongva, an interpretive ranger at Grand Canyon National Park, had just finished her talk about "The Hopi Connection" and was answering questions from the audience when a man asked, "Where can I see a real Indian?"

"Hello!" Phyllis, a Hopi/Apache from the Eagle/Bear Clan, smiled as the audience laughed.

"I mean a real Indian with head dress and feathers," he persisted.

"You can go to Hollywood!" Phyllis explained, finally getting her point across.

Phyllis has fielded this question many times. "I get that question frequently," she said. "They've seen too many cowboy and Indian movies."

Phyllis has lived at the Grand Canyon since she was twenty-two days old.

"My parents were on their way to San Francisco where Dad had gotten a job," Phyllis said. "My mother began having labor pains and I was born in Safford, Arizona." Three weeks later Phyllis' parents, Homer and Nina Yoyetewa, came to the canyon to say goodbye to her father's parents, Donald and Edith Longhoma.

"My grandmother said I was too little to take to California so she kept me. My parents came back after me later but my grandmother wouldn't let them have me," Phyllis said, and so she was raised by her grandparents. "My mother is Apache and my father is Hopi. My grandparents were both Hopi so I was raised as a Hopi," she explained.

Phyllis' grandchildren—Tateyonna and Melisha Jeter, Nassir Donald Keen, and Melaki and Savannah Longhoma—are the fifth generation in her family to live at the Grand Canyon. "My great-grand-father was hired by Mary Elizabeth Jane Colter (see Chapter 2) to work on the construction of Hopi House and later Desert View Watchtower," Phyllis said. "When they celebrated the opening of Desert View Watchtower, he arranged for the Hopi dance group to perform."

"My grandparents met at the Grand Canyon," Phyllis went on. "She was working as a salad girl at Bright Angel Lodge for six cents an hour and he was a bellhop at El Tovar. He made nine cents an hour!" The engaged couple went by train to Williams, Arizona, to get married. "When they returned the community had a dance at the community building to celebrate their marriage."

Phyllis Yoyetewa Kachinhongva shares her knowledge of the Hopi use of plants native to Grand Canyon National Park. *Photograph by Betty Leavengood.*

Phyllis attended school at the canyon. While she was a junior and senior in high school she worked in the afternoons for the National Park Service in dispatch. "I took care of the switchboard and all the mailings," she explained. She attended college in Prescott, but didn't finish. "I had a car wreck and injured my arm so much that I couldn't work for two years," she said. "Then I had my oldest daughter Monica and came back to the Grand Canyon to live."

Phyllis raised her three children, Monica, Kimberly, and Kendall, Jr., on her own. "I held several jobs at once," she said. "I was a teacher's aide and then worked weekends and holidays as a fee collector for the park service. When the fee station closed I would work at gift shops outside the park and, in between all that, I cleaned the magistrate's and telephone company's offices."

Her hectic schedule ended in 1985 when she started working full time in fee collection for the park service. "When I started, the entry fee was fifty cents," Phyllis said. "It went up to two dollars three weeks after I started." Today the entry fee to the Grand Canyon National Park is ten times that.

Phyllis worked in fee collection for thirteen years. In 1996 Grand Canyon National Park Superintendent Robert Arnberger decided to move some Native Americans into interpretation. He offered Phyllis a position. "I had to ask my elders for permission to take the job," Phyllis said, "because Hopi women do not do public speaking." The elders gave their permission for Phyllis to become an interpretive ranger, but she soon had to confront another obstacle.

"The park service wanted me to give tours down Bright Angel Trail to just past the tunnel where you can see rock art on the wall above the tunnel," she recalled. "As Native American women we are taught at a young age that we cannot enter the Grand Canyon. We believe that there are spirits that live down there—spirits that will take you away or prevent you from having children. My elders wrote letters to the superintendent and my supervisors respect my beliefs."

Phyllis began to prepare for her presentations. "I had to do my own research and prepare my own talks," she said. "In the summer we do three presentations a day. At first I was very nervous about speaking before the public, but now you can't shut me up. I love my job."

As I entered the auditorium at the Shrine of the Ages to listen to her talk about the Hopi connection with the Grand Canyon, Phyllis was standing near the stage chatting with some folks in the front row. The auditorium was filling up fast and I hurriedly claimed a seat.

She introduced herself and her seven-year-old granddaughter, Tateyonna, who was seated in the front row. "My grandchildren are the fifth generation of my family to live at the Grand Canyon."

Phyllis started her presentation by talking about growing up at the canyon. "I had a big playground," she said. "My grandmother would dress me up in a little Indian dress and I would wander along the rim by El Tovar and Bright Angel Lodge. The tourists wanted to take my picture and they'd give me nickels and dimes. I'd come home with my pockets full of change."

Her younger brother, Darrell, came to live with them when he was around four years old. "We had quite a time," Phyllis said. "We tried selling Kool Aid at the head of Bright Angel Trail, but that didn't work out too well." They had better luck selling petrified wood and pottery. "We found some pottery clay, so we made little pots to sell," she explained.

Phyllis and Darrell played tricks on the tourists. "We climbed over the rim between Bright Angel Lodge and El Tovar," she said. "People got all excited and yelled for us to be careful. What they didn't know was that there were animal trails right over the wall and there are some caves under the rim that we could hide in. We were perfectly safe!"

One of their activities would have annoyed her grandparents had they known. "In the summertime, my brother and I would run down the Bright Angel Trail to Indian Garden," Phyllis explained. "We'd play around most of the day and then get back before my grandmother came home."

Had they been caught, they would have been disciplined in the traditional Hopi way. "The Hopi are very family oriented," Phyllis stated. "The mother is the head of the family and the father is there to provide for the family. They do not provide discipline to the children." Contrary to the Anglo way, Hopi children are disciplined by their uncles on their mother's side. "If my granddaughter Tateyonna does something bad, her Uncle Kendall will discipline her. That way he becomes the boogey man and her mom and dad provide comfort."

Phyllis explained to us that the Grand Canyon was a special place for the Hopi tribe. "We believe that the Grand Canyon was once a large sea," she related. "When the Hopi started to migrate to the east, the chief of the village at Old Oraibi sent word to the Hopis at Desert View that he needed their help. A little boy named Pokanghoya lived with his grandmother at Desert View and she gave the boy a jar to hold; he was told not to open it and to take it to the chief at Old Oraibi. Being a little boy, he opened it. There was a loud noise and he dropped the jar. Three lightning strikes created the Grand Canyon, the Colorado River, and the Little Colorado River. "

The Grand Canyon has even more significance for the Hopi. "We believe that it was our place of emergence into this, the Fourth World," she said. "Sipapuni, which is upstream from where the Little Colorado enters the Colorado River, is the actual place of emergence. Our ancestors lived in the canyon before leaving to build their homes at the base of three high mesas east of the canyon. We believe that in the afterlife our spirits will return to the Grand Canyon."

Phyllis said that the Hopi were trying to hold on to their traditional ways and language.

"We believe that we are guarded by kachinas that live on the San Francisco Peaks," she said. "In the summer months they come to the mesas for ceremonial dances. Ceremonial doings are when the Hopi wear their traditional dress."

Holding onto the Hopi language is more difficult. "Language use starts at home," Phyllis said, "and many parents don't try to teach their children to speak Hopi." Phyllis is teaching her grandchildren to speak and understand the Hopi language. She asked her granddaughter to come to the stage. "Tateyonna can count to ten in Hopi," Phyllis said. We listened as Tateyonna shyly counted to ten in Hopi. "She is also learning the parts of the body in Hopi," the proud grandmother added.

"Today," Phyllis continued, "most of the 14,000 Hopi live on the Hopi reservation 140 miles east of the Grand Canyon. The Hopi reservation is completely surrounded by the Navajo reservation. The actual boundaries have been debated for years."

Young Phyllis' backyard was the yawning Grand Canyon. *Photograph courtesy of Phyllis Kachinhongva.*

After her talk was over, Phyllis responded to questions from the audience and then invited everyone to meet her at 9:00 A.M. the next morning at Bright Angel Lodge for a walk along the rim of the canyon.

Despite inclement weather the next morning, a small group joined Phyllis. "What would you like to do?" she asked. "We can go to the right and I'll tell you about the historic buildings, or we can go left and learn Native American uses for the plants." The group opted for plants.

As we walked along the rim of the canyon, Phyllis told us that the canyon had a lot to offer. "There are so many remedies in nature and we don't have to take many pills. We really don't need a Wal-Mart," she laughed. "We have everything out here that we need."

Phyllis stressed that you need to know a lot about plants before using nature's remedies. "If you pick the wrong tree or herb you may do yourself more harm than good."

We stopped before a large Utah juniper tree. "If you put some of the leaves in

Phyllis was raised by her grandmother, Edith Wadsworth Longhoma. *Photograph courtesy of Phyllis Kachinhongva.*

a pan and cover them with water and bring to a boil," she explained, "it makes an excellent cough syrup. It has a bitter taste, but it's high in Vitamin C and it works." Phyllis said her boss had a cough and cold for almost three weeks and nothing he took worked. "I kept telling him to get some Utah juniper," she said, "but he wouldn't listen. Finally, he pulled me outside and we got some juniper branches and made some syrup. He got well and then he said, 'Phyllis, why didn't you tell me this a long time ago?'"

In addition to helping with a cough, the Utah juniper has several other uses. "Pull back the outer bark and the brownish material underneath makes great diapers," Phyllis explained. "It also can be used to line shoes." She pointed out some little blue berries that remained on the tree. "Any ideas?" she asked. No one knew. Then I suddenly remembered. "It's gin!" "Right," Phyllis laughed, adding that the dried berries are also used to make jewelry. Lastly she explained, "The Hopi believe that the Utah juniper tree branches burned in the home keep away evil spirits. The ceiling beams in the Hopi House are Utah juniper."

Next we stopped beside a yellowish, pale green bush. "This is a rabbit brush," Phyllis said. "It grows to be a very big bush and it's everywhere. That suits the Hopi just fine because we use the stems to weave baskets. We cut the stem, peel off the bark, and dry it before it is ready for use for basket making. The Navajo use the rabbit brush to dye wool. Boil the branches and you get a yellow color."

As the sun began to break through, a white, misty fog rose out of the canyon. Phyllis gave us a moment to look at the canyon before picking up a small cone off the ground from underneath a tree. "Every four to seven years the pinyon tree gets these little cones," Phyllis said. "Nuts grow in the cone and in the fall the cone drops to the ground." She pulled the cone apart, looking for a nut. "Looks like the squirrels beat me to this one!" she laughed. The pine nuts, she continued, "are very high in calories and cost seven to eight dollars a pound. We use the nuts to make pesto."

The Anasazi, who lived in the canyon from 600 to 1200 A.D., used the sap of the pinyon tree to waterproof baskets and make pottery airtight. Phyllis paused to point out that Anasazi is a Navajo term meaning "ancient enemies." "The Hopi Tribe doesn't like to use the word 'enemy' because we are descended from the Anasazi. We prefer the term *Hisatsinom* which means 'ancient ancestors' or 'old ones.'" She explained that the pine sap is heated until it melts. "A piece of a yucca plant is used as a brush," she said. "Be careful not to get it on your fingers. It's just like super glue."

Phyllis pointed to a spiny plant with a dried stalk, a yucca. "Break off one of the spiny leaves and peel back the edges and you'll have a good paintbrush," she said. "Nampeyo, the famous Hopi potter, used yucca to paint her designs." The yucca plant also provided material for weaving. "Pulling the leaves apart produces a strong fiber that can be woven," Phyllis explained. Archeologists have found mats, ropes, and sandals woven from the yucca plant in caves in the Grand Canyon dating as far back as 1200 B.C. Phyllis added that when the above-ground parts of the plant were entirely used up, the roots were dug, cut up into little pieces, and boiled in water. "This makes a great shampoo," she said, "but be sure and rinse your head well or it will itch all day long."

Our last stop was a short distance from the rim under a large ponderosa pine. "Anyone know what this tree smells like?" Phyllis asked. I remembered from many hikes in ponderosa pine forests that if you pull a little piece of bark away gently, there's a distinct odor of vanilla. Everyone tried it and agreed. Phyllis held up a long needle from the tree. "The needles were used to make baskets," she said. "In the basket this black part that holds the needle to the branch overlaps and makes a design. This type of basket is difficult to weave and few people make them anymore. If you do find a pine needle basket, it will be extremely expensive."

In conclusion, Phyllis asked us to take care of the canyon. "The Grand Canyon is my home," she said.

Phyllis and I headed to the Bright Angel Lodge restaurant for a late breakfast. As we lingered over coffee, Phyllis reemphasized that she truly loved her job. "I've met people from all over the world," she said, "and helped them understand the Hopi culture." In addition to giving talks at the canyon, Phyllis has appeared in a video, *Echoes Through Time*. She has been featured in two children's books and a children's scholastic publication, *The Weekly Reader*.

"I give thanks to my grandparents for where I am today," Phyllis said. "They raised me to know the Hopi traditions and beliefs. I am trying to do the same with my children and grandchildren. Who is going to pass on our cultural history if we don't?"

CHAPTER FOURTEEN

Weaving a Life

JEAN MANN
(1933—)

M y first rug was the size of a Bluebird bag, about twelve by seventeen inches," Jean Mann said, referring to the size of a Bluebird flour sack—Bluebird being the popular brand Navajos use to make fry bread. "The rug was a beginner's rug with a striped pattern. I was seven years old when I made it. I traded it for ten pounds of sugar," she laughed. "I didn't know then that weaving rugs would be my livelihood." Jean, a widely known Navajo weaver, demonstrated weaving for twenty-five years—ten at Grand Canyon National Park and fifteen at Cameron Trading Post in Cameron, Arizona.

"The Grand Canyon Natural History Association (now Grand Canyon Association) was looking for a Navajo woman to demonstrate weaving," Jean explained. "Ingrid Garrison, the association's business manager, had heard about my weaving and offered me the position." Jean was hesitant about accepting the offer. "I asked my second oldest daughter, Marie, if I should take the job and she encouraged me to do it. I was paid a salary and allowed to keep the proceeds from my rug sales."

Jean, a single mother raising her children, moved to Grand Canyon Village in 1970. At first she lived in an apartment but later moved into a house. Her children were away in boarding school, but they came to the canyon on weekends and during the summer. "All my children grew to love the canyon," Jean said. Her loom was set up in the visitor center (now park headquarters) on the South Rim. "I talked to people from all over the world," Jean said. Luckily, through her children, she enhanced her ability to speak English.

Jean Mann weaving at her home in Cameron, Arizona, 2003.
Photograph by Betty Leavengood.

Weaving is very much a part of Navajo culture. According to the Diné, or "the People," as the Navajo call themselves, they were led to the Southwest from the underworld by supernatural spirits called the Holy People. One of the Holy People, Spider Man, taught the Navajo to make a loom using sunshine, lightning, and rain. Spider Woman taught them how to weave.

Anthropologists say that an Athapascan-speaking people, ancestors of the Navajo, crossed into Alaska from their homeland in Asia across a land bridge formed during the Ice Age some 25,000 years ago. Sometime between 900 A.D. and 1400 A.D. their wanderings brought them to the Southwest, where they found people living in towns built of adobe and stone. Those Ancestral Puebloans called the Athapascans *Navaju*, a Pueblo term meaning "great planted fields." Over time, *Navaju* became Navajo.

The Navajo ceased their wandering and remained in the Southwest, primarily in the present-day Arizona and New Mexico. While they continued their traditional lifestyle of hunting and raiding, they learned from the Pueblo Indians how to plant fields of corn, cotton, and other crops. In time the two groups intermarried, and Navajo women learned to weave from the Pueblo men. By the fifteenth century, Navajo women were weaving blankets and garments using cotton grown by Navajo farmers.

That would change with the entry of the Spaniards into the Southwest. In 1540 Coronado led the Spanish Conquistadors into what is now Arizona and New Mexico. By the time Coronado arrived, the Pueblo people had abandoned their great stone dwellings and resettled in other villages and pueblos.

The Spaniards brought horses and sheep with their expeditions. Navajo raiders attacked their settlements and acquired large numbers of livestock. After a few years, the Navajo had large flocks of sheep, which they used for food and for weaving. By 1700 all Navajo weaving was done with wool from the sheep.

Political turmoil in the mid-nineteenth century brought disaster to the Navajo. In 1821 Mexico won its independence from Spain. Twenty-five years later, Mexico gave up the territory of New Mexico to the advancing American army. The United States government sent Colonel Christopher "Kit" Carson to stop Navajo raiding and make way for Anglo settlers.

Carson's measures were harsh. He and his soldiers destroyed Navajo homes, crops, sheep, and horses. In 1865 he and his army force-marched nearly eight thousand Navajo to Bosque Redondo, a desert area southeast of Albuquerque that was totally unsuitable for farming. During their internment, more than two thousand Navajo died from starvation, smallpox, and other diseases.

In 1867 responsibility for the Navajo was transferred from the army to the Bureau of Indian Affairs. In 1868 the Navajo were sent back to their homeland to a newly created 3.5-million-acre reservation that covered parts of Arizona, Utah, and New Mexico. Much had changed. They returned to destroyed homes and a lack of any way to earn their livelihood. Before Carson's campaign, the Navajo owned more than 200,000 sheep but were now left with fewer than one thousand. They were able to rebuild their flocks, so much so that by the 1930s the federal government instituted a livestock reduction program. All this history affected the quality of Navajo weaving for generations.

Jean Mann was born in 1933 on the Navajo Reservation east of Grand Canyon near Cameron, Arizona. Her parents were Roy and Betty Huskon of the *Dzilt aadi Kinyaa aanii* ("near the mountain towering house") clan. A cowboy and Indian movie was being filmed at the time, and "my father supplied the cattle for the movie. She added, "We lived like pioneers. We had one big cabin with no water or electricity. We cooked in an outdoor oven."

Jean attended boarding school in Tuba City, Arizona. While she was there, the Bureau of Indian Affairs began a program whereby Indian children were sent to live and work in Anglo homes to help them assimilate into American society. Jean lived in California with a foster family for several months. She remained at the boarding school for two years. Her mother died when she was eleven years old, and Jean returned home to help take care of her younger sisters.

When Jean was seventeen, she married Henry Mann. "It was a marriage arranged by my husband's side of the family," she said. "It was agreed by my side of the family too." Jean and Henry had thirteen children. "Three of the children passed on. Now I have ten children, ages twenty-seven to fifty-two, and I am thankful for all of them. They are a blessing."

Navajo women are noted for their weaving. "I learned to weave at home," Jean said, "by watching my mother, grandmother, and sister. To weave, you start with the sheep."

The first Navajo weaving with wool was done with the wool of churro sheep, which were introduced into the Southwest by the Spaniards. Churro sheep have long, straight, greaseless wool, ideal for hand spinning into white, brown, and grayish yarn.

When the Navajo returned from Bosque Redondo, they found that their churro sheep had either been slaughtered or had wandered away. To replace the churros, the United States government introduced 15,000 merino sheep to the reservation in 1870. Merino sheep had short, curly, greasy wool that did not make good yarn. By 1880 even the best Navajo weavers were using commercially spun yarns.

"Fortunately," Jean said, "my father had churro sheep. We also had several other kinds of sheep that gave us a variety of natural colors such as brown, beige, gray, and white. I helped herd the sheep and, in May, I helped shear the sheep. It was hard work. We would get hot and sweaty and tired."

Shearing takes place in late spring or early summer when the wool is the thickest. One adult sheep produces eight to ten pounds of wool. It requires wool from two to three adult sheep to make a three-by-five-foot saddle blanket.

Jean Mann did weaving demonstrations at the Grand
Canyon National Park visitor center for many years.
Photograph courtesy of Jean Mann.

Jean did not use commercially prepared yarn for her weaving, and instead
prepared the wool in the traditional manner. After shaking out the dirt, she went
through the wool and picked out burrs and twigs or anything entangled in it. If the
wool was very dirty, she washed it, and then rinsed it several times, especially if it
were to be dyed. The early weavers used the root of the yucca plant as soap.

After the wool dried, it had to be carded. "A carder is a flat metal-toothed brush
measuring about four by nine inches," Jean explained. "I used two carders and
pulled the wool between the carders to get rid of the debris from the wool so it
would be smooth to spin." Early weavers used rows of thistle burrs lashed to a stick.

When she finished carding, Jean piled the wool on the floor in preparation for spinning. "Several of us would work together. We'd sit on the floor with spindles in our laps." A spindle is a stick about twenty-four inches long with a small round wheel about six inches from the bottom. "You pull the wool over the spindle, until it becomes thread of the consistency you want to use for your weaving," Jean explained. "You wind the thread around your feet or hands into a loose skein. At this point the skein is washed, colored, and dried."

Dyes were originally made from wild plants. The indigo plant, which grew in Spain, produced a rich blue color. The leaves of the indigo plant were fermented, dried, and cut into cubes before being exported to the New World. Indigo required the addition of a strong alkaline solution. For this, the Navajo stored and fermented urine to add to the indigo blocks. The dye looked green, but after the yarn had soaked for several days and was hung out to dry, it turned a rich blue.

Nineteenth-century Navajo weavers favored the color red. Before 1863 the only way to obtain red was to ravel a pre-dyed woolen bayeta cloth and use the yarn. This cloth was dyed using one of two insects—lac and cochineal—or a combination of the two. The secretions of the lac, a Near Eastern beetle, provided a dark red dye. The cochineal beetle lives on prickly pear cactus and is native to the Southwest. The Spaniards discovered the cochineal beetle and took prickly pear cactus back to Spain where it still grows today. For a time only Spanish kings had red garments, and red was known as the "color of kings." By 1880 synthetic red dyes had replaced that obtained from lac and cochineal beetles.

Yellow was obtained by boiling down the flowers of rabbit brush and adding native alum. Combining yellow dye with indigo blue dye produced shades of green. A mixture of boiled-down native sumac or pinyon pitch and native yellow ochre mineral made a very dark brown, nearly black dye. A deep black color was obtained by overdying the natural brown wool.

By 1900, most Navajo weavers had begun using the newly developed commercial synthetic dyes. The colors were harsh and tended to fade or bleed. In the 1920s there was a return to the native vegetal dyes. In 1940 the tribe distributed a booklet listing recipes for making scores of colors from native plants. Some 250 native vegetal-dye colors using stems, roots, nuts, berries, leaves, and flowers have been discovered to date.

When she first started weaving, Jean used primarily vegetal dyes. But she shifted to mostly aniline dyes for red, dark blue, and blue, and still uses vegetal dyes for the other colors.

After the wool has dried, it is wound into balls and is ready for the loom. Jean uses a vertical loom similar to the ones used by the tenth-century Pueblo Indians that is portable and easy to assemble.

The final step in weaving is choosing a design. Designs have evolved since Navajo women first began to weave. At first rugs, blankets, and garments were made using simple stripe designs. Later weavers varied the stripe pattern by using different widths of stripes or making triangular- and diamond-shaped designs. Beginning in the 1870s, designs became more elaborate, partially because of the influence of traders and trading posts.

One of the most influential traders was John Lorenzo Hubbell who became a licensed reservation trader in 1879 when he took over the trading post at Ganado, Arizona. Hubbell encouraged the weavers who lived in the Ganado area to make high-quality rugs and blankets and discouraged use of all synthetic dyes except black, blue, and red. He insisted that weavers use a double portion of red dye to produce a rich color that became known as Ganado red. Hubbell also had an influence on rug designs. He encouraged the use of crosses, diamonds, and stripes within a border.

Although Hubbell sold many rugs at his trading posts, it was not until he contracted with the Fred Harvey Company that his sales soared. Fred Harvey had hotels and gift shops along the route of the Santa Fe Railway. In 1902, Hubbell sold $20,000 worth of weavings to the Fred Harvey Company. By 1912, that number had grown to $60,000.

Sales increased in the 1920s when weavers began using a sand painting design in their rugs depicting the Yei— the Navajo Holy People. Sand painting is part of a Navajo ceremony performed by medicine men. Navajos believe the ceremony is only effective if the sand painting is destroyed immediately after the ceremony. The sand paintings on rugs were permanent, and rumors circulated that weavers using the ceremonial designs on their rugs would go blind, go insane, or even die. When this did not happen, a wide variety of pictorial rugs became hugely popular. Contemporary rugs not only use sand painting designs, they also depict cattle, trains, birds and animals, even pickup trucks and automobiles.

Jean is known for weaving the Storm design. The origin of the Storm pattern is often attributed to trader J. B. Moore, who featured a Storm pattern rug in his 1911

Jean and a helper holding a Storm pattern rug that she has just completed. *Photograph courtesy of Jean Mann.*

catalog. Some say that the style is sacred. The central rectangle represents the Navajo hogan, and the rectangles in each corner represent the four sacred mountains of Navajo legend. Connecting lines between the central rectangles and the corner rectangles are said to be lightning bolts carrying blessings between the mountains and the hogan. Others think the Storm pattern is based on designs found on flour sacks at trading posts. Alice Kaufman and Christopher Selser suggest in their book, *The Navajo Weaving Tradition: 1650 to the Present*, that "the symbolism credited to the storm pattern rug is a product of imaginative Anglo marketing."

Although she has Parkinson's disease, Jean Mann still weaves today. Her only concession to her illness is buying skeins of wool prepared by other Navajo carders who've spun it ready for use. "I still love to weave," Jean says, "even though my eyes get tired, my fingers get tired, and my back gets tired."

Watching Jean's fingers move quickly across the loom, I was amazed. "Do you have the pattern marked on the warp?" I asked. "No," Jean replied. "It's all natural and in the mind. It naturally comes to mind as I go along. No two rugs are ever the same." Her daughter Philomena (Mindy Nez) and I marveled at her ability. "Mom tried to teach me," Mindy said, "but I never could learn."

"My oldest daughter, Lisa Mann Adams, has learned the basics of weaving but as with all my daughters, due to their full time careers, it is hard to maintain the techniques suitable to demonstrate the art. Marie Ann had woven a rug when she got out of high school and she sold it for $85 in Flagstaff," Jean said. "She too said that it was hard for her to maintain good consistency in the strokes of the batten and the rhythm was tough to achieve and maintain. Another daughter, Henrietta (Etta) Martinez learned how to weave sash belts as a young girl. The art of weaving the sash belt is somewhat different as the warp forms the design rather than the yarn."

Mindy said that her mother taught them something that proved as valuable to them as weaving. "Mom said we should study the ways of the white man," Mindy explained. "She said we had to learn to function outside of the reservation, to go to school, and to get a good job." Mindy has worked as a visitor use assistant at Desert View at the East Entrance of Grand Canyon National Park. She has also presented Elderhostel programs. "My sister Etta and I talk about weaving and the Navajo culture," Mindy said. "We talk about Southwestern crafts, jewelry, baskets, pottery, dream catchers and cradleboards."

All of Jean's children have learned the lesson well. They are working in several cities in the West, but they all return home to the reservation whenever they can.

"We have a big Christmas reunion the weekend before Christmas," daughter Lisa Adams said. "We all go back to the reservation to celebrate. In August we all hike down to Havasupai for a week of camping."

Jean left Grand Canyon National Park in 1980 after ten years of demonstrating weaving, but not before she had a couple of canyon adventures. "Lisa and I flew in a small aircraft down into the canyon when I was thirty-seven years old," she said. This was in the days before low flying aircraft were banned from the park. She also rode a mule down the Bright Angel Trail to Plateau Point. "I did that when I was forty-five years old," she laughed.

Jean left the Grand Canyon because she wanted to be closer to her home in Cameron. After moving back, she began demonstrating weaving at the Cameron Trading Post, a position she held for fifteen years.

Jean also traveled extensively giving weaving demonstrations and teaching others how to weave. She has been to Tucson, Yuma, and Northern Arizona University in Flagstaff. She went to North Carolina twice, Hawaii four times, Albuquerque twice, and once to Fort Lauderdale. "I took one of my daughters with me on every trip," Jean said. "After the demonstration, I would show those interested how to weave. Before I left, someone would always buy my loom."

Jean voiced concern about the future of weaving. "There aren't as many sheep as there used to be," she said, "and there aren't as many weavers either. The older weavers still tend to card and spin their own wool, but most of the younger weavers tend to use commercial yarn. There aren't many younger weavers either."

There are, however, still many talented Navajo weavers. A stop at Cameron Trading Post on Highway 89 in northern Arizona will show that to be the case. An assortment of beautiful rugs hangs on the walls of the restaurant and in stacks in the rug area of the trading post, many selling for several thousand dollars. And, sitting at the large loom just as Jean Mann did more than twenty years ago, a Navajo woman weaves an intricately designed rug.

Rowing a River, Rowing a Life

LOUISE TEAL
(1946—)

When Louise Teal talks about the Grand Canyon, her eyes glisten and the shadow of thoughtfulness washes over her face. A river guide, or "boat-woman," for twenty-five years, Louise has spent countless hours on the portion of the Colorado River that snakes its way through the canyon. With each trip she has taken on that river, the essence of it has penetrated her soul more deeply.

When Louise was in high school in the San Francisco Bay Area, her father introduced her to the Colorado River on a commercial trip through Glen Canyon, just upstream of the Grand Canyon. That trip affected Louise profoundly. "Being in Glen Canyon was a spiritual experience for me," she explained. "I was raised Presbyterian, but it always had seemed so limiting in that it didn't cover all the bases for me. Seeing the canyon walls, immense, awesome, awe-inspiring, full of possibility and mystery, I lost any belief that I had been taught in church. I mean that. I distinctly remember the time and place where this happened, sitting alone, looking straight up at the walls in a narrow, now flooded side canyon of the Glen. My dad would have died on the spot," Louise admitted, "if he'd known that the trip, which he took me on, had had that effect, but I know that today he'd be glad of where that realization eventually led me back to spiritually."

It would be another seven years before Louise returned to the Colorado. "My husband, Roger, and I were living in Seattle under grey skies, when I saw a magazine article about the Grand Canyon. Some of the pictures showed boats, and I wrote to the

park to see who ran river trips. I signed
Roger and myself up for the longest,
cheapest trip," Louise recalled. "When
it came time to go, Roger couldn't go,
so I went alone. The canyon was beautiful and intense, a completely fulfilling
place to be. I wanted to stay. Simple,"
she thought. "I'll convince Roger to
become a boatman."

And so she did. It helped
immensely that Roger had burned out
at his job as a stockbroker and was as
ready to leave Seattle as Louise was
eager to head to the Southwest. Louise
observed that the women working on
the river during the early 1970s were
more or less assistants to their river
running husbands or boyfriends. "I
later realized that for most women,
breaking up with their boatman boyfriend meant the end of going down the river."

Louise Teal exploring a side canyon of the
Grand Canyon. *Photograph courtesy of
John Annerino © 1998.*

It turned out that no one wanted to hire a former stockbroker as a river guide,
so Louise and her husband enrolled in the American River Touring Association's
(ARTA) first river running school. "The next year, Roger was running motor trips
down the Grand Canyon, and I was working as his assistant, a soul in bliss." Louise
found she didn't like motors and wanted to learn to row. The following summer,
she and Roger purchased a raft and helped other boatmen give free trips to kids on
the Stanislaus River in California. "I learned to use oars that summer," Louise said.
At the end of the summer Roger went fishing in Alaska, and Louise managed to get
on a canyon "snout" boat trip. A snout is a twenty-two-foot, one-ton boat equipped
with thirteen-foot oars. They are configured from a four-foot-wide steel and wood
frame set between two inflated military surplus pontoons. Learning to row a snout
is hard for anyone, man or woman. "I learned to use the current as much as possible," Louise said, "looking way ahead in order to have time to make any needed
maneuvers. Making tight eddies right above a rapid like the small entrance to Mat-
katamiba Canyon was the biggest challenge."

Louise got the chance to row her own boat when Rob Elliott and his wife, Jessica Youle, bought ARTA and changed the name to Arizona Raft Adventures (AZRA). "They wanted to start women rowing. I was a likely candidate because I was already working there as an assistant and I had learned to row in California. Then, although Roger and I broke up, I continued rowing."

As with anyone who is an outsider of sorts, Louise did feel left out some of the time during her early years on the river. "After years of being a tomboy, of playing fighter pilot instead of house, it was still pretty obvious that I wasn't a guy. When I worked on crews as the only girl, it could get a little lonely. It took me a while to realize that I didn't want to be a guy anyway! Being in this great place surrounded by these vibrant men was a great deal. . . . They were superb, intelligent, and caring people, and how they made me laugh!"

Apart from a brief stint in real estate in Los Angeles in 1979—a bad career move brought on by a panic attack, where Louise convinced herself she had to work a "real" job in order to live a meaningful life—Louise was lost to the Grand Canyon. Talking with her, it is hard to picture her in a business suit and high heels, clutching a clipboard and steering clients from one ranch-style house to another; she seems at home sitting in a boat, oars in hand, rowing river-soaked passengers between cavernous canyon walls.

Louise enjoyed the exhilaration of river running, including reading the water correctly, maneuvering into a tight eddy successfully, and surviving a dowsing at Lava Falls without flipping. But the quiet moments were equally gripping, and it was those moments she still holds sacred. The beauty of the canyon astounded Louise continually. It is what kept her there, what she wanted to share with her passengers.

"When I first started working here, I was beyond eager to learn everything about the place. I'd go to libraries and read old journals and books. I still find the science and history fascinating, but more and more, it's the feeling of the place that astounds me, the beauty. The shape and color of a rock, the flowing water, and always, the light . . . the light. The light down there is like nowhere else. The canyon has a glow, salmon, rose, and orange."

It was important to Louise that her passengers experience this glow. "All a guide ever asks from the passengers is that they are blown away by the Grand Canyon, that they appreciate the place. That's all. I don't care if they ever help in the kitchen, leave a great tip, or whatever. Just so they fall in love. So they realize where they are and aren't just floating through the canyon sitting on the boat, talking about the next vacation they're going to nab."

And more often than not, passengers did fall in love; they did connect on some level with the ineffable beauty of the canyon. Much of this may well have had to do with Louise's own profound connection to the river, for she always encouraged her passengers to take notice. "I joke sometimes about telling the passengers to shut up and look at the canyon. Like when they want to know how far, when will we get there, what mile, and so on—reasonable questions, but sometimes asked just to fill the air with distracting facts. Distracting from what they are feeling and seeing and hearing."

Louise bid her passengers to listen to the river's voice—the roar of the rapids, as well as the soft bubbles that follow to tell you calm is restored, giving the listener permission to rest and think. And everything in between. "On my last trip with a group, we were being quiet and we heard a deer rustling in the reeds before we ever saw him. He was a big buck, and we would have missed him entirely if we'd been jabbering."

Louise Teal's devotion to the river was evident the moment she began talking about it. She expressed a profound respect for its beauty and its power, both of which she has experienced firsthand. "You're not going to realize the power of the river until something goes wrong," a veteran boatman once told her. "And he was right," she said knowingly. "It is not until you're up against a rock and the river is folding your boat, or you've flipped and you are rolling around like a washing machine in the water, and the water is pounding you, and then you will realize the power of the river."

On a trip some years ago, after a particularly strenuous day of into-the-wind rowing, Louise set up a tarp because it looked like rain, and then she collapsed, exhausted. When she awoke later, she realized immediately that something was different. "I was in the middle of the river, with another boat tied to me, heading downstream toward Lava Falls. My story would have a different ending if I'd stayed sleeping until the jet engine roar of Lava Falls woke me up. As it was, I managed to pull the boats to shore well before that noisy thirty-seven-foot drop. Still, it's a story I always tell as we row down to run Lava, and I always mention that I was naked, in the thunder and lightning, except for my life jacket. On one trip, this gave a group of women riding on my boat an idea: 'Let's run Lava naked!'"

Despite some initial concerns, Louise agreed to go along with her passengers.

"At the scout above Lava [the place where guides study the rapid from shore], we parked a little away from the other boats so they wouldn't see us until we pulled out to run it. We put our life jackets on, and at the last minute I realized that I was going to slip all over the seat without pants on, so I put a scarf on the seat.

"We had a wild run and slammed into the top wave, slid down into the V-shaped wave and just got pummeled. Even with the scarf, I almost slid off the seat. I lifted myself back into some semblance of control over the boat, but we weren't going to be straight for the first big wave. I yelled, 'high side'" (meaning everyone gets on the high side of the boat to prevent it from flipping).

"We all leaned into the big wave and went up and over it. Then we just got absolutely hammered by the second wave behind it. It was like trying to hold on with a fire hose blasting you, and it was absolutely incredible. But, amazingly, no one fell in. The wave finally spit us out. We looked around and couldn't even see our boat. The tubes were literally under water, but they slowly wallowed up as we started bailing," Louise remembered. "One girl had blood all over her face because she'd been hit, probably by someone's elbow, but she didn't realize it. She was okay. I've decided it was a safety measure not to have clothes on, because no one was about to let go and get picked up naked. We were about as high and happy as you can get. We'd felt the full force of the river."

A river that can toss and pummel you is a force to respect. People lose their lives when they fail to discern this one fundamental distinction. But when people meet the water's force for the first time, especially when their lives are in danger, they often perform remarkable feats. "People perform way beyond their capabilities—or what they perceive as their capabilities," Louise explained. "There was a sixty-year-old lady named Grace on a boat that flipped in Sockdolager. She got caught under the boat, but she did exactly what she was taught—looked for the light and walked her way out with her hands from under the boat. All this in the middle of a big rapid! She was so excited. Grace said she'd always wondered how she would react in an emergency, and she was really proud of herself. It was great to be part of her excitement."

In 1978, Louise and AZRA planned the first all-women's trip through the Grand Canyon. "A passenger on one of my trips came up with this idea," she said. "Pulling an all-woman crew together for the trip was tough. That's how few qualified women were canyon guides then." Louise was to lead the trip though she'd only led one other trip before. Her boss, Jessica Youle, and fellow guide Suzanne Jordan would run two other snouts, and Barbara Thomas guided the smaller paddle raft.

"We finally got it all organized and were at Lees Ferry with our snouts tied up to the shore," Louise said. "We had three snouts and one paddle raft to carry twenty-two women. I'd just finished my introductory safety speech, and we began to untie and shove our high and dry boats into the river, when the ranger decided we needed another spare life jacket. We had to stall while our truck driver went to borrow one from a nearby river company's warehouse. I took the group back to the shade of the tamarisk trees and talked more about safety tips and taking care of the canyon, totally forgetting that the water was due to come up thanks to the workings of the [Glen Canyon] dam.

"We hung out under the trees for a while and then started walking back to the river. Whale, a Hatch River Expeditions motor boatman who was also putting in, grinned at me and said, 'Louise, I tied up your boats for you. They were starting to float away.' So . . . oh, my God . . . the first Grand Canyon women's trip in history came pretty close to becoming a great river story in which all our boats floated downriver without us!" After telling this story, Louise suggested that all boatwomen working today should be glad that Whale wasn't one of those boatmen who thought women shouldn't be guides in the canyon. He could have had a heyday by letting their boats drift away. Instead, he had the good grace to cut the women a break—Louise in particular. She learned from Whale and others like him.

Louise arrived on the river at the time that Americans—indeed, people across the globe—were at a cultural crossroads. Women were just beginning to assert themselves in the male world, and she unwittingly championed the role of women working on the river not as assistants but as full-fledged river runners and guides. Louise recognized early on that her opportunities were possible because of the courage of her contemporaries, both men and women.

"I wanted to honor the women I'd worked with and met on the river," she said, and she did so by writing *Breaking Into the Current: Boatwomen of the Grand Canyon*, a compelling collection of biographies of the canyon's boatwomen. Writing the book, she said, "was a way to show my love for the people and the place." Though the issue of sexism was not the motivating factor, it necessarily surfaced in her research because it was a sizable part of the experience of those she interviewed. "The book became not only a story of people in love with a place, which I feel it primarily is, but also of women struggling to be in a place they loved. I wanted to honor that struggle." As Louise wrote in the preface to her book, these

Louise masterfully negotiating Crystal Rapids. *Photograph courtesy of John Annerino © 1998.*

first boatwomen "were only following their hearts amidst the pressures and possibilities facing all women in our particular era."

The evolving role of women on the river has been the hallmark of the quarter century Louise spent on the river. Boatwomen have made incredible strides, with more working as guides today than ever before. "They're no longer oddball or working jobs on the periphery. They're acknowledged contributors. In 1869, John Wesley Powell made his first exploration in the *Emma Dean*. Robert Brewster Stanton's survey crew rode the rapids in the *Sweet Marie* and the *Bonnie Jean*. Now we're rowing the boats!"

Louise has witnessed a lot of changes in the Grand Canyon and among the people who visit, some not so agreeable. The days of high adventure and the thrill of the unexpected have been diluted by movies, books, and magazines. The clientele has changed as the trips become more and more expensive. The river has become increasingly crowded, more and more regulations have been established, and (thanks to the Glen Canyon Dam) beaches have disappeared and the riparian habitat considerably altered. Most disturbing to Louise, however, has been the growing popularity of "interchange" trips, where visitors run only short sections of the river. "It takes folks three or four days to really be there," she explained, "and if they leave on day five or six, they miss the opportunity to immerse themselves in the experience, to become a tribe traveling through the Grand Canyon." Without this complete immersion, visitors are missing the true magic of the place, the mysterious effect it has on body and psyche. It is a rare gift, she said, to disappear into one of the earth's deepest crevices and to escape cars and phones and televisions.

Louise lamented the passing of earlier days, where adventure and discovery of the unknown were what drew people to the Grand Canyon. She wished she could have gone down the river before the Glen Canyon Dam controlled its flow. "Can you imagine being with Elzada Clover and Lois Jotter? Being the only trip in the canyon? Never knowing what was around the next bend? What an adventure that would be!"

Despite the less agreeable changes, Louise Teal's own connection to the Grand Canyon and the spiritual renewal she has found there have remained constant. And she said she plans to keep on "rowing the boats. It's still absolutely the coolest thing to be down there. Even with the changes, the place is always there. The beauty and magnificence is solid. I can't imagine not being there. I plan to keep doing it as long as the body's willing."

CHAPTER SIXTEEN

Raising a Family in the Grand Canyon

MARY AIKEN
(1951—)

I carried Mercy into the Grand Canyon for the first time in 1973 when she was ten months old," Mary Aiken said as we were having dinner at El Tovar on the South Rim. "I never thought that it would be a long-term thing!" But thirty years later, there she was.

Mary grew up in Seattle, Washington. "I was a zombie looking for sunshine," she laughed. "My body took me to Arizona. I thought I was in heaven." Mary was studying nursing in Phoenix when she met her future husband, Bruce Aiken. "I didn't expect it to work out," she said. "Bruce had studied geology, he was born in Greenwich Village in New York, and his mom was an artist. Plus, he wanted to live in the Grand Canyon!"

Bruce first saw the Grand Canyon when he was three years old. By the time he returned at age nineteen, he knew that he wanted to paint views of the canyon. What better way than to live there?

Bruce and Mary lived five and a half miles down from the North Rim of the Grand Canyon on the North Kaibab Trail at Roaring Springs. Bruce worked for the National Park Service, maintaining the pump that delivers water to the North Rim. A pipeline from Roaring Springs also carries water by gravity down to Phantom Ranch, across the river, and up to Indian Garden where it is pumped to the South Rim.

Mary met the challenge of raising three children in a setting unlike any other. She learned to cope when groceries ran low and the helicopter was late, when a child was sick, when injured hikers showed up at the door needing help, and when myriad crises arose. She learned to be flexible and not be disappointed when things

Mary Aiken raised her family in a very unusual setting. *Photograph courtesy of Bruce Aiken.*

didn't happen as planned. She learned to love the Grand Canyon. "It's the only place I have ever lived that you have time to really live," Mary said.

The National Park Service constructed the pump station and house for the manager in 1928. "We lived in that house until 1978," Mary said. "We had electricity, a telephone, and indoor plumbing. I loved that house. The bathroom had a claw foot tub." In 1978 the park service constructed a new house at the same time they built a new pumping station. "They brought in backhoes and tractors in a sling dangling from a helicopter," she said. "The new house was built of redwood and painted brown. When we moved into the new house, they tore the old one down. It made us so sad."

The Aiken children did not find their house by the side of the trail unusual. To them it was home. Mercy was born in Seattle, a few months before they moved to the canyon. "I named her Mercy because God had been merciful to me," Mary said. "When Shirley came along we were on winter furlough on the South Rim. It was snowing hard and our truck wouldn't start. Bruce borrowed a neighbor's truck. It was so low on gasoline that we thought we wouldn't make it to Williams in time for her delivery, but we did."

When the time approached for Silas' arrival, Mary decided to hike out of the canyon a week early. "There I was, nearly nine months pregnant and hiking out of the canyon. People gave me horrifying looks!"

Mary made many adjustments to life in the canyon. The supermarket was not around the corner. "The first year we lived in the canyon, I could call Babbitt's Supermarket on the South Rim and order groceries," she recalled. "They would arrange for the National Park Service to bring the groceries down by pack mule. By the time the mules got here, the eggs were always broken."

When a new manager at Babbitt's refused to deliver their groceries, Mary arranged to have the park service bring them into the canyon by helicopter. "I would coordinate delivery of groceries when the chopper was coming down for a water sample or to bring chlorine," she explained.

The new process took two days. "I would hike out to the North Rim to get the car," Mary said. "That would take three to four hours. Then I would drive to Flagstaff, another four hours. I would buy the groceries and take them to the South Rim airport where they would be wrapped, weighed, and our name put on the package for delivery to us. Then I would drive back to the North Rim and hike home. At least our eggs weren't broken!"

There were times when the helicopter would not come into the canyon for several weeks. "I learned to make do," Mary said. "I'd make homemade bread, Mercy and Shirley would collect watercress for salad, and Silas would catch fish out of Bright Angel Creek."

Silas became quite adept at catching fish with his hands. "One time I put my hands under a rock and caught a fish," he said. "I got pretty good at it. I'd see people fishing with a pole and they were always getting their line caught in the bushes. It wasn't until I was about ten that I understood why people used a pole."

In the summer, the Aikens raised a garden to supplement their food supply. "The garden was a family project," said Mary. "The kids and I took wheelbarrows down to the mule corral at Cottonwood Campground [one and a half miles down the North Kaibab Trail] and brought back manure to fertilize the plants. We fought an unending battle with wild creatures, especially deer."

The heliport near their house played an important role in the Aikens' life. Besides delivering food to them and supplies for the pump station, the children, and sometimes the entire family, slept on the helipad. At first they used old sleeping bags, but later they got good mattresses and blankets.

Daughter Shirley remembered that Mary used to tell bedtime stories to them out there. "One of her themes had to do with the helipad taking off," Shirley said. "We loved that story. Mom had many versions. One night while we were sleeping on the helipad, we heard a huge roar. We started screaming. I looked over and saw this huge white cloud coming toward us. We started freaking out and screaming. We ran inside."

"The noise woke Bruce and me," Mary said. "It sounded like a train wreck or an earthquake. The house shook. The children were so frightened. Shirley thought the world was coming to an end. Mercy thought it was a flood and began pulling sleeping bags off the helipad. Silas had just watched the movie *Ghostbusters* and he thought the cloud of dust was a ghost." The noise was actually a huge rock slide. "The slide covered the trail and dammed Bright Angel Creek," Mary said. "Before the NPS could get it cleared, we had a lake!"

Although the children were frightened by the rock slide, it was one of the few times in the canyon that they were afraid. "When I first came down in the canyon I was afraid of heights," Mary said. "I didn't want the children to be that way. Our house is surrounded by cliffs. I'd look out the window and see the children playing way up high. I'd be nervous, but I didn't say anything to them. They have no fear of heights."

Neither did they have any fears about hiking in the canyon. "Whenever we went anywhere," Mary explained, "we had to walk up to the North Rim to get our car. When the children were small, we put them on our back, but by the time they were three, they were too heavy. Age three was our carrying cut-off date. After that they had to walk by themselves." This meant that what would normally be a three- or four-hour walk would take five or six hours. "The children would sit down in the middle of the trail and play with rocks," Mary said.

Silas remembered one of his first hikes out when he was three or four years old. "My legs were quivering," he said. "I remember thinking 'This is one of the hardest things I have ever done in my life.' Mom was really patient. It wasn't until I was around twelve that I accepted the hike out as not a big deal. I'd hike out in the summers to play Little League baseball."

The hike is definitely a challenge. It is five and a half miles from the where the Aikens lived to the North Rim, with a 3,500-foot elevation gain. But Silas mastered the hike. "The last time I visited my parents, I did my best time ever," he bragged, "one hour and thirty-five minutes!"

On the hike out someone would occasionally fall down and skin a knee or scrape an arm. Mary kept a first aid kit handy for such minor injuries, but on one hike out the kit wasn't adequate. "The kids and I were hiking out," she recalled. "Mercy was sixteen, Shirley thirteen, and Silas ten. Mercy and Shirley were exploring and fooling around when Shirley stepped on a boulder and broke her ankle." Shirley tried to walk, but she limped badly.

"Two Swiss hikers came along," Mary said, "and one said, 'I carry little girl if you carry my pack.' The pack weighed eighty pounds. We were past the tunnel and about a mile and a half from the top." By the time they made it out of the canyon, Shirley didn't

Shirley Aiken (left) and sister Mercy outside the family garden at Roaring Springs, ca.1978. *Photograph courtesy of Bruce Aiken.*

have any feeling in her toes. "I drove her to the South Rim Clinic and they sent me on to Flagstaff. Shirley was in a cast from her knee down for a long time."

Shirley's cast gave the children material for one of their many hoaxes on tourists. "We dressed in weird costumes and walked down to Cottonwood Campground," Shirley explained. "Since I had my leg in a cast, Mercy put me in a wheelbarrow," she said. "I remember I wore a nightgown with a bra on the outside. Silas put on women's makeup. We walked all the way to Cottonwood singing very loud. People said, 'Are you crazy?' Later people stopped at our house and asked if we saw that crazy family at Cottonwood."

Mercy said that one of their favorite things was to play tricks on hikers camped at Cottonwood. "We would wear dumb outfits, with one sandal and one shoe, and walk down to Cottonwood. When we had friends down we would go in a large group and tell the campers at Cottonwood that we were all related and that we were being cared for by nuns. We did this stuff just for the fun of it."

Silas laughed as he remembered the time they "freaked out" a group of Boy Scouts. "We pretended we were eastern Europeans," Silas said. "My sisters wore evening gowns. I put one of Mom's bras over my shirt. We all went barefooted down to Cottonwood and asked, 'Where's the hotel?' The totally prepared Boy Scouts went crazy. 'Where are your shoes? Do you have any water?'" Silas said they always made friends with the ranger at Cottonwood who overlooked their shenanigans.

Mary laughed as she recalled the children's escapades. "Sometimes they would all carry guitars," she said. "They would put on weird hats and funny robes and tell the campers at Cottonwood that they were a singing group."

Interacting with the hikers was part of the children's life in the canyon. "We would act out stories for the hikers that came down the trail,"

Silas Aiken knew how to use canyon resources to advantage and gravitated toward water. *Photograph courtesy of Bruce Aiken.*

Mercy said. "One time I needed two ugly stepsisters so I dragged these two hippie men with long hair off the trail to be the stepsisters!" Mary remembered that play. "The children had just read *Hansel and Gretel*," Mary said. "Luckily the men Mercy dragged off the trail were French and didn't speak a word of English. They didn't know they were portraying ugly stepsisters!"

While the children enjoyed playing tricks on hikers, there was a more serious aspect to living beside a major trail in Grand Canyon. "We were Bright Angel Rescue," Mary said. "We had people stop if they were injured. I'd tape up sprained ankles and bandage cuts. People would hike from the North Rim to the Colorado River and back in a day. Some even try to hike rim to rim to rim. They'd stop at our house on the way back, too exhausted to go on. We'd have them spend the night. People still send us presents and cards years after we helped them. We felt totally lucky to live there and to be able to help," Mary said.

I remember well my first hike across the canyon. If it hadn't been for the Aikens I might not have made it. A friend and I started on the South Rim and spent the night at Phantom Ranch. Our plan was to hike fourteen miles to the North

Rim in one day. We started at daybreak. It was mid-summer and unbearably hot. I couldn't believe my eyes when I came around the bend and saw the lemonade stand in the Aikens' yard. The cold lemonade gave me the strength to make it to the North Rim.

Mercy remembers her parents laughing about having a lemonade stand when she was around six or seven. "One day we just dragged out a little table and it was an instant success," Mercy said. Shirley said that working at the lemonade stand helped her become outgoing. "People think that if I grew up in the canyon I would be introverted but it was just the opposite. I talked to people all the time."

Even after the children were grown and gone, Mary still put out the lemonade stand as a service to hikers; she and Bruce noticed there was less heat exhaustion when the stand was out. "People will stop in the yard for a drink, then rest, and continue on to the North Rim in the shade," she said.

Although the children enjoyed the lemonade stand, one of their memories was of scorpion hunts. "One summer scorpions seemed to take over the house," Mary said. "They were *Centruroides* scorpions and were poisonous. We were all stung, but Shirley had the most serious sting."

"Shirley was stung when she was about three," Mary recalled. "She nearly died. She had a high fever and went into convulsions. It was the middle of the night and they couldn't get the helicopter down. They told me over the phone how to get her fever down and we flew her out the next morning."

Shirley never got over her fear of scorpions. "I wouldn't join in on the scorpion hunts," she said. "At midnight someone would yell 'Scorpion Hunt! Scorpion Hunt!' and Mercy and Silas would scream and run around with a flashlight looking for scorpions. They'd come back and report how many they had found."

As the children grew older, the question of schooling arose. During Bruce's winter furlough, the Aikens spent time in Ajo, Arizona. "We bought a house in Ajo," Mary explained, "and for three years we spent the furlough in Ajo. I'd put Mercy in preschool so she had some interaction with other children. I assumed that we would leave the canyon when Mercy was old enough for school," Mary said. When she discovered that Mercy had taught herself to read, she decided to home school the kids. "I took a basic skills test to qualify for home schooling. In those days, home schooling was not as accepted as it is now."

Mary spent three hours in the morning in formal teaching. They studied reading, English, history, biology, and math. "I couldn't get them to sit still any longer," she laughed. "In the afternoon, we would go into the canyon on field trips. We'd study geology. Also, I encouraged them to read books. I would pack books into the canyon on my back," Mary said. "Mercy read so much that I had to limit her to one book a day. Her eyes would be red and swollen by evening."

Mary had what she called Creative Time. "We'd gather in the kitchen and bake bread or make crafts," Shirley said. Mary had the children keep journals. She encouraged drawing and writing poetry.

Mary credits the children's imagination and creativity to the fact that they did not have television. "Looking back, this is the best thing I ever could have done for them," she stated.

Music, not television, was the family's passion. "We all love music," Mercy said. "We grew up singing." Mary remembered that Mercy walked up and down the trail singing. "When she was at Northern Arizona University in Flagstaff, I walked into a Wal-Mart and heard Mercy singing," Mary said. "All the kids play instruments and write songs." Shirley said that music was on all day long. "We listened to all kinds of music—music of my parent's generation, Spanish music, everything."

Silas remembered another kind of music. "As long as I can remember we sat around in the evening playing instruments and singing," Silas said. "During Dad's time off we used to go to San Miguel, Mexico, and work with missionaries. Back home we'd sing Christian songs in Spanish. Mercy, Shirley, Dad, and I played the guitar. I also played the drums. Our family has a strong faith even though we did not go to a formal church. Bible study was part of our schooling."

As the children got older, Mary realized that she could not teach them all the subjects they needed. "I couldn't remember algebra, chemistry, and geometry well enough to teach them," she said. "I knew that I would have to come out of the canyon so they could attend school on an everyday basis. Besides, the kids were begging to go to school. Silas wanted to participate in sports. Mercy said, 'I think I need some social interaction.' Shirley wanted to be with her friends. I had to bring the kids out," Mary stated.

Bruce and Mary were assigned a house on the South Rim in Grand Canyon Village. "Bruce and I saw each other every other weekend except for the four months in the winter when he wasn't in the canyon," she said. "I got a job at the airport. For a while I worked as a tour guide. I had a commercial driver's license. I'd meet the planes as they came in from Las Vegas and put people in a van and take them on a three-hour tour of the canyon."

The Aiken family at Roaring Springs, Thanksgiving Day, 1988. *Photograph courtesy of Bruce Aiken.*

Shirley now realizes that it was difficult for her mom to live away from her father. "I know she missed my dad," Shirley said. "It was really strange to see them separated. Mom wanted to go back down, but she couldn't. She had to work and stay up with us. I was so happy to be in regular high school, though. All I thought about then was being with my friends."

Mary didn't like living on the South Rim. "Down in the canyon, I had time to do things I wanted," she said. "I painted watercolors. I watched the storms in the canyon, the lightning and the rainbows. I read books. Up here, I didn't have any time. When I got home from work, I didn't have time for anything."

As the children left for college, they began to realize how much the canyon meant to them. When she first went to Northern Arizona University in Flagstaff, Mercy dreamed that she was hiking down in the canyon, going home. "It was winter and everything was beautiful," she said. "There was a black gospel choir singing 'Sailing on the Sea of Your Life' . . . over and over again. When I got home we were all little again. Mom had just made enchiladas. I remember the skirt she was wearing. The canyon is always a part of me and it will be that way for the rest of my life."

Shirley used to complain about living in the canyon. "All I thought about was being with my friends," she remembered. "I didn't think about the canyon at all. Now it means so much to me. Whenever I have time off, I go back down."

Silas looks forward to coming back to the canyon. "I can't imagine my parents not being there," he said.

Mary is proud of her children. Mercy earned a degree in English from Northern Arizona University, and works with a Christian ministry. Shirley received a degree in art from the University of Arizona. Silas finished his Master's Degree in Education from Arizona State University and teaches elementary school physical education.

Mary moved back to Roaring Springs when Silas left for college. I asked what she would do when Bruce retired, and she said she planned to take a few classes, "like blowing glass and sculpture and physics and astronomy and physiology and acupuncture and painting and poetry and massage and herbology . . . you know, the usual."

That time came in May 2006, when the pump station at Roaring Springs was computerized. The house in the canyon near Roaring Springs that was home to the Aiken family for thirty-three years became the base for a preventative-search-and-rescue ranger to carry on the Aikens' tradition of assisting hikers.

The Aikens have moved to Flagstaff, Arizona, where Bruce maintains a painting studio downtown. And Mary? "I've been certified as a caregiver and plan to work with hospice patients," she said. "But I haven't forgotten about the classes." She is doing "You know, the usual."

"I do have one complaint," Mary laughed. "I made a rule not to lay guilt on the children; however, I have been waiting a very long time for grandchildren!" But, that wish has now been granted.

CHAPTER SEVENTEEN

A Voice in Washington

ETHEL JACK
(1908—1977)

M y mother had an unusual dream," Bernice Watahomigie, daughter of
Ethel Jack, said, as we talked over coffee at the cafe in Supai.

"In the early forties she was bitten by a black widow spider and she got
very sick. Her father called for the medicine man to heal her. She got a little better
and then she got worse again. On the fourth visit he placed an eagle feather in my
mother's hair and admitted that he could do no more," Bernice continued. "She got
worse and became unconscious. That's when she had the dream."

In the dream Ethel Jack heard horses coming up the path from Havasu Falls.
They stopped at her door. "Her father was holding a beautiful gray horse," Bernice
said. "He put the horse in front of the door and said to my mother, 'My daughter,
get up on this horse."

"My mother replied, 'I can't get up. I'm too weak.' Her father insisted, saying, 'Get
up!' My mother struggled and got out of bed and went to the door," Bernice went on.
"The horse knelt down on his front legs and she was able to get on the horse."

"Her father told her to ride the horse toward the rocks as he pointed to the
Grand Canyon walls to the east. The horse took off and soon was flying," Bernice
told. "They flew for a long time until the horse came down in front of the White
House flower gardens in Washington, D.C. My mother told us that she looked at
the flower gardens through a parking meter. Then she woke up. Her body was well
and she had no more pain. She never got sick again. My mother told us about that
dream so many times. She didn't understand the meaning of the dream for thirty-
one years."

Ethel Jack was born in the village of Supai in Havasu Canyon in 1908. Bernice said her mother was a tomboy. "Her older brother taught her how to ride untamed horses and how to chop wood," Bernice said. Ethel married Clark Jack, who later became tribal chairman and they had had seven children, four of whom died of measles.

Ethel was an outstanding basket weaver. "She sold baskets to tourists and a few to the Smithsonian," Bernice said. Ethel also worked in the South Rim lodges at Grand Canyon as a housecleaner. "She took care of Emery Kolb when he got older," Bernice added, "and my dad worked for the Santa Fe Railway." Bernice remembered living in a brown house in Supai Camp, near Grand Canyon

Ethel Jack with Arizona Senator John J. Rhodes in Washington, D.C., on October 11, 1974, during the Havasupai campaign to regain their rim lands. *Photograph courtesy of Bernice Watahomigie.*

Village, while her parents worked at the South Rim. "My mother and I moved back to live at Supai permanently in 1972," Bernice said. "She was getting older and wanted to retire. She enjoyed working in the fields."

The Havasupai have inhabited Havasu Canyon and the southern portion of Grand Canyon National Park and the Tusayan District of the Kaibab National Forest since around 700 A.D. In summer, Havasu Canyon is a garden spot in the western end of the canyon. The Havasupai are known as the people of the blue-green water because of the color of the water that flows in the stream and that creates several spectacular waterfalls on its way to the Colorado River.

Traditionally the Havasupai lived in the canyon from April to mid-October, planting corn, beans, and squash. In the winter the sun penetrates the steep-walled canyon for only a few hours a day, and the lush canyon becomes a damp and dismal place. So as winter approached, the Havasupai went to live on the plateau in semi-permanent homes. They subsisted by hunting mule deer, pronghorn, and smaller game, and gathering pinyon nuts, the fruits of barrel and prickly pear cactus, and wild grapes.

By the middle of the nineteenth century, white settlers and ranchers began moving onto Havasupai plateau lands and blocking their water supplies. Confrontations occurred with increasing frequency. The United States government decided that the best way to deal with the Havasupai on the plateau was to confine them to a reservation.

President Rutherford B. Hayes created the Havasupai Reservation on June 8, 1880. The reservation was twelve miles long and extended two and one half miles on each side of the creek. A surveying party sent in the summer of 1881 to mark the boundaries of the new reservation found that they could not place boundary markers on the high cliffs. Also, there were three claims being mined by Anglos in the area between Havasu and Mooney Falls.

Lieutenant of Engineers Carl F. Palfrey consulted with Navajo, Chief of the Havasupai, and argued that the reservation be diminished to include the land between the canyon walls and above the rim of Havasu Falls.

Chief Navajo agreed to decrease the size of the reservation because he was afraid that if he did not agree, the tribe would be forced to move—as had happened in 1874 to the Hualapai—or be exterminated. President Chester A. Arthur confirmed the reduction in the size of the Havasupai reservation on March 31, 1882.

The Havasupai Reservation contained only 518.6 acres. Rim lands were no longer theirs, but the Havasupai did not understand that they were limited to the reservation and continued to spend their winters on the plateau for many years. The Havasupai apparently believed that the creation of the reservation was to protect that land from encroachment forever and that the rim land was still theirs to use. However, increasing encroachment by ranchers and the granting of grazing and hunting permits to outsiders gradually forced the Havasupai to abandon their winter homes.

A few Havasupai, including Ethel Jack's grandfather Billy Burro, and Swedva, known to the Anglos as "Big Jim," lived and planted gardens at the "Place Below the Spruce Trees." Today that place called Indian Garden, the green area visible from Grand Canyon Village, is now a park campground.

When President Theodore Roosevelt came to visit the Grand Canyon, he rode a mule down to Indian Garden and explained to Billy Burro and Swedva that a national park was soon to be created in the canyon. He urged them to leave the inner canyon and make room for the park. Swedva moved to a cave near the rim along the present Bright Angel Trail, but Burro refused to leave.

On January 11, 1908, President Roosevelt created by proclamation the 1,279-square-mile Grand Canyon National Monument. Eleven years later, on February 26, 1919, President Woodrow Wilson signed the bill establishing the Grand Canyon National Park. Still, Billy Burro remained at Indian Garden.

In 1928 two park rangers went to Indian Garden and told Burro he would have to go. When he refused, they ushered him out. Burro died in Supai the following year. His wife died in 1930.

It was not until the winter of 1942–1943 that a Havasupai lived at Indian Garden again. Ethel's husband, Clark Jack, Sr., was hired by the National Park Service to maintain the Bright Angel Trail and to take tourists on mule rides down into the canyon. He stayed at Indian Garden. Ethel grew up there, and Clark wanted his wife to spend a final winter there. It was not as she remembered. She missed the laughter of her grandfather Burro and his family. To Ethel, Indian Garden was now a lonely place.

A number of Havasupai lived at Supai Camp, a 160-acre plot west of the railroad station on the South Rim that was set aside for Havasupai who worked at the Grand Canyon. Assistant Chief Ranger Carl Lehnert met with the Havasupai in 1955. Lehnert told the tribe that he had received a paper from Washington instructing the Havasupai to move their families and horses from Supai Camp unless they were employed by the park.

Shortly after the meeting, Grand Canyon National Park and its concessioners began terminating the employment of the Havasupai. A Bureau of Indian Affairs truck hauled the people and their belongings to Topocoba Hilltop where everyone, including old people and children, were left in the snow at the head of the trail. They had to walk the fourteen-mile trail that led down 2,300 feet to Havasu Canyon. Park officials demolished the homes of those who lost their employment.

On August 7, 1971, the Havasupai Tribal Council brought the elders of the tribe together to discuss what they must do to remedy their problems. Believing that a return to their traditional lifestyle would improve conditions in Supai, they decided to renew the fight to regain their land on the plateau.

Ethel Jack played a prominent role in the struggle. She had learned the culture and traditions of the Havasupai people from her parents and grandparents. She lived at the drift fence on the plateau in the winter and at Indian Garden in the summer as a child. She could speak for her people.

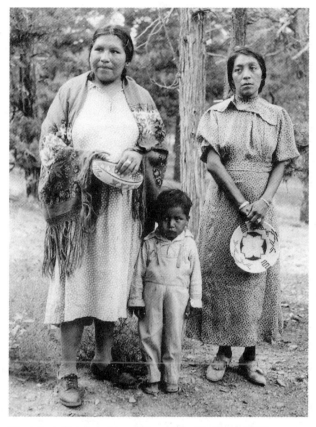

Ethel Jack (right) and her sister, Viola Crook ca. 1937.
*Photograph courtesy of the Barbara McKee Collection, Cline
Library, Special Collections and Archives, Northern Arizona
University. NAU.PH.95.48.1137.*

On October 11, 1972, the Tribal Council unanimously approved resolutions
demanding the restoration of 78,720 acres from the Kaibab National Forest and
166,522 acres from Grand Canyon National Park. The Tribal Council conducted
discussions with the National Park Service and the U. S. Forest Service regarding the return of their traditional lands, to no avail. In the process, however, they
gained the support of Arizona Congressmen John Rhodes and Sam Steiger, as well
as Senator Barry Goldwater. When the council learned that Senator Goldwater was
preparing to submit a bill for the expansion of Grand Canyon National Park, they

invited him to come to Supai.

Senator Goldwater met with the Havasupai Tribal Council on January 27, 1973. Before the meeting, the council passed Resolution 1-73, which superseded any prior resolutions regarding restoration of the former tribal lands. Resolution 1-73 requested:

> The return of all Havasupai allotments and permit areas presently under the U.S. Park Service and U.S. Forest Service control, including the 160 acre Havasupai residency area at Grand Canyon; the return of the 1866 Atlantic and Pacific Railroad indemnity-grant lands; and the return of the Havasu campground to the Havasupai Tribe as part of the Havasupai Reservation.

Senator Goldwater promised to include their demands in his forthcoming bill.

On March 20, 1973, Senator Goldwater introduced the Grand Canyon National Park expansion bill, S. 1296. Arizona Congressman Morris K. Udall, who was convinced that the Havasupai cause was just, introduced the House of Representatives version of the bill on the following day. Initial hearings on the Senate bill were scheduled for June 20, 1973.

Senator Goldwater briefly introduced the bill at the June 20 hearing. When he referred to the Havasupai he said, "When we consider that about 300 Indians live on a little over 500 acres, I don't think that is exactly fair in anybody's book and I do hope you can work out some solution which will help this fine people to survive."

A number of witnesses followed the Senator. The Interior Department had released its opinion earlier in the day, stating in part:

> . . . We also strongly recommend that any decision on transferring land from the National Park System, as well as other Federal land, to the Havasupai Reservation be deferred for a year until the department is able carefully to review this proposition.

National Park Service Director Ronald Walker said the park service opposed withdrawing any lands from the park. Thomas C. Nelson of the U. S. Forest Service said they planned to study the Havasupai claims and present recommendations at a later time. The Sierra Club's Southwest representative reported that the Sierra Club of Arizona was opposed to expanding the Havasupai Reservation.

Finally, Havasupai Tribal Council vice-chairman Clark Jack, Jr. and council-man Augustine Hanna spoke before the committee. They were the only ones in favor of the bill.

Clark Jack said, in part:

We ask for these lands to give our people a home again on the plateau. Many of our people were born there. We love these lands where we gave birth, built our lives and returned our old people to the earth. Our old homes and burial grounds lie on these lands. Our historical, emotional and legal ties and claims to these plateau lands we have outlined are so powerful they are undeniable to any who view them.

Councilman Hanna spoke next, saying in part:

We've had these permit lands all our lives, before most of us in this room were born. We have to have these lands returned to our people. . . . Not too many of you would stand the humiliation we stand every day; we live in a Park Service zoo. . . . We are the only ones who don't seem to matter, and we are human beings who have to support ourselves on this land. And we used to own it.

The Senate passed S. 1296 with some modifications on September 24, 1973.

The House of Representatives did not hold its hearings until November 12. Again, most of the witnesses spoke against the enlargement of the Havasupai Reservation or recommended further study. To counteract these statements, the Tribal Council had sent the fiery and eloquent Lee Marshall, chairman of the Tribal Council in the early 1970s. He said that no more studies were needed, adding:

No other lands except our permit lands are available to us. Our permit lands are the heart of our homeland, and we are not leaving our home. . . . So hear us now and remember. We will go on grazing our animals on all our permit lands forever. We will go on keeping our homes on them forever. We will not be pushed from the plateau for Sunday recreation, ever. We have never stopped using these lands, and we will not go from them now. They belong to us.

Then the tide began to turn. The Arizona chapter of the Sierra Club asked to meet with the Havasupai in Flagstaff, Arizona, on December 2. Despite a heavy snowstorm, twenty-eight Havasupai came to the meeting, making the long trek in the few trucks owned by tribal members. After much discussion and communication among the various chapters of the Sierra Club in the state, the executive committee resolved on January 26, 1974, that the Arizona Chapter of the Sierra Club supported enlargement of the Havasupai Reservation.

William Byler of the Association on American Indian Affairs contacted the Tribal Council on March 4 with an offer of help. Byler suggested that the council contact Joe Sparks, a young Scottsdale attorney known for his work with Indian land cases. Sparks came to Havasu Canyon to talk with the Tribal Council. He told the council that they faced a difficult struggle but he was willing to help. The council hired Sparks immediately and sent him to Washington.

Two weeks later the Tribal Council sent Ethel Jack, Councilman Leon Rogers, Clark Jack, Jr., and Augustine Hanna to join Sparks in Washington. The group took a taxi to the old Capitol Hill Hotel across the street from the White House. Ethel stood and stared in disbelief. There were the beautiful gardens, the White House, and the parking meters that had appeared in her dream thirty-one years ago. A few weeks later, the Tribal Council sent Daniel Kaska and council member Earl Paya and Issa Uqualla to help in the campaign.

Under Attorney Joe Sparks' direction, the group spent weeks talking to government officials and congressmen. They explained in detail how environmental groups such as the Sierra Club and Friends of the Earth had misrepresented their cause. No, the Havasupai did not have an agreement with the Marriott to build a resort complex on the land, nor did they plan to put a highway across the plateau and two tramways down into Havasu Canyon.

Ethel Jack, Leon Rogers, and Attorney Sparks showed pictures of the remaining homes in the Pasture Wash area on the plateau to substantiate the tribe's claim to the area. Ethel Jack explained the traditions and beliefs of the Havasupai people. Her presentations were very effective and she became the primary Washington spokesperson for the Havasupai Tribe.

As the Havasupai representatives made their case, the tribe began to get support from several sources. The influential *Washington Post* ran an editorial on April 18, 1974, supporting the return of the land to the Havasupai. The powerful senator from Minnesota, Hubert H. Humphrey, spoke in favor of the Havasupai land acquisition on the floor of the Senate in early July, saying, "The Havasupai are simply asking Congress to grant them the security that most Americans have—legal title to their lands." President Richard Nixon announced that his administration would urge Congress to support enlarging the Havasupai Reservation. After the airing of a Columbia Broadcasting System documentary, *Grand Canyon Shadows*, thousands of letters arrived in Washington urging congressmen to support the Havasupai cause.

House Speaker Carl Albert scheduled the Grand Canyon expansion bill for a vote on October 11. Ethel Jack, who was alone in Washington at the time, sat in the gallery and watched. After an hour's debate, Speaker Albert called for a voice vote on the Havasupai land return amendment. When it appeared that the nays had it, Arizona Congressman John Rhodes called for a recorded vote. The amendment passed the House by 180 to 147. The entire expansion bill passed by a voice vote.

The next step was the appointment of a conference committee to iron out the areas of disagreement between the House and Senate versions of the bill. The process moved slowly. Not until December 12 and 13 were the conferees named.

Ethel Jack and Leon Rogers sat in the House Interior Committee room all day on December 17 waiting and asking, "Is it ready yet?" as the committee staff worked on the final version of the bill. They waited until 6:30 P.M. Finally, the conference committee report was complete and ready for a vote in both houses the following day.

"My mother waited in the lobby all the next day," Bernice said. "People offered her coffee and told her she should go rest. She told them, 'This isn't for me. It is for the younger members of the tribe.'" Ethel Jack waited for twelve hours.

Congressman Morris Udall was not able to present the conference report to the House until 6:00 P.M. on December 18. Speaker Carl Albert called for a voice vote, and by a large margin the ayes had it. The report was rushed over to the Senate where it received final approval.

"When she received word that the bill had passed, she jumped for joy," Bernice said. "185,000 acres of rim land were returned to the tribe."

President Gerald Ford signed the bill, P. L. 93-620, on January 3, 1975.

Back in Supai, Ethel Jack sat in the center of a group of schoolchildren, singing an ancient song. The children joined hands and danced around her to the beat of a great drum. Ethel Jack had been chosen to tell the children about the land. She said, "I'll tell them that the land is our grandmother and our grandfather, for it feeds us and provides for us. Then the land was taken from us, and we were alone for many years. But now we have our grandmother and grandfather back. I'm just so very happy."

The Tribal Council asked Ethel Jack to help prepare the land use plan required by the federal government. Her influence shows in the completed plan which emphasizes maintaining "their ancient beliefs and the ways of their old people toward the earth in every way possible. . . ."

Given her love of the land, Ethel must have played a part in banning tract type housing on any part of the upper reservation, as their rim lands were now called. Homes, to be conical shaped earthen houses that blended in with the landscape, were restricted to four areas—Pasture Wash, south of Hualapi Hilltop, Moqui Tank, and east of Topocoba Hilltop. No doubt Ethel, remembering the sadness of her days at school in Riverside, California, encouraged setting aside a school site on the upper reservation so that all Havasupai children could attend school close to home.

Ethel Jack, her work finished, passed away in 1977. She is buried in Supai. On her grave a small plaque reads:

Havasupai Ambassador to Congress 1974
Havasupai Land Use Planner 1975-76
A true daughter of the Havasupai,
she realized her dream and ours.

Bernice Watahomigie spoke highly of her mother. "My mother was very strict and she had a good heart, always ready to help. She taught my brothers and me right from wrong and to always respect and do unto others, as you would want them to do unto you. Her teachings were good. She was a little lady but she had strong wisdom."

CHAPTER EIGHTEEN

Saddle Up! Lady Mule Wranglers of the Grand Canyon

PATTY NOLAN, BERNICE REEVE, KITTY MARR

For more than a century, wranglers (folks who work with mules and horses) have guided dudes (city folk pretending they are cowboys) into the Grand Canyon. Mule rides are a favorite pastime for canyon visitors, and most agree that exploring trails while atop a mule is the most exciting way to see the canyon. Not only have they been brought face to face with the canyon's exquisite beauty, but also the "dudes" have had a true western experience.

Mules are crafty animals, known for being sure-footed and stubborn, yet safe. In the more than one hundred years that mule wranglers have been taking dudes into the Grand Canyon, they've never lost a dude! That's because mules have a special set of breeding requirements. A male donkey is called a jack, and a female donkey is a jenny. In horses, the male is a stallion, and the female, a mare. Breed a jack with a mare and you have a mule. The result of this breeding is an animal with the shape and surefootedness of a large donkey and the disposition of a horse, making it an ideal animal for trips along steep, narrow ledges like those found in the canyon.

Mules were the work animal of early prospectors like John Hance and William Bass (see chapter 1), who used them to haul ore from their mines in the canyon. Both men soon learned that putting a dude on the back of a mule was more profitable than hauling out ore, and by the mid-1880s both men offered trips into the canyon.

197

In the early years, women rode into the canyon wearing long skirts and proper hats, but none was counted among the ranks of the wranglers. That is until William Bass's daughter Edith came along. She rode her own mule down to Shinumo Camp at age three and a half, and by age thirteen she could wrangle a mule better than most cowboys. Edith's outgoing personality and skill with mules made her a natural with dudes, and she can rightly be called the Grand Canyon's first woman wrangler. (Edith married Bert Lauzon in 1916 and lived at the canyon until her untimely death in 1924 after gallstone surgery.)

Wrangling was incredibly hard work, and it remains so even today. No modern devices substitute for the personal touch of the wranglers.

Mule wrangling at the canyon spans generations for some families, including wrangler Patty Nolan, pictured here with her father, Bud Dunagan. *Photograph © by Sue Bennett, 1999.*

Today at the Grand Canyon, a mule wrangler's day begins much the way it always has: with a cold splash of water on the face at 4:00 A.M. and a quick, hearty breakfast. The wrangler is in the stables before the sun crests the horizon. Stalls are swept clean, and fresh hay replaces the matted, day-old pile. The wranglers haul grain for the mules' breakfasts and then brush, comb, and check the animals head to heel for cuts, bruises, or other injuries that may not have been apparent the night before. All the animals are then saddled, cinched, and led off to the corral to await the day's dudes.

Guiding dudes requires more than being a good rider. First and foremost, the wrangler is responsible for each rider's safety. In addition, the wranglers give talks about the canyon in an entertaining style, contend with every personality type known to the human race, react in a split second to an emergency, and do it all with a smile. Not much has changed in the past hundred years except one difference: the mule wrangler of today is just as apt to be named Patty, Bernice, or Kitty as Joe, Curley, or Carl. Now, nearly half the wranglers at the Grand Canyon are women.

Ron Clayton, livery manager for Xanterra (as the Fred Harvey Company is now called) and an admitted chauvinist, was at first reluctant to hire women wranglers, but he changed his mind: "My women wranglers are great. You don't need brawn to be a wrangler—it's the knowledge of the animal and skill with people that counts! Patty is one of my best wranglers."

He referred to Patty Nolan, who was in her sixth year of wrangling dudes when I met her on the South Rim. "My mom always told me, 'Don't learn to cook or type,'" Patty laughed as she explained how she came to the canyon, "but I didn't listen and worked as a legal secretary in Flagstaff for several years. Finally, when my kids were out of the house, I decided to do what I'd always wanted to do, and I came here to work. My dad worked here as a wrangler in the 1960s before becoming a deputy sheriff. I've been around horses and mules all my life."

It's hard to imagine Patty, an attractive brunette with a long ponytail and soft voice, working as a wrangler. "I do have a problem being female sometimes," she explained with some annoyance. "Although I have the most seniority here, the male dudes will walk right by me and ask the male wranglers a question!"

Patty also had trouble convincing men that she could get them on the mule. "They'll come up to me and say, 'You can't possibly get me up there.' It's real easy. You just use your brain instead of your back. I drop the stirrup down real low so they can reach it, then I get down and lift with my shoulder at the same time they are pulling themselves up. It works perfectly," she said.

The concern didn't end once the dudes were saddled up. "For about the first twenty minutes of the ride they are really nervous about whether I can take care of them or not, but I have this sense of calmness when I go down the trail because I have done it for so long," Patty added. Her weekly schedule was one overnight trip to Phantom Ranch, two day rides to Plateau Point, and a day in the barn sweeping, cleaning, and loading hay into the chutes. "I love it," she said, sweeping her hand toward the canyon and patting her mule. "I have the greatest office in the world and the best desk." What could be better than having a movable desk that takes you where you want to go—into the Grand Canyon?

"I love the canyon, and I love to show it off. All I ask is that people really look at the Grand Canyon and love it too," Patty commented. "I hate when I am with people who signed up because it was the thing to do or because someone else insisted." However, people who don't want to do the ride are usually willing to follow instructions, unlike "experienced" riders. Of the latter, Patty pointed out,

"They may be experienced, but they are not experienced in the canyon. One morning I was tightening cinches and came to a man wearing a movie logo jacket. He told everyone that he was working on a movie and that he was famous, but I didn't recognize him. He also said he had done a lot of trail riding and told me, 'Young lady, if you need any help today, you just let me know.' I thanked him politely and cinched him up, and we took off down the trail."

The Bright Angel Trail starts off gradually but quickly becomes steep, with some abrupt turns and sheer drop-offs. "Everyone else was a little nervous and was sitting up straight and paying attention and doing what I had told them to do, but this guy was hanging back and taking pictures. He had his bridle reins over the saddle, and the mule stumbled a little, and this guy bounced off into the ditch because he wasn't holding on," Patty recalled. "We were near the top, and I could have called someone to come after him. He insisted he could go on, but he was terrified after that, and he swore every time the mule made a little stumble and yelled, 'Patty, he's bucking on me.' On the way back up he got off and led the mule."

When an accident like this happens, it's nearly always the dude's fault. Patty explained that the mules that carry dudes are very trustworthy. "We get new mules once a year, and the guides ride the new ones to see how they will do. They come broke to ride, but they have to get used to the Grand Canyon and the hikers. If they scare us, we turn them over to the packers. It is a common myth that the mules pack first and then go to the dudes. This is not true. We pack them when we don't trust them. Our 'duders'—the mules that carry guests—are solid gold. I have seen people get off, catch their foot in the stirrup and fall, and the duder mule just stands there and looks bored."

Patty had worked as a wrangler for nearly nine years when the National Park Service began requiring the owners of the mule operation, Xanterra, to repair the damage done to the trails by the mules. "I had become very conscious of the condition of the trails," Patty said, "and tried to convince my boss, Ron Clayton, to put me on the trail crew. I wanted to help with the trails and it was a pay increase. Finally, he agreed."

Patty worked on the trail crew for three and a half years. "I liked repairing trails," she said, "but I left the Xanterra Corporation when an opening became available with the National Park Service to service the outdoor compost toilets, I applied for the position and got it." Patty then began going all over the canyon taking care of the composting toilets.

"It doesn't sound interesting," Patty laughed, "but it is. I enjoy packing my equipment on the mule, tying the hitches and getting to know the government mules. Every day I get to get on a mule and ride into one of the most beautiful places on earth."

The job is more complicated than it sounds. There are composting toilets on the main trails and also in the remote backcountry. "There are places that are so remote that we have to arrange for the compost to be floated on the river or taken to a place where a helicopter can pick it up and fly it out," Patty explained. "There is an ongoing controversy about allowing helicopters in the backcountry. There may come a time when helicopters are forbidden. Then we will have to find alternative ways to get the compost out."

Bernice gets Elvis under control when he is frightened by Betty Leavengood taking a picture, 1996.

Patty has found her job satisfying and rewarding. "I can't imagine being anyplace but the Grand Canyon," she said.

Mule wranglers seem to have a special sense of humor. Like Patty, Bernice Reeve, a wrangler on the North Rim of the Grand Canyon, often saw the humorous side of the job. I first met Bernice when I went on one of her mule rides several years ago. "Don't let your horse eat," Bernice instructed us firmly. A dude asked, "Why not?" In her most serious manner, Bernice replied, "There's a lot of buckin' weed down there." She starting laughing, and we realized that Bernice was kidding. She had me fooled. I've watched too many Western movies not to believe in "buckin' weed."

Becoming serious, Bernice explained, "The real reason we don't want them to eat is that we want them to stay bunched up because it's safer. Plus, if you let them eat, they will eat all day." Keeping the mules close together is so important that Bernice told us to give the mules a whack with our quirts if they stopped. When someone asked, "Why do I have to hit the mule?" Bernice explained patiently, "This is what mules understand. It's for the mule's safety and yours."

Bernice had been giving instructions to dudes on the North Rim for seventeen seasons when I met her. "It wasn't my life's ambition to be a dude wrangler," she said, when I asked how she came to the North Rim of the canyon. "I came out here under protest. I was in college, pre-vet [veterinarian], and training horses in the summer. One summer when I got out of college, the man I worked for didn't have anything for me to do. He knew the man who did the mule rides off the North Rim, so he sent me to the Grand Canyon to work," she explained. "When I got here, I liked it. I've been here ever since. This canyon

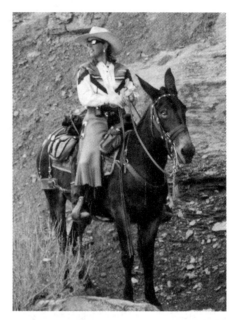

Kitty Marr on a ride into the canyon, ca. 2003. *Photograph by Gale Dvorak.*

has a draw; it has some type of magical draw to it. You see the same things, but there is always something different that you haven't seen before that you notice."

For the five months the North Rim is open each year, Bernice rode almost daily into the canyon. All mule day rides go to Roaring Springs, a 3,200-foot drop over four miles of steep terrain. Half-day rides end two miles into the canyon at Supai Tunnel. "People from all walks of life and all different backgrounds come to ride. You never know what will happen," Bernice said. "We had a guy with an artificial leg below his knee. We got him on the mule, and the wrangler walked around to adjust the stirrups, and the leg fell off. So we got him all back together and sent him out of the corral, and he got one hundred yards away and that leg fell off again! So we gave up and tied it on the mule. Everyone was laughing, including the man with the artificial leg!"

Bernice could make people laugh, as I discovered when we rested at the Supai Tunnel during our half-day ride. Someone asked, "Where do you get the mules?" In her most serious manner, Bernice replied, "These mules come from Tennessee, but some owners get their mules from Missouri." After a pause, she asked, "Do you know the difference between a Tennessee and a Missouri mule?" When no one responded, Bernice explained, "About 600 miles!"

It wasn't all work at the North Rim especially on the Fourth of July. "At the end of the work day a parade is organized by the National Park Service in which all the North Rim employees participate," Bernice noted, "and the wranglers come loaded with all the water pistol firepower they can pack on their mules to ambush dudes and each other during the parade." Bernice remembered an exceptionally hot Fourth. "We wranglers developed a mighty thirst and, with no place to tie our mules, we rode up the steps and into the saloon and ordered beers. My mule, Elvis, and I were right in the middle of it," she laughed. Tourists watched in awe, cameras clicking, but the park service did not see the humor in the situation. "We pleaded for forgiveness and headed for the barn," Bernice said, "and then Judy, the park's head ranger, 'lightened up' and ambushed us with the fire truck. One of the other wranglers yelled, 'Bernice, rope her!' I jerked down my rope and built a loop. By this time Judy was at the other end of the fire hose, aiming at me and Elvis. Elvis pulled his ears back, and I ducked my head and let the loop sail. When I pulled my slack, all of a sudden the water stopped. I looked up to see that the rope had settled on my intended target—Judy—who was calling a truce!"

Bernice's sense of humor would get her through the season, but by mid-October, when the North Rim closes, she was ready to return to her family's ranch on the Arizona Strip and train horses, not people. When spring rolled around and the snow melted on the North Rim, she was back to the canyon, the dudes, and another summer with her friend and fellow wrangler, Kitty Marr.

I first met Kitty in 1992, when she was in her eleventh year at the North Rim. Like Bernice and Patty, she spoke of her love of the Grand Canyon. "I think the canyon has a hold on me. I really love it here, and I enjoy working with the mules and meeting new people. It's fun taking people from all over the world [down into the canyon], but mostly I love the canyon itself."

That year, I'd arranged a backpacking trip across the Grand Canyon from the South Rim. Our packs were to be picked up at Roaring Springs and carried to the North Rim. We were happy to drop the packs by the hitching rail after the long haul from Phantom Ranch. When I saw a woman—a short, slender woman to boot—coming into camp and leading three mules, I'll admit I was a bit worried, but without cause. Kitty made sure we had the thirty-pound packs properly packed, and then she lifted and arranged them like they were bags of groceries. She took time to chat with us and answered our questions about the trail ahead, and then, with a wave and a smile, left us to climb out of the canyon, thankfully without the packs.

The way Kitty handled the mules showed she was no stranger to riding. "I've been around animals since I was a kid," she said, "showing horses in breed shows in all classes and in 4-H. I still enjoy teaching kids how to ride." Kitty worked at a livestock auction for a few years before she started wrangling mules.

She grew to know the individual personalities of the mules in her care. "Some are very affectionate and love to be petted. Some prefer to be left alone. Some mules like being ridden by women, others like men, and some are good for children." Some of the mules even have a sense of humor: "I've seen them go around a corner on a switchback and pause just to see if they can get a thrill out of people." And, Kitty added, they were usually successful. "I've taken hundreds of people down in the canyon, and every trip is different. The youngest we take is eight years old. I took a woman who was eighty-three years old. Once, I had this lady who was wearing sunglasses and a baseball cap, and I wondered if she was television star Sandy Duncan. When she started to talk, I knew it was her. She was a really neat lady, and I enjoyed taking her into the canyon."

Kitty answered questions, even the comical ones. "We have a half-day ride down to the Supai Tunnel. Once, I had a lady ask, 'When we get there, is there a shuttle bus that brings us back to the top?' I laughed to myself and explained to her that there are no roads into the canyon and that she would have to ride a mule both ways." When she worked at the sign-up desk inside the lodge she would frequently be asked, "How long does the one-hour ride last?"

At the end of the season, with no more questions to answer, Kitty, along with Bernice and the other North Rim wranglers, celebrated with—what else?—a twenty-seven-mile ride across the canyon to meet the wranglers on the South Rim. "We have a great party!" Kitty said. The next day they ride back, close up the barn, and leave the North Rim for the winter.

For Patty, Bernice, and Kitty, it has been the Grand Canyon, the people, the camaraderie of their fellow wranglers, and the mules that have kept them throwing saddles on their mules for another day with the dudes. No longer a curiosity in the Grand Canyon, women wranglers, with hard work and skill, have risen to the call of the canyon's beautiful surroundings.

CHAPTER NINETEEN

Protecting the Past

LORETTA JACKSON-KELLY
(1958—)

M y father gave me my Indian name—Hakama Misi—when I was thirteen
years old," Loretta said. "It means 'river girl.' The naming is taken very
seriously. It depicts how your future will be. My father named me before
I was involved with the Colorado River."

As Tribal Historic Preservation Officer for the Hualapai tribe, Loretta Jackson-
Kelly has been very much involved with the Colorado River. She has been down
the Colorado River through the Grand Canyon many times, identifying sites in
the canyon that are sacred to the Hualapai. "I scoped the tribal elders, doing eth-
nographic interviews and oral histories," Loretta explained, "so I would be able to
locate the sites and study the impact people and the Glen Canyon Dam have had
on the sites."

Loretta said that, while there is evidence of damage from the operation of the
Glen Canyon Dam, all impact has not due to the dam. "Archeologists have impact
when they do studies," Loretta explained. "Sometimes vandalism is done by people who do not realize what they are doing. For example, people don't know they
should cover their footprints when they leave a site. Also, people should not pick
up artifacts or stones at a site."

She has taken the information and created a data base of management recommendations for the sites for the tribe. "This will help in determining where camping can
occur, where people can hike, or where to stop and look," Loretta said. "We share this
information with the National Park Service and they can relay it to outfitters." She
added that the sites are continually monitored and evaluated throughout the original

Loretta Jackson-Kelly at work in her office at Peach
Springs, Arizona, 2003. *Photograph by Betty Leavengood.*

territory of the Hualapai, which extends from below Lees Ferry to Hoover Dam.

Loretta was born in Kingman, Arizona, in 1958. Her parents, Robert "Bobby"
Jackson (deceased) and Jeanie Jackson belong to the Pine Springs and Milkweed
bands, respectively. "I have four older sisters and two older brothers," Loretta said.
"I am the baby of the family. It took awhile for me to mature because everyone was
always looking after me!" Now she has her own family—three daughters and two
grandchildren.

Loretta attended various Indian boarding schools including, in her high school
years, the Phoenix Indian School in Phoenix, Arizona.

"When I was past the teenage years, I became more aware of the environment," Loretta said. "In the 1980s there was a proposal to do uranium mining on

the reservation. The company was Energy Fuels Nuclear, Inc. (EFN). I went to all these environmental impact statement public scoping meetings and had input as far as public comment. The tribe made a resolution to ban uranium mining on the reservation, therefore opposed and terminated the proposed studies and mining."

All of Loretta's first jobs were in the outdoors. "I was in on the beginnings of tourism," she said. "My first job was as a swamper on river trips."

"Having been on a commercial Colorado River trip, I learned to appreciate the swampers. As the raft pulled into the shore, the swampers swung into action, jumping off the raft into the water and securing the raft to trees or rocks. Next they grabbed the port-a-potties and put them away from camp somewhere in the bushes. Then it was set up the tables, cook the food, serve the food, and, when everyone is finished eating, the swampers washed the dishes and put everything away."

"My next job was as a lumberjill," Loretta laughed as I did a double-take. "I worked for the Tribal Forestry Department. We thinned the ponderosa forests on the reservation, taking everything out that was below eight inches 'dbh' (diameter breast height)," she explained. "I learned to operate and maintain a chainsaw. I ran a chainsaw and thinned trees for a living."

Just in case she hadn't had enough adventurous jobs, Loretta became a firefighter. "I was a crew boss for fighting wildland fires for the Bureau of Indian Affairs," Loretta said. "I fought lots of fires including Yellowstone National Park, Stanislaus National Forest in northeastern California, and near Johnson City, Tennessee." Loretta was the first Hualapai woman to obtain certification to be a crew boss in the Southwest Indian Fire Fighters (SWIFF) in wildland forest fires throughout the Kaibab National Forest headquartered in Williams, Arizona.

Loretta began taking college courses through the Internet and finally completed her last four required classes from Mohave Community College, receiving an Associate Degree in Applied Science in December 2003.

"I realized that if I didn't have a degree, I could not get a better job," Loretta said. "The tribe is encouraging people to get a degree and is hiring people with degrees." Part of that encouragement is paying for the costs of advanced education. She's also pursued a bachelor's degree at Northern Arizona University in Flagstaff, Arizona.

In 1991, Loretta was hired by the tribe as a cultural resource trainee. One of her first tasks was to obtain funding to secure that position, which she did with the aid of the tribe. As a trainee she learned the job skills required for conducting archeological surveys and the concepts of cultural resources management and preservation. She became aware of the importance of protecting sacred sites and significant cultural resources based on traditional values and beliefs of her tribe. Loretta realized that there was a subtle double standard for protecting historical and prehistoric properties, as opposed to protecting vast landscapes of tribally significant resources such as traditional cultural properties (TCP).

TCP issues became Loretta's forte in her early training. These issues stemmed from a federal guideline called Bulletin 38 of the National Historic Preservation Act, which included tribal concerns for cultural resources that may be affected. These tribal concerns were only effective through "consultation processes" that agencies and project entities exercised in meeting with tribes.

"Protecting sacred sites of Hualapai ancestral homeland has been a constant fight for our tribe," Loretta explained. "Sacred sites include spiritual aspects of our traditional beliefs; they include the philosophical views of our ancestors passed down through the generations; they include oral history of our creation of the world that we know now; and they include the sacredness of archeology sites where our ancestors' spirits still reside. It is most important to vocalize these viewpoints to ensure that the Hualapai culture continues to thrive."

Loretta found that many people and even politicians view Grand Canyon as an important landmark and heritage site. "For my people it is the lifeline," she explained. "The Colorado River signifies the backbone of our people. Without it we could not survive. These concepts strengthen our tribal sovereignty as a unique nation within a nation."

Loretta became a Program Manager for the Department of Cultural Resources and the Tribal Historic Preservation Officer (THPO) for her tribe. "I thoroughly enjoy it," she said.

Part of her responsibility as THPO has been to educate the public about Hualapai culture. She has been actively involved in public school programs teaching students in the greater Mohave County about the Hualapai Tribe.

"There is more than what meets the eye," Loretta explained. "During the precontact era dating thousands of years ago, there were fourteen bands, or clans, of 'the people' or better known as the 'Pai.' We covered seven million acres of northwest Arizona and portions of Nevada. Our people never had full contact with Anglos until the mid-1850s and wham!, just like that, we were steamrolled over quite literally by the 'Manifest Destiny' and gold rush of the period."

"The 7th U. S. Calvary collected all our people together after consistent warfare,"

Loretta continued. "At Fort Beale Springs (now Kingman, Arizona) my people were force-marched to Fort La Paz, in La Paz County in the lower Mohave desert. This occurred on April 21, 1874, and the march became known as the Hualapai Trail of Tears, the Forced March. There are vivid historical accounts of this march and of the monstrous acts inflicted onto my people that will make you cry. Many died along the trail—men, women, children, grandparents, and infants. They died by the hand of the United States Cavalry. Once at La Paz, the imprisonment lasted for a year until the remaining people simply walked away from the degrading fort."

In addition to educating the public about Hualapai culture, Loretta has also become a protector of that culture. As Tribal Historic Preservation Officer, Loretta has confronted many issues.

Loretta Jackson-Kelly and her youngest daughter, Justine Kelly. *Photograph courtesy of Loretta Jackson-Kelly.*

A major issue is rock mining for decorative rocks and boulders used in landscaping by private land owners in Hackberry, Crozier Canyon, and Truxton along historic Route 66 close to the Hualapai Reservation near Peach Springs. "Why are we tearing down a beautiful canyon like this for landscaping materials for people who live in the city?" Loretta asked.

"This land is sacred to the Hualapai," Loretta explained. "The area contains the cremated remains of Hualapai ancestors and should be afforded protection under state, federal, and tribal laws," she said. "Back in the '80s we would take field trips to those areas. We would visit the rock writing sites, which are sacred. We never imagined these things we held in high esteem would be destroyed in the manner they are now."

The Hualapai tribe unsuccessfully asked the landowners to stop mining along Route 66 between Kingman and Peach Springs. The Cultural Resources Department then issued a three-page press release in February 2003, calling for county and state government to end rock quarrying in the canyons, contending that rock mining in the canyons scars the landscape and threatens ancient burial grounds.

Loretta and other tribal members attended a meeting of the Kingman Area Chamber of Commerce to try to gain support, but without success. After much discussion, Beverly Wiles, chamber president said, "It is private property. That is the bottom line."

Feelings ran high. Loretta said that tribal members tried, but failed, to reach an agreement with landowner Fred Grigg who operated a major rock mining operation. Grigg contended that rock mining serves an environmental purpose by encouraging water preservation. "We are doing everything we can to conserve water and give people something to be proud of in their yard," he said. "There is no agreement to reach," he continued. "It is private property and that's all I've got to say. The Indians don't control it. We pay taxes on the property. We have owned it for years and years." Grigg since sold his property, but the present owner continues rock mining.

Loretta and other tribal members argued that a moratorium be placed on mining so that Hualapai cultural experts could inventory all burial sites in the area, but again the landowners refused. "Before European settlement and the influence of Christianity in northern Arizona, the remains of Hualapais were typically cremated and placed in unmarked sites with many of their belongings," she explained. "If time was short, the remains were scattered."

Although Arizona state law protects conventional Native American burials on private land, it doesn't address cremated remains. The tribe does have authority through the National Historic Preservation Act, Section 106, to protect and preserve its historical resources, even if the sites are not on the reservation, but they cannot go onto private land.

Loretta has not given up. "My husband and I have two daughters, and my brothers and sisters live here. My father taught us to value the cultural resources God has given us, so our children and our children's children will know their cultural heritage. They will come to know this place and sing the songs."

Another area that is in danger is Red Lake, near the reservation boundary. Dry and dusty for part of the year, Red Lake is a playa—a temporary shallow lake formed after a heavy rain. Even though Red Lake has water only part of the year, it serves an amazing variety of wildlife.

"Red Lake is an important area culturally," Loretta explained. "There are things you can't touch or see. There are spirits. Whirlwinds dance on Red Lake. Whirlwinds can be a good deity or a malevolent deity if not prayed to. These are things ingrained in our beliefs."

Tribal leaders believe that the proposed Red Lake Gas Storage Project, which would use underground salt caverns to store natural gas in the mile deep salt dome that sits under the lake, threatens to deplete the water supply and endanger cultural resources.

"My ancestors once inhabited Red Lake," Loretta said. "It is a place where bands of Hualapais came together to hunt and gather, and a meeting place where they came together in peace to pray." Before any construction was to start, the Hualapai Nation is guaranteed input under the National Energy Policy Act.

"We have concerns about air quality and the cultural resources that will be destroyed," Loretta said. "We want to preserve this cultural site for our children and the rest of the world, so that we can preserve the history." Loretta added that petroglyphs in the Red Lake area are a written history of the Hualapai Tribe dating back to prehistoric times. "The rock writings are interpretive pictures that depict burial sites, trails, how to find water sources, and actions of the bands," she said. At this writing, the environmental impact statement for the project had been postponed due to the technicalities of the report.

Another of Loretta's concerns has been saving historic properties. "Since I act on the behalf of the Hualapai Tribe as their Tribal Historic Preservation Officer, one of my duties is to maintain a list of historic buildings that may be eligible for the National Register of Historic Places," Loretta explained. "I also maintain the tribe's own Hualapai Register of Heritage Places per the tribe's ordinance: Hualapai Cultural Heritage Resources Ordinance enacted on Feb 18, 1998 through Tribal Resolution No. 13-98. With the THPO established through the enactment of the ordinance, I have the authority and responsibility to nominate such buildings or properties to the Keeper of the Register in Washington, D.C. who then places such nominations to the National Register of Historic Places."

Two historic buildings have been placed on the National Register of Historic Places—Truxton Canyon Training School and the historic trading post at Peach Springs.

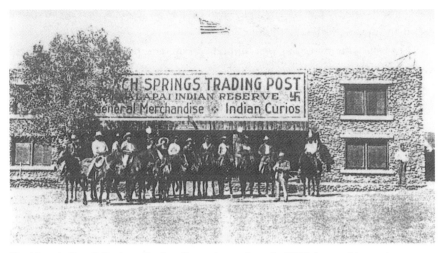

The historic Peach Springs Trading Post, shown here in 1936, is used for various Hualapai Tribal departments. *Photograph courtesy of Loretta Jackson-Kelly.*

Hualapai parents objected to their children being sent to the boarding school at Fort Mohave. Not only did the parents not want their children living away from home, but they also had bitter memories of the Hualapai confinement near the fort. In 1891 school administrators sent twelve Hualapai children to the Albuquerque Indian School without their parents' knowledge. Two of the children died.

Hualapai leaders and the Mohave County Deputy Sheriff demanded that a school be established closer to the students' homes. The Massachusetts Indian Association responded by founding a day school at Hackberry in 1894. Hualapai families lived in the hills around Hackberry and soon fifteen students were attending daily. By 1895, when the school was transferred to federal control, the Hackberry School had an enrollment of sixty-nine students. The school did not have the facilities to handle that many children; what buildings did exist were in need of major renovations. A new school was needed.

In 1898, President William McKinley issued an executive order creating the "Hualapai Indian School Reserve" on 795 acres near the Hackberry School. Congress appropriated $60,000 to begin construction of the Truxton Canyon Training School. Construction began in 1900. Even though the school was not totally complete, students moved from the Hackberry Day School to the new boarding school on April 1, 1901.

At first Truxton Canyon Training School consisted of three buildings—a dormitory, teacherage, and schoolhouse. By 1930 the campus had expanded to include a superintendent's office, laundry building, heating plant, an infirmary, cottages for faculty and staff, a reservoir, a dairy barn, and a detention house.

The training school, built to accommodate 150 Hualapai students, had near capacity enrollment in the early years. By 1906 enrollment began to decline as many Hualapai parents moved away from the reservation to find jobs. By 1922, only eighty-five students were enrolled.

The Office of Indian Affairs (OIA, now Bureau of Indian Affairs) decided to increase enrollment by admitting non-Hualapai students. By building a second story on the schoolhouse, expanding the dormitory, and adding new cottages for the faculty and staff, the OIA increased the capacity of the Truxton Canyon Training School to two hundred students, recruited from the Navajo, Apache, Havasupai, Hopi, Tohono O'odham, Pima, and Yavapai tribes. Enrollment remained above capacity until the school closed in May of 1937.

The Truxton Canyon Training School closed as a result of the Indian Reorganization Act of 1934. The act abandoned the policy of assimilation and gave the tribes the authority to write constitutions and organize their own tribal governments. The federal government urged individual tribes to start their own day schools, and Indian boarding schools across the country were closed. In the mid-1930s a day school opened in Peach Springs.

The remaining buildings stand empty. According to Loretta, discussions began to determine what to do with the buildings. "If the tribe can obtain the funding to renovate and rehabilitate the school, we certainly will use it as facilities for public education purposes and a museum with a gift shop," she said.

The Historic Peach Springs Trading Post, located on Route 66 in downtown Peach Springs, met National Register requirements under Criterion A as a place of historical significance in the areas of Commerce and Government. Erected in 1928, the modest stone and concrete building was associated with the substantial 1920s era commercial expansion of the small trading community of Peach Springs, brought on largely by increased automobile tourism and the development of U. S. Route 66. The building's early history as a trading post illustrates important links between Native American and Euro-American culture and commerce during the period.

The site was acquired by the local Hualapai Tribe, marking a significant era of growing economic and political maturity for the tribe, during which the Hualapai people secured increased economic self-sufficiency and political autonomy. Today the Historic Trading Post houses two departments—the Grand Canyon Resort Corporation's River Running and Wildlife Conservation Department and the Hualapai Tribal Forestry Program of the Natural Resources Department.

Hualapai prosperity has increased. Several tribal-owned businesses provide employment for tribal members. Hualapai River Running is the only rafting company on the Colorado River that is owned and operated by Native Americans. Hualapai Lodge in Peach Springs offers excellent facilities to tourists and travelers. Tourists from Las Vegas fly into the tribal-owned airport near Grand Canyon West where they are taken by helicopter into the Grand Canyon. Once they've landed by the Colorado River, they board rafts for an exciting ride on the river. Hualapai Wildlife Conservation sells big-game hunting permits for Rocky Mountain bighorn sheep, trophy elk, antelope, and mountain lion.

Yet while the Hualapai Tribe has moved into the twenty-first century, it hasn't abandoned its past. Loretta Jackson-Kelly has helped them remember.

CHAPTER TWENTY

With a Pack on Her Back

DENISE TRAVER
(1956—)

Y ou won't need this!" laughed Denise Traver as she pulled a hammer out of Jane Marshall's pack. "We'll use rocks to pound in tent stakes." Jane, New York City born and bred, was on her first backpacking trip ever, and like most people in her situation, she was seriously overloaded. "Most people come with more equipment and food than they need," Denise explained. "That's why I spend an entire day in orientation."

Denise, a slender woman with light-brown hair and a ready smile, started back-packing classes for women for the Grand Canyon Field Institute in 1995. She has introduced women to the outdoors and relished the camaraderie that develops among the women she has led on trips.

Contrary to what one might think upon first meeting her, Denise did not grow up outdoors. "The closest I came to outdoor activities when I was young was that my grandparents had a cabin in the mountains of Washington state," Denise said. "We would visit, and I would always pretend that I was a deer running through the trees. I loved it!"

Denise's parents divorced when she was only twelve. When Denise was fifteen, she moved with her mother from Yakima, Washington, to San Diego, California, when her mother remarried. Shortly after that, she met John Marroquin. "His parents lived next door. I was sixteen, and he had just returned from Vietnam. I had a tremendous crush on him and used to hang around watching him design and build a forty-one-foot sailboat," she said. "When my mom moved back to Washington,

Denise Traver at Hualapai Hilltop, March 1997.
Photograph by Jo Haslett.

I moved in with John. I was only seventeen. We got married when I was nineteen and he was twenty-eight."

Denise worked as a secretary for an engineering firm and helped John build his boat. "We were about three-fourths of the way done when John went to Alaska to help his friend Ray get a commercial abalone fishing venture started," Denise said. "I had gone on a business trip to Hawaii for a week, and when I got back to work, I was called in to the president's office. I was terrified and thought I must have done something wrong. When I got to the office, Ray's mother was there, and I knew right away something horrible had happened. She said, 'Denise, there's been an accident. John's dead.'"

"For several days I didn't know what had happened. It was a pretty rough time, and I was only twenty-four. I learned that John and Ray were scuba diving in thirty-five feet of water. Ray came back up to the boat, and when John didn't surface after forty-five minutes, he went back down. John was on the bottom. His mask was filled with blood. He had had a massive embolism. He went up too fast, and they didn't know why. His air hose was disconnected, one of his fins was off, and his face was bruised. The Coast Guard investigated but never did find out what happened," Denise explained.

The loss devastated Denise, and she spent the next several months surviving in a thick fog of grief. "I had read that you don't do anything different for at least a year after you lose your spouse, because you could get into lots of problems by rebounding. I definitely wasn't looking for a relationship, so I stayed low and kept working very hard." She did leave her secretarial position to work as a waitress. "I made lots of money, and a year and a half later, in 1982, I sold everything I owned and bought a little Toyota truck and a fifth-wheel trailer."

Denise spent the next few months traveling, visiting family in Washington and British Columbia, and eventually ended up in Arizona. "I fell in love with Arizona," she said. "I got a job doing boat tours at Canyon Lake east of Phoenix. In the evenings I would sit on the pier and watch the moon rise over the desert. It was so beautiful. This is where I met Charlie, the man who taught me to backpack."

Charlie was a musician from New Orleans who had left the music scene and was working in maintenance at the lake. "He did a lot of hiking and backpacking. Finally, I persuaded him to let me go on a backpacking trip with him. He taught me all the things to do to make it nice. He would set up a shower and make camp very comfortable," Denise explained. "I love doing things that are physical and seeing what is beyond the roads, but still, I want to be comfortable. I don't want to go out there and not brush my teeth for two weeks. I want to go out there and enjoy myself and live in style!"

Denise spent the next few years working at Canyon Lake in the winters and at a resort in the Verde Valley in the summer months, always finding time for solo backpacking trips. She first hiked the Grand Canyon in 1988. "The women I worked with were going to hike to Phantom Ranch, spend the night, and hike out, and I went along. I got dehydrated and sick. I didn't even get a chance to enjoy the cabin. I had a headache and couldn't eat dinner or breakfast. I was sick for two days after hiking out. I said I was never coming back to the canyon as long as I lived!"

But Denise, like many, did return to the canyon. "I kept having people say to me that as much as I liked the outdoors and liked to backpack that I should be a ranger, so I filled out an application to work as a 'seasonal.'" Denise was hired; she spent most of 1989 at Mather Campground collecting fees. "I wasn't meant to be in fee collection," she laughed. "On my days off I would backpack alone in the canyon, just on the corridor trails that first summer. On lunch hours I volunteered in the backcountry office and eventually joined search and rescue." In her search and rescue work, Denise met Patty Thompson, the supervisor at Phantom Ranch Ranger Station, who mentioned that there would be an opening the next year at Cottonwood Campground, Denise's favorite place in the inner canyon. Denise went to Santa Rosa Ranger Academy, where she got her commission and learned advanced first aid, and in spring 1990 became the ranger in residence at Cottonwood.

Cottonwood Campground is seven miles from the North Rim down the North Kaibab Trail. Named for the tall cottonwood trees that shade the area, the campground is a favorite stopping place for hikers on cross-canyon trips. The small ranger station there, built in 1934, had no electricity but did have running water with propane lights, a refrigerator, and water heater. Denise thrived there.

"At Cottonwood you can be an old-fashioned ranger," she said. Unlike many rangers, whose jobs are primarily to enforce regulations, Denise spent her days and nights there doing the more traditional tasks people associate with park rangers. "Law enforcement was such a small part of what I did at Cottonwood. I worked on campground revegetation, painted the ranger station, made curtains, and even crocheted." She visited with campers, answering questions while checking permits.

"Some wanted to know [about the park's] geology or had questions about backpacking. Because of the effort required to get there, the people that come to Cottonwood tend to be more prepared and experienced than the people that come down to Indian Garden," she recalled.

There were exceptions to this, though. One night at midnight Denise got a call from the North Rim night dispatcher concerning a husband and wife who had not shown up for dinner with his parents at the lodge at the North Rim. The woman was six weeks pregnant, and the man had bad knees, yet they were hiking down to the Colorado River and back in one day—a total of twenty-eight miles. Denise put on her clothes and headed up the narrow ledges of the North Kaibab Trail calling the couple's names every few minutes.

"At the top, I called the dispatcher and told her I had not found anyone, but that I would rest for two hours and go back down to the river," Denise said. "After taking a quick nap, I called to see if anything had been found out about the couple. The

Denise enthusiastically shares her knowledge of the Grand Canyon with anyone who shows an interest. *Photograph by Mike Buchheit.*

dispatcher was incredulous as she told me they were on the South Rim! They had gone down to the river and were talking to someone who told them they should do the Bright Angel Trail instead of the Kaibab because it wasn't as steep and had water. Now these were educated people, but they didn't know that the Bright Angel took them to the wrong rim!" Their confusion may have occurred because there are two Kaibab Trails: North and South. They had come down the North Kaibab Trail to the Colorado River, but their well-meaning adviser was talking about the South Kaibab Trail.

Denise enjoyed being at Cottonwood. "I would work nine days on and be off for five days. On my days off I would go rock climbing, hiking, backpacking, or kayaking. I'd been widowed for eleven years, and I had no intention of getting married or even getting into a serious relationship. I was just having fun."

Fun, that is, until a chronic bout with tick fever proved dangerous her first year at Cottonwood. "I felt tired all the time towards the end of the summer," Denise explained. "The nurse at the North Rim diagnosed my tiredness as relapsing tick fever. After a course of tetracycline I finally got better."

That Labor Day weekend, Denise was sent to Thunder River on patrol. She drove out to Monument Point and hiked down the rigorous Bill Hall Trail. "I really got tired, but I thought I was just out of shape," she said. "It was raining by the time I got to Upper Tapeats Creek, and I had to ford the creek." The tick fever had relapsed, and Denise quickly became very sick. "I spent the night in the Upper Tapeats Campground and then started back up to Thunder River. I sat under a boulder to keep out of the rain, and I was so sick. There were rockslides all around me, and I kept thinking this boulder would go too, but I was so miserable, I almost wished it would."

Denise struggled toward Surprise Valley, nearly a mile above Thunder River. She didn't make it. "I set my tent up partially on the trail and spent the night. My radio signal couldn't get out. The next morning, I dragged myself up the trail, and I found a cave near the top," Denise remembered with a shudder. "I stayed there all day. I didn't know what I was going to do. My radio didn't reach anyone, and I was wishing I would die in that cave."

Just when Denise had almost given up, she saw two people coming up the trail from Thunder River. "You are not going to believe this," she told them, "but I'm a ranger here and I am very sick." One of the hikers, who turned out to also be a ranger, took Denise's radio up to Surprise Valley and was able to make contact. "He called for a helicopter and got me out of there. That experience killed all my pride as a backcountry ranger!" Denise was prescribed another series of tetracycline. "By the time I went back down to Cottonwood for my second season, I was much better."

Early that season Denise had some unexpected visitors. "I'd been suggesting that solar power might work at Cottonwood, and a group of division chiefs were hiking through the Grand Canyon, checking on projects that needed to be done. Jim Hutton, the corridor supervisor, said, 'If you want solar power here, Brad Traver is the one to talk to.'" Denise went over to talk to Brad, and "he blushed so easily that I loved ribbing him." The next day some of the group walked to Upper Ribbon Falls, including Brad and Denise. "We realized that we had common interests, and as he left, he shocked me with a hug. I said he would have to come down to dinner sometime."

A couple of weeks later a helicopter came down with a bunch of people to check on mouse-proofing Denise's living quarters. It had been determined that all the people suffering from relapsing tick fever lived in the old buildings around the Grand Canyon. Park officials wanted to mouse-proof them without destroying their historic value.

"I was watching the helicopter land, and there in the front seat was Brad. I had no idea he was coming down," Denise said. "We talked, and he was considering building a solar-powered, self-contained house, and I was fascinated. Before he left, he pulled out a brown bag with a bottle of Bailey's Irish Cream. When I first met him, someone had said they wanted a beer, and I had remarked that I preferred Bailey's Irish Cream, and he had remembered. I said, 'I'll open this when you come and help me drink it.'"

Denise didn't have to wait long. Brad hiked in on a July full moon. "We had a nice dinner and walked in the moonlight to Ribbon Falls. It was very romantic, and we talked all night long. It was quite an experience, and I fell in love." Once again, the Grand Canyon and the moon had worked their exquisite magic, helping two souls find each other.

A canyon courtship is always a bit unusual, and Brad and Denise's was no exception. Logistics and accessibility made getting together in the canyon something of a challenge. Brad worked on the South Rim while Denise continued her work at Cottonwood Camp. Thursday night after work, Brad would hike down from the South Rim to Phantom Ranch. Denise would hike the seven miles down to Phantom Ranch, and together they would hike back to Cottonwood. Brad would stay for the weekend. On her days off, Denise would hike out to the South Rim.

After a year of this strenuous dating effort, the two decided to marry. But even after they wed, they still spent time apart so each could work at the canyon. Denise accepted a position as an interpretive ranger at Phantom Ranch, which got her seven miles closer to Brad.

But, she said, "It didn't work out, because I finished my last talk at 9:00 P.M., and it was too late to hike out," Denise said, "so I [transferred] up to the rim and worked in fee collection." She subsequently met John Frazier, director of the Grand Canyon Field Institute, who asked her to teach backpacking for the institute. "You know," Denise replied, "I would love to teach women's backpacking classes."

Frazier thought a separate backpacking class for women was an excellent idea, and he encouraged Denise to design a class. "I'd been thinking about it after observing people at Cottonwood," Denise explained. "Most women start out hiking with guys. Men hike differently than women. Most men are out to conquer things—to be able to say that they did this; but women want to stop and see the flowers and stop in the creek and wiggle their toes. If you are talking to a man, they will say, 'How long did it take you?' and not 'What did you see?' Men don't take as many breaks."

Denise (seated left) has introduced scores of women to backpacking through her women-only classes. *Photograph by Mike Buchheit.*

Denise claimed that women can be excellent hikers if given a chance to go at their own pace and style. "Women are the mules of the human race," she explained. "We are slow, steady, and have the endurance. Don't make us go faster than we want. Let us do it in our own way, and we are very strong. Women are tough." She also thinks women are more relaxed on backpacking trips done without men. "Women together are very comfortable. There's no sexual tension. Women act differently around men. They worry about their make-up and how they look."

She described the typical woman who signed up for her course: "Most are in the thirty-five- to fifty-five-year range. Their children are grown, and they are looking for new challenges. Almost every class has at least one nurse. They tell me it is a way to release the stress from their jobs. Ninety-five percent of the participants are married. Most of their husbands are excited about it, and some of the women are doing it so they can go backpacking with their husbands."

Over the years, Denise has seen repeatedly that the women who took her backpacking trips got more than exercise and a chance to make friends while exploring an incredible place. Time and again, women gained confidence, self-esteem, and spiritual renewal. In a rugged and unassuming environment, the women learned to challenge themselves and have their own expectations. It was often a life-changing experience, and Denise was thrilled by the chance to offer such an experience to them.

"I spend the first day just getting acquainted and orienting them to the Grand Canyon. First we introduce ourselves and tell why we are taking the class. I help fit their packs. Most of the weight has to be on the hips," Denise explained. "Then we go through what they have brought, and invariably they have too much, even though I have sent them a list of things they need. I tell them that I will stay with the slowest person." This policy once resulted in a seven-hour hike to do the four miles up from Indian Garden to the rim. "One lady was so worn out, but determined to make it on her own," Denise said, "that it took her seven hours. I actually crocheted while I was walking."

Denise said staying behind prevented any conflict or any feeling of inadequacy. "If the fast people had to stay slow, or the slow people had to try and keep up with the fast ones, it just wouldn't work. I tell them of spots where we should all meet, and this works real well. I like to be alone at times and understand someone else's need to be alone for a while. Allowing people to hike at their own pace gives them the opportunity to be alone if they wish." She always included a layover day on her hikes. "Women like to set up home for a couple of nights and not have to carry a pack."

Evenings in camp were wonderful as the light leaves the canyon and the backpackers relaxed around dinner. "I don't do backpacking foods," Denise said. "I fix mashed potatoes and gravy, angel hair pasta with pesto sauce, and refried beans and tortillas. You can eat all you want when you are out backpacking because you are working so hard."

Denise has felt that backpacking can often be a retreat of sorts, where women could resolve personal problems or come to terms with some inner conflict. "One of my backpackers was raped thirteen years before, and she was still dealing with it," Denise explained. "It has helped me as well. I didn't used to be nearly as confident as I am now. About twice a year I go on a solo backpacking trip. I'll go off for two weeks at a time, and you can't believe what that does to your confidence. I feel strong and good when I come back."

Denise and Brad eventually moved to the Tonto Basin in central Arizona, when Brad became superintendent of Tonto National Monument. Brad went on to become superintendent of Petrified Forest National Park, while Denise began to concentrate on web design and management, including two sites related to Grand Canyon: www.hitthetrail.com and www.phantomranch.com.

Denise continued leading tours, both in national parks and to Mary Elizabeth Jane Colter's structures at the South Rim and her La Posada Hotel in Winslow, Arizona. Denise has also kept doing those solo backpack trips.

The women-only program Denise Traver started has proved successful for the Grand Canyon Field Institute. Women-only classes comprise nearly 20 percent of all backpacks the institute conducts in a year. Institute director Mike Buch- heit said the trips are unique in several areas. "Women are very loyal as clients, coming back again and again, often as a group. Women tend to work as a team, helping each other with equipment and loads," he added. "Plus, judging from the laughs, tears, and farewell hugs during the wrap-up sessions, women-only groups have more fun."

CHAPTER TWENTY-ONE

Ambassador for Kaibab Paiute Culture

ILA BULLETTS
(1955—)

"I became interested in our culture because of my parents," said Ila Bulletts. "My mother, Crissy Roger Bulletts, and my dad, Dan Bulletts, worked with Dr. Richard Stoffle, research anthropologist at the Bureau of Applied Research in Anthropology at the University of Arizona in Tucson, to record the history and culture of our tribe."

Ila is a member of the Kaibab Paiute tribe, and the tribe's former acting cultural resource program director. By giving talks in schools, at scientific workshops, and at professional conferences, Ila has worked to promote understanding of her tribe's history and culture because, she said, "Most people know very little about our tribe."

The Kaibab Paiute were one of fourteen bands of the Southern Paiute Tribe that lived in southern Utah, northern Arizona, a corner of southeastern California, and the Great Basin of southeastern Nevada. There is linguistic and archaeological evidence that the Southern Paiute spread across this territory shortly after 1000 A.D. The territory of the Kaibab Paiute Band ranged across the Arizona Strip (that portion of Arizona north of the Colorado River), from the Grand Canyon on the south, to Kanab Creek on the west, Paria River on the east, and the northeast drainages of the Virgin River on the north. Their land went from a high elevation of 9,000 feet where pine, spruce, and fir forests thrived; to plateau lands covered with sagebrush, mesquite, juniper, and pinyon; to the depths of the Grand

Canyon. Prior to 1492, an estimated 5,500 Kaibab Paiute lived in this area. Today 250 tribal members live on the 120,413-acre Kaibab Paiute Reservation located north of Grand Canyon National Park.

Ila was born in St. George, Utah, in 1955. Her mother belonged to the Shivwits Band and her father to the Kaibab Band of the Southern Paiutes. Ila grew up in southern Utah, at Enterprise.

"In the second grade I was sent to the Latter Day Saints (LDS) Indian Student Placement Program," she said. The goal of the program was to give Native American youth better opportunities for education and to promote greater understanding

Ila Bulletts looks over her ancestral lands. *Grand Canyon Association photograph by Todd R. Berger, 2004.*

between Native and non-Native Americans. Children had to be at least eight years of age, baptized members of the LDS church, and in good health. "My parents placed a lot of emphasis on education and they thought the placement program would be good for me."

The Indian Placement Program began in 1947 in Richfield, Utah, and by 1972, nearly 5,000 Native American students were participating in the program. The child's parents had to request the placement, and then foster parents, who were recommended by the bishop, provided free board, room, and clothing for the child. Ila stayed with foster families for nine months of the year and then returned home for the summer. "I stayed in Utah in Ogden, Clearfield, and Sunset," she recounted. "I went for the education and to try to get along with other kinds of people. My foster parents were very helpful and I really enjoyed them because they really wanted to help me."

Ila participated in the placement program until she was in the tenth grade. "Then my dad wanted to move back to the reservation in the early seventies because there were some new homes built," Ila explained. "I finished high school in Fredonia,

Arizona." She took some additional training in a boarding school in Lawrence, Kansas. "I didn't like the boarding school," she said, "so I came back to this area and took additional courses at Dixie State College in St. George, Utah. Later I spent a year at Utah State in Logan taking general courses."

When Ila finally came back to the reservation to live, she worked at various jobs for the tribe —as a community health representative, a secretary in Social Services, and as comptroller of the tribe's casino, now closed.

Ila's parents were then working with Dr. Stoffle. "My mother went down the Colorado River with Dr. Stoffle," Ila said. "She had a small stroke on the river which was the beginning of a series of strokes. She died the following year. For two years I was grieving and I couldn't think of going down the river." By 1997, Ila had decided that she wanted to go down the Colorado River through Grand Canyon. "Two older ladies of the tribe went with me and helped me understand the river and the canyon," she said. "It was an amazing experience I won't forget. They told me what was important."

Shortly after that trip, Ila received a call from Diane Austin, a colleague of Stoffle's in the Bureau of Applied Research in Anthropology. "She was writing a grant to help our tribe and she told me she had a job for me," Ila said. "I applied for the position of Outreach Educator and got it!" She worked in that position until she became Acting Cultural Resource Program Director. In that position, Ila continued efforts to educate tribal members and the general public in several areas of Southern Paiute history and culture—ethnobotany, the Southern Paiute homeland, and the Colorado River and the Grand Canyon.

One of her primary responsibilities was monitoring sacred sites in the Grand Canyon. "To us, the entire Grand Canyon is sacred," Ila explained. "We have twenty sites in the canyon that we monitor as a sample of the condition of the canyon. I have been down the river six times checking on these sites. They include rock art, burial places, and other sites."

Along with checking on sacred sites, she monitored beach erosion along the river. One site is endangered because of erosion due to varying flows out of Glen Canyon Dam. Ila found changes each time she went down the river.

Teaching Southern Paiute youth about the meaning of the canyon, its water, vegetation, animals, and beaches, has been one of Ila's primary goals. Young people have been included in the monitoring programs, and at times the challenge was to get them out of the water long enough to do their monitoring tasks—especially at their favorite stop where the Little Colorado River joins the main Colorado. Ila recalled one year when "It started with a circle. Then one of the boys said, 'Hey, we should do that thing where they all swim in a circle.' None of them could remember the name until one of the university students remembered it was synchronized swimming. Then they appointed a leader and soon the hairy legs and big sandals went up together. It was funny."

The elders of the tribe used to accompany the trips but now almost all of the elders have passed on.

Ila also teaches about the history of her tribe. The Kaibab Paiute were primarily hunter-gatherers, moving in small family bands for food and game animals. If they were near a permanent water source, they cultivated corn, beans, potatoes, wheat, and squash, staying long enough to harvest their crops. They lived in temporary shelters called wickiups that were easily dismantled and moved or rebuilt at the new location. Clothing consisted of an apron of skin or vegetable fiber during the warm months and buckskin ponchos during the colder months. Rabbit skin blankets provided extra warmth if needed.

In the fall, several bands would camp together in the forests near the plateau to prepare for the winter months. The men would choose a leader to organize deer hunts. The women made pemmican by mixing lean dried deer or other meat with melted fat. They added berries and currants for flavor, and then pressed the mixture into cakes which were stored for the coming winter. As winter came, the individual bands separated, many moving to lower altitudes for the winter—some as far south as the rim of the Grand Canyon. Others moved into rock overhangs or the mouths of caves, where they blocked off the entrances with juniper branches to keep out the cold. The Kaibab Paiute followed this seasonal pattern for hundreds of years, maintaining a steady increase in population.

This would change with the advent of Europeans. Although the Kaibab Paiutes had no direct contact with the Spaniards, after 1520 their population was greatly affected through indirect contact through their Hopi neighbors. Smallpox and measles, both highly contagious, spread north along trade routes, affecting the Hopi and through them the Kaibab Paiutes. It is estimated that the Kaibab Paiute population fell from 5,500 to around 1,175.

Beginning in the early 1860s, Mormons expanded their planned "nation of the desert" to the fertile grasslands of Kaibab Paiute territory. They established ranches near artesian springs in Short Creek, Moccasin, and Pipe Springs by 1863. The following year more ranches were built up in the foothills of the Utah mountains to the north and at the present site of Kanab. In a period of two years, the Mormons took over the major water sources within Kaibab Paiute territory.

In a short time, large herds of horses, cattle, and sheep overgrazed the grasslands. The Mormons cut thousands of pinyon and juniper trees to build corrals and fences and to use for fuel. No longer could the Kaibab Paiutes rely on hunting and gathering food, and starvation further decimated the tribe. One elderly tribal member who was a child when the Mormons first came said, "After the Mormons come, all the Indians died." Within ten years, the Kaibab Paiute population declined from an estimated 1,175 persons to a total of 207 persons in 1873.

To avoid starvation, some of them stayed close to the newly established Mormon communities in hopes of obtaining employment or handouts. Some made agreements to help the Mormons fend off attacks from the Ute and Navajo tribes in exchange for access to water and land for farming. A few chose to join with the Navajo in attacking Mormon communities.

Colorado River explorer John Wesley Powell first met the Kaibab Paiutes in September of 1870. He talked with Chuarumpeak, who impressed Powell as a possible leader of the tribe. Powell and Mormon missionary Jacob Hamblin, who was highly respected by the tribe, worked together to obtain some relief for the people. In December of 1870, Hamblin suggested that Powell request supplies for the Kaibab and other Paiute bands from the Superintendent of Indian Affairs in Salt Lake City, which he did. The shipment did not arrive until April of 1872. Powell arranged a meeting of the Shivwits, Santa Clara, and Kaibab bands for the distribution of "blankets, shirts, cotton cloth . . . blue flannel, butcher knives, some hoes, axes, and shovels." Hamblin encouraged the Paiutes to attempt farming.

Creating additional hardship for the Kaibab Paiutes was the discovery of gold at the mouth of Kanab Creek in January 1872, by a member of Powell's party. When a Salt Lake City newspaper published the discovery, hundreds of prospectors and miners flocked to the region. Since gold was usually found at the confluence of creeks and rivers, the prospectors and miners settled on the nearby alluvial plains, taking away the last tillable land available to the Kaibab Paiute. With no consistent help from the Mormon Church or the United States government, the Kaibab Paiutes' situation became more desperate; many died of starvation.

Powell's 1872-1873 expedition revealed the plight of the Kaibab Paiute. In an 1873 report, Powell recommended that the Kaibab Paiute be placed under federal jurisdiction so that they might have access to farmland and food to eat. Seven years later, no assistance had been provided and the condition of the Kaibab Paiutes worsened. In November 1880, Hamblin wrote to Powell, who by then was director of the Bureau of Ethnology at the Smithsonian Institution:

> The Kanab or Kaibab Indians are in very destitute circumstances; fertile places are now being occupied by the white population, thus cutting off all their means of subsistence except game, which you are aware is limited. They claim that you gave them some encouragement in regard to assisting them eak [sic] out an existence.

Powell recommended that the Kaibab Paiutes go to a nearby reservation—either Uinta or Muddy Valley—where government assistance would be available. By this time their population had been reduced to ninety-nine by the passage of Mormon settlers who spread smallpox and measles through Paiute country in 1877.

The situation grew so desperate that the Indians turned to the Ghost Dance movement for relief. In 1889 a Northern Paiute ranch hand from Yerington, Nevada, named Wovoka (known to the Americans as Jack Wilson), learned in a trance that the old ways would be returned if certain rituals were practiced. Their lives would return to the time before the arrival of the white man—the whites would disappear, Indians who had died fighting the whites or from their diseases would be brought back to life, and deer and other game would live in abundance once again in the wild.

The Kaibab Paiute participated in several Ghost Dances beginning in 1890, but the results were not as promised, and they had to find other ways to survive. One way was to cooperate with the Mormon policy of "peaceful penetration." Mormon leaders had learned that moving into Kaibab Paiute territory too rapidly antagonized them, so they sent missionaries to establish a foothold in new areas to acquire converts and access the economic potential of the area. The missionaries made friends with the Kaibab Paiute people by giving gifts and assisting them in various ways. Settlers followed and usurped the Indians' resources for their own use. To regain access to some of their resources and those of the Mormons, many Kaibab Paiutes accepted baptism in the Mormon faith.

Another survival strategy was to accept Powell's urging that the Kaibab Paiute select a chief. Powell had already chosen Chuarumpeak as the person through

In this John K. Hillers photograph from 1874, young Kaibab Paiute women carry water in baskets suspended from their foreheads by tump lines. *Photograph courtesy of the Cline Library, Special Collections and Archives, Northern Arizona University. NAU.PH.91.3.*

whom messages were passed and goods distributed. In the late 1870s, the Kaibab Paiutes finally acknowledged Chuarumpeak as their chief, making it easier to negotiate with the invading Americans for resources. A group of about a hundred Kaibab Paiutes had settled around Moccasin Spring southwest of Kanab. In 1906 the Mormon Church persuaded the white residents of Moccasin Spring to allocate one-third of the artesian water flow to the tribe. A government inspector visited Moccasin in 1907 and observed that "A group of about eighty Paiutes . . . have a fenced pasture of several thousand acres and some ten to fifteen acres of tillable land watered by a spring on Moccasin ranch of whose flow the Indians own one third."

Finally, on October 16, 1907, the Kaibab Paiute Reservation was established by an order of the United States Department of the Interior.

Much of this land was claimed by five Heaton brothers, who had been ranching in the area prior to the establishment of the reservation. After the reservation was established, the Heatons continued to occupy and use 3,000 acres of land within the reservation. As a result of numerous lawsuits, the boundaries of the reservation were changed several times. It was not until July 17, 1917, by executive order of President Woodrow Wilson, that the present boundaries were finally established. Not until 1925, after a federal lawsuit, were the Heatons forced to remove their fences from the 3,000 acres they once controlled.

In an attempt to help the Kaibab Paiutes achieve self-sufficiency, the Bureau of Indian Affairs issued cattle to the tribe to supplement their farming efforts. While this worked for a time, by 1916 the herd was decimated. The bureau issued another lot of cattle, this time with more success. In 1922, Bureau of Indian Affairs inspector John W. Atwater visited the Kaibab Paiute Agency and Schools. Atwater reported that about fifty acres were under irrigation. He stated that an additional five acres could be irrigated for an expenditure of two to three thousand dollars. He pointed out that the Kaibab Paiute had no other resources other than working for white settlers during the summer and autumn months. He said that the tribe appeared healthy but had not increased in number because of epidemics such as flu and whooping cough. The school, he reported, was in good repair and could accommodate twenty students. The tribal livestock herd consisted of 662 good quality Herefords, he noted, and by raising a small amount of produce and working for the white settlers the Kaibab Paiutes managed to eke out a precarious existence.

Ila Bulletts' family has raised cattle since the early 1900s. "My dad was born in 1906 and was a cowboy and boxer all his life. He worked with the Civilian Conservation Corps and did calf roping in local rodeos." Every year in late spring the entire Bulletts family has gotten together to brand the family herd.

With the Indian Reorganization Act of 1934, Congress mandated that the tribes could write their own constitutions. This was a step in the direction of self-sufficiency for all Native American tribes. The Kaibab Paiute adopted their constitution in 1951. With the subsequent election of a Tribal Council, the Kaibab Paiute began to have more control of their own affairs, although it would be several decades before they were able to exert real control.

In 1946 Congress established the Indian Claims Commission to receive claims from Indian tribes for a period of five years concerning the loss of their traditional homelands and to compensate the tribes for that loss. The Kaibab Paiute filed suit against the United States government claiming restitution for the loss of the lands that had been wrongfully taken from them. The case dragged on and was bitterly argued before the Indian Claims Commission in 1956. It was not until 1970, however, that the Kaibab Paiute finally received a judgment in the amount of one million dollars.

The Kaibab Tribal Council distributed the funds as follows: 15 percent of the total payment was distributed to individual tribe members, giving each member slightly over one thousand dollars; an additional 15 percent was allocated to families to pay off past debts, purchase household furnishings, and for other household needs; 10 percent was budgeted for education; tribal enterprises received 35 percent of the total; community development was allocated 15 percent; and administration received 10 percent.

After distributing the judgment, one goal of the Kaibab Paiute was to create enough on-reservation employment so that any tribal member who desired could live on his or her traditional homeland.

Further economic development involved opening a tribal casino, which operated from 1994 to 1996. Ila Bulletts was comptroller for the short-lived enterprise. Though the casino closed, the Kaibab Paiute Tribe still owns and operates a convenience store and gas station, along with an RV park and campground.

In line with the tribe's emphasis on tourism, on May 31, 2003, the National Park Service and the Kaibab Paiute Tribe opened a joint visitor center and museum at Pipe Spring National Monument, which is located on the reservation. Pipe Spring National Monument was created on May 31, 1923, to honor pioneer Mormon ranchers. The stone building known as Winsor Castle, which was erected by the Mormon Church in 1872 as a refuge against the Indians, is the main historical building at the monument.

Under the joint agreement, Kaibab Paiute history is told alongside that of Mormons. Tribal members were hired to guide tourists through Winsor Castle, and Ila worked there during summers while she was in high school. She recalls having to dress up like a Mormon pioneer woman in a long dress and bonnet. None of the young Paiute women liked the job, but it provided income for their families. "The tourists would ask us why we were dressed like pioneers when we were Indian," Ila said. "We would tell them it was just a job."

Ila has been pleased that the museum tells more of the history of the Southern Paiute people, and that Paiutes are no longer asked to dress up as pioneer women to work there. "Now I am still trying to understand Paiute history and share it with others," she said.

The tribe holds the "Sounds of Thunder" powwow each fall at the Te'Angwavaxant Pow Wow Grounds fourteen miles west of Fredonia. "We did not want to celebrate Columbus Day," Ila said, "so we celebrate our own heritage." The powwow varies each year but generally includes a parade, an art show, drum competition, softball and horseshoe tournaments, demonstrations by tribal elders, dancing and singing, a five kilometer walk/run, and a feast.

By celebrating its heritage, the Kaibab Paiute tribe does not forget its past. "We have a language revitalization program that is going well," Ila noted. "We have elders who want to pass the language on. They work for no pay. They do it from their hearts." And Ila too works from her heart, looking to a brighter future for her tribe.

Bibliography

I. PRIMARY SOURCES

Interviews

Adams, Lisa. Interview by author, numerous telephone conversations, November, December, 2003.

Baker, Ruth Stephens. Interview with Julie Russell, Tucson, Arizona, November 3 and 5, 1978. Grand Canyon National Park Museum Collection, Catalog #GRCA 36152.

Baker, Ruth Stephens. Interview by author, Tucson, Arizona, July 30, 1996.

Baker, Ruth Stephens. Interview with Karen Underhill, Grand Canyon, Arizona, May 29, 1994. Grand Canyon National Park Museum Collection, Catalog #GRCA 63378.

Bulletts, Ila. Interview by author, numerous telephone conversations, 2004.

Burak, Gale. Interview by author, North Woodstock, New Hampshire, September 5-8, 1995.

Clayton, Ron. Interview by author, Grand Canyon, Arizona, July 11, 1996.

Davis, Dan. Interview by author, Tucson, Arizona, May 5, 1995.

Hinchliffe, Louise. Interview by author, Sedona, Arizona, November 1, 1995.

Hinchliffe, Louise. Interview with Julie Russell, Grand Canyon, Arizona, November 18, 1980, Grand Canyon National Park Museum Collection, Catalog #GRCA 35957.

Jackson-Kelly, Loretta. Interview by author. Peach Springs, Arizona, November 6, 2003.

Kachinhongva, Phyllis Yoyetewa. Interview by author, Grand Canyon, Arizona, November 12, 2003.

Lee, Katie. Interview by author, Jerome, Arizona, October 31, 1995.

Lee, Katie. Interview with Roy Webb, Jerome, Arizona, April 14, 1984, University of Utah, Marriott Library Special Collections.

Mann, Jean. Interview by author, Cameron, Arizona, November 10, 2003.
Marr, Kitty. Interview by author, Grand Canyon, Arizona, July 14, 1996.
Meyer, Elizabeth Kent. Interview by author, Phoenix, Arizona, March 27, 1996.
Nez, Mindy. Interview by author, Cameron, Arizona, November 10, 2003.
Nolan, Patty. Interview by author, Grand Canyon, Arizona, July 11, 1996.
Patraw, Pauline Mead. Interview with Julie Russell, Santa Fe, New Mexico, August 3, 1981, Grand Canyon National Park Museum Collection, Catalog #GRCA 35736.
Patraw, Pauline Mead. Interview with Mike Quinn, Santa Fe, New Mexico, September 4, 1995, Grand Canyon National Park Museum Collection, Catalog #GRCA 65559.
Reeve, Bernice. Interview by author, Grand Canyon, Arizona, July 14, 1996.
Teal, Louise. Interview by author, Durango, Colorado, May 23, 1995, and subsequent correspondence.
Traver, Denise. Interview by author, Rock Springs, Arizona, June 18, 1996.
Traver, Denise. Interview with Mike Quinn, Grand Canyon, Arizona, May 12, 1996, Grand Canyon National Park Museum Collection, Catalog #GRCA 66189.
Vaughn, Margaret. Interview by author, Peach Springs, Arizona, November 8, 2003.
Watahomigie, Bernice, daughter of Ethel Jack, interviewed by the author on February 10, 2003, in Supai, Arizona.

Diaries and Journals
Bass, Ada. Diaries and Manuscripts. W. W. Bass Collection, Manuscript Number 1065, Arizona Historical Society, Tucson, Arizona.
Clover, Elzada. Diary, Elzada Clover Collection, Bentley Historical Library, University of Michigan. (Copy also at Grand Canyon National Park Museum Collection, Catalog #GRCA 58957.)
Cutter, Lois Jotter. Diary, Lois Jotter Collection, Northern Arizona University, Cline Library Special Collections, Manuscript 69.
Lee, Katie. "Journal of Katie Lee, made during the traverse of the Grand Canyon from Bright Angel Creek to Temple Bar, July, 1955," Otis T. Marston Collection, Huntington Library, San Marino, California, Box 116, Folder 5.
Nevills, Norm. Diary, University of Utah, Marriott Library Special Collections. (Copy in *Some Colorado River Journals and Diaries* by Otis Marston at the Grand Canyon National Park Museum Collection, Catalog #GRCA 54981).

Collections
Martin J. Anderson Collection, Northern Arizona University, Cline Library Special Collections, Flagstaff, Arizona.
Georgie Clark Collection, Northern Arizona University, Cline Library Special Collections, Flagstaff, Arizona.

Delphine Mohrline Gallagher Collection, Northern Arizona University, Cline Library Special Collections, Flagstaff, Arizona.

Fred Harvey Collection, University of Arizona Library Special Collections, Tucson, Arizona.

Emery Kolb Collection, Northern Arizona University, Cline Library Special Collections, Flagstaff, Arizona.

Otis R. Marston Collection, Huntington Library, San Marino, California.

II. SECONDARY SOURCES

Books

Anderson, Michael F. *Living at the Edge: Explorers, Exploiters, and Settlers of the Grand Canyon Region.* Grand Canyon: Grand Canyon Association, 1998.

Anderson, Michael F. *Polishing the Jewel: An Administrative History of Grand Canyon National Park.* Grand Canyon: Grand Canyon Association, 2000.

Babbitt, Bruce, ed. *Grand Canyon: An Anthology.* Flagstaff, Arizona: Northland Press, 1978.

Blair, Mary Ellen, and Blair, Laurence. *The Legacy of a Master Potter, Nampeyo and Her Descendants.* Tucson:Treasure Chest Books, 1999.

Brian, Nancy. *River to Rim.* Flagstaff, Arizona: Earthquest Press, 1992.

Brower, David, ed. *The Place No One Knew.* San Francisco: Ballantine Books, 1968.

Clark, Georgie White, and Newcomb, Duane. *Georgie Clark: Thirty Years of River Running.* San Francisco: Chronicle Books, n.d.

Cook, William. *The* Wen, *the* Botany, *and the* Mexican Hat. Orangevale, California: Callisto Books, 1987.

Courlander, Harold. *Hopi Voices, Recollections, Traditions, and Narratives of the Hopi Indians.* Albuquerque: University of New Mexico Press, 1982.

Dobyns, Henry F., and Euler, Robert C. *The Walapai People.* Phoenix: Indian Tribal Series, 1976.

Euler, Robert C. *The Paiute People.* Phoenix, Arizona: Indian Tribal Series, 1972.

Euler, Robert C. *Southern Paiute Ethnohistory.* Salt Lake City: University of Utah Press, 1966.

Fradkin, Philip L. *A River No More.* Tucson: University of Arizona Press, 1981.

Goldwater, Barry. *Delightful Journey.* Tempe: Arizona Historical Foundation, 1970.

Grattan, Virginia L. *Mary Colter: Builder Upon the Red Earth.* Grand Canyon: Grand Canyon Natural History Association, 1992.

Hirst, Stephen. *Havsuw 'Baaja: People of the Blue Green Water.* Supai, Arizona: The Havasupai Tribe, 1985.

Iliff, Flora Gregg. *People of the Blue Water.* Tucson: University of Arizona Press, 1954.

Inskip, Eleanor, ed. *The Colorado River Through Glen Canyon Before Lake Powell.* Moab, Utah: Inskip Ink, 1995.

James, Harry C. *Pages From Hopi History.* Tucson: University of Arizona Press, 1974.

Kabotie, Fred, and Belknap, Bill. *Fred Kabotie: Hopi Indian Artist.* Flagstaff, Arizona: Northland Press, 1977.

Kaufman, Alice, and Selser, Christopher. *The Navajo Weaving Tradition: 1650 to the Present.* Tulsa/San Francisco: Council Oak Books, 1999.

Kramer, Barbara. *Nampeyo and Her Pottery.* Tucson: University of Arizona Press, 1996.

Kroeber, A.L., ed. *Walapai Ethnography.* Menasha, Wisconsin: American Anthropological Association, 1935.

Lamb, Susan, ed. *The Best of Grand Canyon Nature Notes.* Grand Canyon: Grand Canyon Natural History Association, 1994.

Lavender, David. *River Runners of the Grand Canyon.* Tucson: University of Arizona Press, 1986.

Lee, Katie. *All My Rivers Are Gone.* Boulder, Colorado: Johnson Books, 1998.

Martin, Russell. *A Story That Stands Like a Dam.* New York: Henry Holt & Company, 1989.

Maurer, Stephen G. *Solitude and Sunshine: Images of a Grand Canyon Childhood.* Boulder, Colorado: Pruett Publishing Company, 1983.

Merriam, C. Hart. *Results of a Biological Survey of the San Francisco Mountain Region and Desert of the Little Colorado, Arizona.* Washington: Government Printing Office, 1890.

Morehouse, Barbara J. *A Place Called Grand Canyon.* Tucson: University of Arizona Press, 1996.

Nelson, Nancy. *Any Time Any Place Any River: The Nevills of Mexican Hat.* Flagstaff, Arizona: Red Lake Books, 1991.

Parischan. Parkersburg High School Annual, Parkersburg, West Virginia, 1924.

Patraw, Pauline Mead. *Flowers of the Southwest Mesas.* Globe, Arizona: Southwestern Monuments Association, 1953.

Poling-Kempes, Lesley. *The Harvey Girls.* New York: Paragon House, 1989.

Powell, J. W. *The Exploration of the Colorado River and Its Grand Canyons.* New York: Dover Publications, 1961. First published in 1895 as *Grand Canyons of the Colorado.*

Sadler, Christa, ed. *There's This River: Grand Canyon Boatman Stories.* Flagstaff, Arizona: Red Lake Books, 1994.

Schwartz, Douglas J. *On the Edge of Splendor: Exploring Grand Canyon's Human Past.* Santa Fe: The School of American Research, nd.

Stein, Pat. *School Days at Truxton Canyon.* Flagstaff, Arizona: Arizona Preservation Consultants, 2002.

Sutton, Imre, ed. *Irredeemable America: The Indians' Estate and Land Claims.* Albuquerque: University of New Mexico Press, 1985.

Teal, Louise. *Breaking Into the Current: Boatwomen of the Grand Canyon.* Tucson: University of Arizona Press, 1994.

Webb, Robert H. *Grand Canyon: A Century of Change.* Tucson: University of Arizona Press, 1996.

Webb, Roy. *Call of the Colorado.* Moscow, Idaho: University of Idaho Press, 1994.

Westwood, Richard. *Woman of the River.* Logan, Utah: Utah State University Press, 1997.

Zwinger, Ann Haymond. *Downcanyon.* Tucson: University of Arizona Press, 1995.

Newspaper Articles

Denver Post, Denver, Colorado, November 20, 1928.

"Reclaiming a Lost Grand Canyon," *High Country News*, Paonia, Colorado, November 10, 1997.

"Planes Seek Six Explorers," *Los Angeles Herald*, July 5, 1938.

"Search by Air, Water for Pair," *Prescott Evening Courier*, Prescott, Arizona, December 18, 1928.

Swinton, Stan. "Faculty Women to Face Danger on Stormy Colorado for Science," *Michigan Daily*, University of Michigan, Ann Arbor, June 5, 1938.

Oraibi, Arizona. *Qua' Toqtil*, July 4, 1974, p. 4.

"Land Show Is On; Wilson Opens It To All Chicago." *Chicago Sunday Tribune*, November 20, 1910, unnumbered page following page 1.

Magazine and Journal Articles

Aleson, Harry. "Colorado River Raft Drift," *Southern Sierran*, August 1946.

Berger, Meyer. "Hunting the Secrets of the Awesome Colorado Grand Canyon," *New York Times Magazine*, September 19, 1937.

Howard, Kathleen L. "Weaving a Legend: Elle of Ganado Promotes the Indian Southwest." *New Mexico Historical Review* 74: 127-53.

Lee, Katie. "Glen Canyon Diary, 1956," *Journal of Arizona History*, Spring 1976.

Sayre, Joel. "The Average Can't Imagine," *Sports Illustrated*, June 16, 1958.

Stoffle, Richard, et.al. "Ghost Dancing the Grand Canyon," *Current Anthropology*, Volume 41, Number 1, February 2000.

Videos

Briggs, Don. *Grand Canyon Mule Ride*, Don Briggs Productions, 398 11th Street, San Francisco, California, n.d.

Williams, Jonathon. *Navajo Weavers: The Unchanging Artists of the Southwest*, Atkinson Trading Post, n.d.

Government Documents

United States Department of Interior. Secretarial Land Use Plan for Addition to Havasupai Indian Reservation, Washington, D.C.: National Resources Library, March 12, 1976.

Pamphlets

Stoffle, Richard W. and Evans, Michael J. *Kaibab Paiute History: The Early Years.* Fredonia, Arizona: Kaibab Paiute Tribe, 1978.

Websites

www.lightplanet.com/mormons/daily/education/indian_eom.htm
www.nps.gov/pisp/adhi/adhi.htm (Pipe Spring NM: An Administrative History).
www.nps.gov/pisp/pphtml/newsdetail7749.html (Pipe Spring National Monument).

Cover Credits

Front cover top: Grand Canyon, photograph by W. Tyson Joye, courtesy of National Park Service

Front inset photographs, clockwise from left: courtesy of John Annerino © 1998; courtesy of Kansas State Historical Society, Topeka, Kansas; courtesy of Jean Mann; courtesy of National Park Service

Back cover inset photographs, from top: courtesy of National Park Service; courtesy of Gale Burak; courtesy of Lois Hirst; courtesy of National Park Service; courtesy of Betty Leavengood

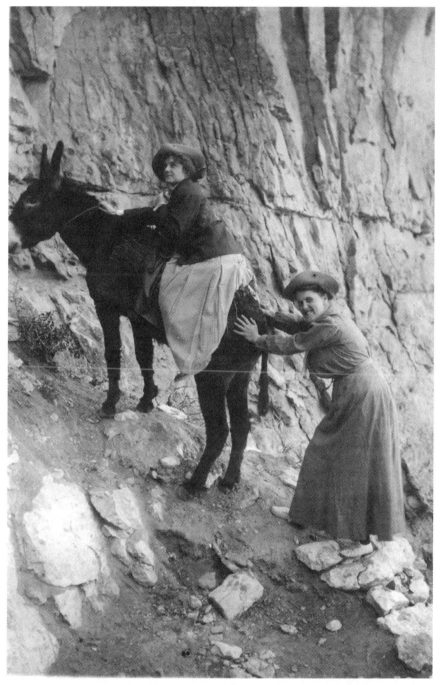

One woman sits on a mule, while another tries to push her up the Bright Angel Trail, ca. 1910. *Photograph by the Kolb Brothers courtesy of National Park Service.*

About the Author

Betty Leavengood was born and grew up in the hills of West Virginia. She moved to Tucson, Arizona, in 1971, where she taught school and later led hiking trips across the Grand Canyon for Pima Community College. Her many hikes inspired her to learn, and write, about other women who were associated with the canyon. Leavengood is also the author of the *Tucson Hiking Guide*, now in its fourth edition. She currently lives in Davidson, North Carolina, but makes frequent trips to Arizona.